FINANCE FOR LIFE

Smart Choices to Make and Save More Money

F.B. Wiseman

Abcor Publishers
New York

DISCLAIMER: While I have taken every effort to verify the accuracy of the information presented in these pages, I cannot accept any responsibility or liability resulting from any misinformation presented or any of the information, opinions, or conclusions set out in this work. Further, this publication is sold with the understanding that the author and publisher is not providing accounting, legal, or any other professional services or advice. Please speak with a trusted, competent attorney or other qualified professional before making any decisions involving personal or business financial and investment decisions.

ISBN # 978-0-9859556-2-5
Library of Congress Control Number: 2012920902

First published in the United States by Abcor Publishers, 2012

In memory of SLR

This one is for the Gipper

Acknowledgements

The completion of this book is due in part to many individuals. I specifically want to thank my editor and designer for their hard work. I also owe great gratitude to my family, friends, and everyone who supported this endeavor. For all your help, I am truly grateful.

Thank you.

Table of Contents

SECTION 1: Credit.......... 7

CHAPTER 1: Good and Bad Credit.......... 9

CHAPTER 2: Benefits of Consumer Credit.......... 13

CHAPTER 3: Credit Cards: The Consumer and Debt.......... 19

CHAPTER 4: The Debate over Payday Loans.......... 39

SECTION 2: Personal Finance.......... 49

CHAPTER 5: A Budget for All Your Needs.......... 51

CHAPTER 6: Learning to Respect Debt: The Reduction Plan.......... 65

CHAPTER 7: Fear of Generic Products.......... 85

CHAPTER 8: Why Banks Nickel and Dime You.......... 89

CHAPTER 9: Leasing vs. Buying...The Discussion Continues.......... 111

SECTION 3: Real Estate.......... 127

CHAPTER 10: Real Estate Investing: Buying a Home.......... 129

CHAPTER 11: International Real Estate Investing.......... 147

CHAPTER 12: Refinancing.......... 159

SECTION 4: Education and Jobs.......... 167

CHAPTER 13: Financial Education for Kids.......... 169

CHAPTER 14: Higher Education 179

CHAPTER 15: Student Loans and Bankruptcy 189

CHAPTER 16: Salary Trends: Compensation in America 207

SECTION 5: Financial Products 215

CHAPTER 17: Insurance Overview 217

CHAPTER 18: Understanding Life Insurance 225

CHAPTER 19: Annuities and How to Use Them 229

CHAPTER 20: Municipal Bonds 233

CHAPTER 21: Government Investments 243

SECTION 6: Financial Planning 253

CHAPTER 22: The Power of Compounding 255

CHAPTER 23: Investment Programs Introduction 261

CHAPTER 24: Traditional IRA Retirement Plans 271

CHAPTER 25: Retirement Plans in the Workplace 279

CHAPTER 26: Investments for Children 301

CHAPTER 27: Bankruptcy and Retirement Plans 307

SECTION 7: Government 311

CHAPTER 28: Social Security Benefits 313

CHAPTER 29: Tax Rates Comparison 323

SECTION I

Credit

CHAPTER 1

Good and Bad Debt

Debt may seem like one of life's necessary evils. It is virtually impossible to go through life without incurring some kind of debt. In fact, today, a good credit history is required to qualify for many loans, housing, and jobs. That means acquiring managing your debt. However, not all debt is created equal. Some debt is necessary to achieve life goals, such as an education, while other debt is frivolous, burdensome, and destructive to your quality of life when it gets out of hand. For debt to be considered good, it should meet four requirements:

1. The debt is incurred as an investment for the future
2. The debt is reasonable in view of your total financial picture
3. The debt payments are manageable
4. The debt is incurred for products that increase in value

This boils down to one question: how do you discern good debt from bad debt? You will find as many answers to this question as there are financial advisors, because everyone has an opinion. The fact is that unless you are independently wealthy, some debt is going to be necessary to make large purchases such as houses and college tuition. Small debt usually takes the form of credit card debt used to buy clothes, food, electronics, and so on.

As a general rule, your debt-to-income ratio should not exceed 35 to 36 percent of your gross income. This percent is just a guideline, but statistics indicate that, on average, a higher debt-to-income level will not leave you with enough money to comfortably pay taxes and afford living expenses. When you total up debt, include such things as:

- Mortgage or rent payments
- Credit card debt
- Car payments
- Other loan payments

Here is an example of debt-to-income ratio:
John and Mary Dowe have a combined monthly income of $7,000.

Their major monthly debt expenses include:

- $1,500 mortgage
- $450 credit card payment
- $300 car payment
- $200 student loan payments

Total monthly debt = $2,450

Total monthly income = $7,000

Debt-to-Income Ratio = Debt divided by Income

$2,450/$7,000 = 0.35 x 100 percent = 35 percent

As you can see, the Dowe's monthly debt level falls within acceptable levels based on their monthly income, but clearly, there is some debt that can be reduced to give them a smaller monthly debt burden. By taking the time to find and make certain reductions in their monthly debt, they can spend more money on other monthly expenses and invest in assets for their future.

Principles of Good Debt

In analyzing good debt versus bad debt, you should keep a few principles in mind. First, you need to maintain cash reserves for emergencies. So sometimes, it is better to borrow for a short term than to spend all the cash you have on hand. Second, you should only take on debt if you can afford the monthly payments. Third, the debt should only be incurred for essential items, like a house, and not for unnecessary things that you cannot afford, like a vacation or expensive jewelry. Fourth, debt may sometimes be justified if the proceeds are *certain* to create more value or an investment return that is higher than the fees and interest you will pay on the debt.

Ideal debt will be used to make investments that are certain to increase in value and do not increase your debt-to-income ratio beyond 36 percent. Typical investments that can produce value include a house, property, stocks, bonds, precious metals, and mutual funds. The key word in all of this is *certain.* Risk is always associated with investments in stocks, bonds, commodities, and mutual funds, because they can increase as well as decline in value. Unless you are investing in a "sure thing," if such a thing even exists, borrowing money to make these kinds of investments is rarely justified.

Good debt may include money borrowed to cover the cost of anything that can make it possible for you to achieve financial gains in the future. According to a US Census Bureau study, college graduates earn twice as much as people with high school diplomas do. (1) Clearly, investing in an education returns a lifetime of value. This is also the kind of good debt that can turn into bad debt. If you graduate college burdened with tens of thousands of dollars of debt, your debt-to-income ratio could grow to higher than 36 percent, depending on your early career income level. One more guideline is to not assume debt for higher education expenses that will lead to post-college loan payments that exceed 8 to 10 percent of your estimated monthly gross income. (2) Therefore, careful thought, research, and analysis are imperative to all investments and debt undertaking. With sound analysis, you will be able to understand the risk inherent in your financial plans, and hopefully, you will not be blindsided by foreseeable events.

Principles of Bad Debt

Bad debt is money borrowed to pay for items that depreciate, living expenses, luxury items, or products that do not bring additional financial value. Though most people do buy vehicles on credit, they are paying interest for a depreciating asset. Also, in another example of good debt that can become bad debt, after the recent housing market collapse (the aftermath of which is still being felt as of this writing) many consumers found themselves owing more on their mortgages than their homes were worth. In other words, the asset value became less than the debt that they owed, which is exactly the same result as a vehicle loan. These loans are commonly referred to being underwater. All investments carry inherent risks, and certain events can create an environment that increases otherwise-dormant risks.

Other examples of bad debt include charging entertainment expenses, taking out an equity loan on your house to pay for a vacation (paying for a one-week vacation for fifteen years will never be a sound investment), charging new clothes, and buying furniture on credit. In every one of these examples, the debt is incurred to pay for something that may offer short-term gratification and usage, but these items also lose value fairly quickly. Sometimes, the item's total value may decrease substantially in less than a year.

Therefore, before taking on debt, it is important to evaluate whether your purchase will appreciate and to consider your debt-to-income ratio. Managing debt takes discipline and sometimes a willingness to do without, whether you do without a bigger house, new clothes, or a trip to Hawaii. Yes, this means sacrificing today for a better tomorrow. This might not be an easy proposition, but in general, you will be glad you did.

CHAPTER 2

The Benefits of Consumer Credit

It is difficult to imagine life without debt. The availability of consumer credit makes it possible to borrow money for just about anything you can think of: cars, houses, jewelry, food, clothes, entertainment, boats, education, medical bills, travel, and so on. Credit refers to a debt incurred with the intent of increasing current goods or services consumption. Consumer credit specifically refers to credit extended regularly by an individual or business that represents borrowing by an individual to be used for household or personal expenses or a family business. This credit is also subject to a finance charge. (1)

Consumer credit is generally used for items that do not increase wealth, which means the credit must be paid back out of existing assets like a savings account or earned income. Going into debt requires you to make a choice about how you will be using your future income, which you have not yet been earned. Most people do not compare their present debt against the future income that will be required to efficiently service that debt load. Yet once you accept consumer credit, future income is committed to something that will not increase your income unless you used the borrowed money to invest in an appreciating asset. Each month, as you pay the monthly installment payment, you are making the choice to use the payment amount for the debt and not for food, gas, clothing, or anything else. You have also given up your ability to put that money into savings or investments. And if you make only the minimum payments each month, the original debt will balloon into even greater debt, costing you more in lost investment and other opportunities.

Consumer credit can be a valuable tool for obtaining needed products and services, but it can also cause you enormous financial stress in the long term if you do not do careful research and analysis of the products and the financial institutions offering these products. There have been cases where unscrupulous lenders committed illegal, greed-induced, and unfair acts, which have resulted in a plethora of laws regulating the consumer credit industry. In other words, the world of consumer credit is a two-way street. Lenders are legally and ethically obligated to treat borrowers fairly, while borrowers are legally and ethically obligated to incur only debt they can afford to repay and to adhere to the contract. Sure, there are regulatory agencies to ensure that lenders are in compliance with the rules, but based upon evidence from the mortgage crisis of 2008, the ultimate responsibility is upon the borrower, who must read and understand the terms of any contract before signing it. Speaking with a qualified financial advisor before entering into financial obligations that will affect your long-term financial goals is always wise.

Types of Consumer Credit

In general, there are two categories of consumer credit: revolving and non-revolving. Revolving credit is usually referred to as open-ended and non-revolving credit is known as close-ended credit.

An open-ended credit transaction is a loan arrangement that allows you to make repeated transactions until you have borrowed up to the amount of the approved credit line. Credit cards, department store revolving charge accounts, and home equity lines of credit are typical examples of open-ended credit.

Here are some types of open-ended consumer credits:

- Credit with a maximum limit that allows the consumer to borrow or charge any amount up to that limit
- Installment loans (signature or collateralized): close-ended loan in which you make payments until the borrowed amount is paid off
- Non-installment credit or short-term credit allows you to borrow money, then repay those funds in a single payment or lump sum, usually within thirty days

Conversely, the non-revolving, or close-ended, credit refers to loans that are issued once and cannot be reissued unless a new loan contract is signed. For example, you get a loan at the credit union to make roof repairs to your house. Once the loan is paid off, the debt is cleared, and you can no longer borrow on the same loan. You must apply for a new loan in order to borrow more funds.

Consumer credit is not per se "bad debt." In fact, consumer credit can help you obtain assets that you could not otherwise afford. Mismanaging consumer credit, however, can lead to a number of problems, including a lower credit score, delinquent payments, and calls from debt collectors.

Understanding the debt you assume is always important. Amazingly, a 2009 survey of American consumers reported that as many as 36 percent of credit cardholders questioned did not know the interest rate on their cards. When consumers were asked questions involving interest rate calculations, only 65 percent were able to answer correctly. (2) Making good consumer credit decisions is difficult if you do not read the terms of the loan or understand the interest rate and fee calculations.

Fees and Interest Rates

Consumer credit fees and interest rates represent the cost of borrowing. The cost of credit or borrowing can vary significantly from account to account. The annual percentage rate (APR) is the rate at which you will accrue interest each year, and this rate must be clearly stated in your loan agreement and on your credit card statements. Most states have laws that govern one or more of the following:

- Maximum finance charges or interest rates
- Maximum delinquency fees for late payments
- Maximum allowed annual fees
- Allowable cash advance fees

Federal law also places a number of consumer protections on credit card accounts. The Credit Card Accountability Responsibility and Disclosure Act, or Credit CARD Act, of 2009 limits retroactive interest rates, restricts when interest rates and fees can be increased, preserves your right to pay off older balances at the last interest rate before a rate increase, and requires payments to be applied fairly. It is important for consumers to know that the law limits when and how rates can be charged by the lender, but it does not prohibit fees and interest. Credit cards and many checking accounts are becoming more expensive to own and use as financial institutions raise their interest rates and up-front fees to make up for revenues that will be lost due to the credit card reform law. (3)

Consumer loans on real estate are also regulated by the Credit CARD Act. Typical fees include the loan origination fee and the points. The loan origination fee is subject to maximum limits set by the federal and state governments. Some FHA loans are restricted to 1 percent origination fees while others may charge a reasonable fee based on regional rates. But the state may cap fees for non-FHA loans for an area, which has the effect of capping FHA loan-origination fees, too.

Points are equivalent to 1 percent of the loan and are usually financed. If you pay the points upfront, you can save a significant amount of money over the life of the loan. Other fees associated with real estate loans include closing costs and prepayment penalties.

When analyzing a loan interest rate, there are two features to consider:

- The actual interest rate.
- The type of interest. Is it fixed or variable?

The details of the loan interest rate are critical to determining the true cost of the loan. Banks will sometimes offer a low "teaser" rate on a credit card and then raise the rate after a period of time. The Credit Card Reform Act now restricts increases in interest rates for the first year, but after the first year, the bank can raise rates on new purchases with proper notice. Variable interest rates can catch you unprepared for higher charges on your loan or credit account. Real estate variable interest increases will make your future payments higher, and that can cause a serious cash-flow problem if you are living paycheck to paycheck.

Government Regulations

Federal and state truth-in-lending laws are designed to ensure that consumers fully understand the terms and costs of their credit transactions. These laws require that certain consumer credit disclosures be made to the consumer. They include: (4)

- Name of the actual creditor
- Loan principal
- Finance charge
- Interest rate, including if it can vary
- Account fees, including periodic and transaction fees
- Cash advance fees (on open-ended credit)
- Total number of payments (close-ended credit)
- Amount of payment and when those payments are due
- Payment grace periods
- Total amount paid after close-ended loan is paid off
- Fees and late payment amounts
- Total sale price minus the down payment or other adjustments (close-ended credit)
- Prepayment penalties (close-ended credit)
- Disclosure of right to raise interest rate and fees

If you have signed a contract, you do have a right to rescind it within three days of signing. This gives people time to experience buyer's remorse. It also allows time to correct a wrong should you discover there are problems with the loan terms.

Some Advice on Credit

The best way to control debt is to make sure you do not accept too much consumer credit. Getting into debt is easy. Walk into a department store to buy anything, and chances are, you will be asked if you want to open an account. The "teaser" usually offers a discount on your purchase right then if you charge it on a new account. Within minutes, you are approved and have a new debt. It is really that easy.

Assuming any kind of consumer debt should not be a mindless decision, no matter how small the approved credit amount or loan amount is. Millions of consumers have black marks on their credit reports due to past-due payments on department store charge accounts. If you do get into financial trouble and cannot make your loan payments, the best thing to do is call your creditor. Most creditors are willing to work with consumers because they know that is their best chance of getting payment. If you cannot come to a resolution with the creditor, then you have other options.

- Consolidate your debt into a single loan
- If applicable, sell the asset and eliminate the debt
- Hire a nonprofit credit counseling service
- File bankruptcy (This should be the option you consider last.)

Getting consumer credit is not difficult. Getting out of debt can be.

CHAPTER 3

Credit Cards: The Consumer and Debt

A credit card is a card issued by a financial institution that allows the cardholder to buy goods and services or get cash advances up to a pre-approved spending limit. Each period, payments are due on the amount borrowed against that account. The credit card represents a revolving line of credit, which means that the remaining unpaid amount rolls forward from period to period, and the unused credit is available for purchases. As the unpaid balance decreases, the available credit increases until it has reached the credit limit. A charge card is a different type of credit card. Holders of this kind of card are required to pay the balance in full each month.

Credit cards are so integrated into today's society that it is easy to assume they have been around for a very long period of time. However, the story of credit cards does not really begin until the 1920s, and the credit card as we know it today appeared in 1951. The earliest credit cards were referred to as "metal money" because the cards issued by Western Union in 1914 were literally made of metal. In 1924, General Petroleum followed suit by issuing metal money cards that could be used to pay for automobile services and gas. The cards were first issued to company employees, then customers, and finally to the general public. Cards were also issued by hotels and department stores so that travelers could buy goods and services without cash.

In the 1930s, the Bell System Credit Card was issued by American Telephone and Telegraph (AT&T). The use of credit would probably have grown quickly at that point if World War II had not led to a prohibition on the use of charge cards and credit. After World War II, credit cards became embedded in the consumer economy as people used credit to buy new kitchen appliances, televisions, and department store goods.

In 1951, Diners Club introduced a credit card that could be used in twenty-seven New York restaurants. Credit cards were being made of cardboard by this time. The Diners Club credit card was not enormously popular, but it laid the groundwork for the introduction of the American Express card and the Bank Americard charge card. In 1958, Bank Americard mailed out 60,000 cards to Fresno, California, residents. The Bank Americard has not changed much since then, except for its name. Now called Visa, the all-purpose charge card became very popular with consumers. In a competitive response, a group of US banks collaborated to issue the Interlink charge card in 1966. The Interlink charge card became MasterCard in 1979. Up to this point, the cards could only be used at the issuers' payment processing outlets, but this quickly changed.

In the 1970s, the paper credit cards were replaced with plastic cards with magnetic strips that could be processed through compatible electronic systems. In the 1980s, the MasterCard and Visa charge cards were changed to credit cards that could be used at any outlet able to process the payments. As expected, the use of charge cards exploded because they could be used anywhere in the world. In 1986, Sears, Roebuck and Co. issued the Discover Card.

With the explosion of credit cards came growing concerns about protecting the public from bad practices that emerged from their widespread use. The Federal Truth in Lending Act passed in 1988 did not address all the issues. However, it was a much-needed start to protecting consumers. This act informed consumers by requiring the disclosure of costs and terms connected with the use of the credit cards. More legislation followed.

During the 1990s, a variety of marketing tactics was employed to encourage charging on credit cards instead of using checks or cash. They included low introductory rates, rewards, incentives, frequent-flier miles, and cash-back offers.

In 2005, PayPal was founded and allowed people to make credit card payments on the Internet. PayPal became popular because it provided a safe and secure method of making payments over the Internet to sometimes unfamiliar vendors and individuals. This is a needed service because the Internet was a minefield of fraudulent and insecure sites that left customers' information exposed to hackers and identity thieves.

The Square, which was introduced in 2010, enhances the security of credit card transactions through mobile phones. This was just another part of the emerging technologies targeting those who wanted to make secure portable payments. These new technologies have also led to processing capabilities like Bling Tag, which links PayPal with a mobile patch; Google Wallet, which is a mobile payment system; and computer chips that permit multiple accounts on a single card.

The success of credit cards lies in the consumers' ability to use them anywhere to buy almost anything and the ability to carry forward a balance each month by paying a minimum amount. The revolving balance has become a double-edged sword for many consumers in that it is easy to keep charging and paying the minimum amount due while incurring significant interest charges and fees. Over the long term, this practice tends to benefit the credit card industry more than it benefits the consumers.

Credit cards are now used extensively, and the five main cards issued are MasterCard, Visa, Discover, Capital One, and American Express. The following numbers represent how large the credit card industry is and show its projected growth:

- Consumers carried $801 billion in outstanding revolving debt as of December 2011 (1)
- Projected number of credit cards issued in 2012 equals 1.167 billion (2)
- Projected number of credit cardholders in 2012 equals 160 million (3)
- The average cardholder's debt is about $5,438 ($870 billion projected for 2012) (4)

There are three major types of credit cards

Unsecured: The credit card balance is not secured by collateral. If the cardholder defaults on the balance, the creditor cannot seize assets to settle the debt. This type of card is generally issued to employed people with a good credit history.

Secured: The credit card balance is secured by collateral, which is usually in the form of a cash deposit held by the creditor. The credit line of the credit card is usually equal to the account balance. Once a deposit is accepted and the credit card is issued, the account works like an unsecured credit card in that you must make payments each month. Secured credit cards are usually issued to people who have a low credit score or are re-establishing credit.

Prepaid: The prepaid credit card balance is based on the amount of money loaded on the card. Technically, the prepaid card is not a credit card because no credit is being extended. As charges are made, those amounts are deducted from the balance. Once the full amount of the money that was loaded has been used for purchases, the card's balance must be reloaded. These cards are issued by major credit card companies and can be purchased in various retail and grocery stores. People who have poor credit and cannot get a secured or unsecured credit card can benefit from prepaid credit cards. These cards allow holders to make purchases and pay bills online. They are also often given as gifts.

Major Credit Cards

There are five main credit cards issued today. These credit cards are issued to certain target consumers and offer a variety of features from small perks to exclusive member-only offers.

Visa

The Visa card is a universal credit card that can be used nearly everywhere, unlike a department store charge card. Visa does not actually extend the credit or the cards and does not set interest rates and fees. Individual financial institutions are responsible for setting these requirements and paying Visa a fee for purchases while also paying licensing fees. Visa is essentially an electronic payment processor offering branded products to banks like Chase, Citibank, and Bank of America.

The financial institutions issuing Visa credit cards target a broad customer base by issuing both secured and unsecured credit cards. Customers range from college students with little or no credit to senior citizens, who typically have a longer credit history. In other words, customers can have average to excellent credit. As of February 2012, the average national interest rate was 14.9 percent. Banks do still issue cards without annual fees, but they are charging fees on a more regular basis in response to the Credit CARD legislation's limits on their ability to change interest rates. The lower a customer's credit rating is, the higher his or her interest rate is. Visa currently accounts for approximately 38 percent of the credit card market.

MasterCard

MasterCard emerged from the launch of the first interbank reciprocal agreement of a member-owned association in 1966. First called the Interbank Card in 1966, its name was changed to Master Charge–the Interbank Card in 1969 and then finally to MasterCard in 1979. Like Visa cards, MasterCards are issued by financial institutions. Now the second largest electronic payments processor, MasterCard has about a 24 percent of the credit card market share. The target market is similar to the Visa market in that people with average to excellent credit can qualify for a MasterCard. Those with poor credit can apply for a secured credit card. Interest rates vary with credit scores and finances. As of February 2012, the average interest rate for the Advance MasterCard (average credit) was 17.9 percent, while the average rate for the Premier MasterCard (excellent credit) was 12.9 percent. Annual fees also vary by financial institution. Annual fees can be as low as zero and as high as $300, depending on the type of MasterCard.

American Express

American Express issues its own credit cards. Thanks to effective marketing and a quality brand image, this card is recognized by most people whether or not they can qualify for one. The company, which was started in 1850 as a valuables and freight delivery service, eventually began issuing money orders and then entered the travel business during World War I. In 1914, US citizens found themselves stranded in Europe after letters of credit were refused, and they turned to American Express for travel money.

In 1922, American Express expanded into luxury steamship travel and issued traveler's checks to high-income customers. Growing on the fees charged, the first American Express credit travel and entertainment charge card was issued and is referred to as the "Green Card." The Green Card has no pre-set spending limit and must be paid off each month. The Gold Card (charge card) was issued in 1966 and also has no pre-set spending limit. In 1984, the Platinum Card (charge card) was launched with an annual fee. The Optima Card, American Express's first credit card, was introduced in 1987, and the Blue "Smart Card" rolled out in 1999. A Smart Card enables customers to consolidate multiple accounts on a single card. The company's target market is made up of consumers and businesses with high purchase volumes and excellent credit history. The company currently has 23 percent of the credit card market share.

American Express charges an annual fee ranging from $0 to $450, and the interest rates vary from approximately 13 percent to 22 percent, depending on the particular card type. Today, the company has its own payment network that issues and manages credit cards. It also licenses a network of financial institutions issuing American Express Cards. The company is projected to have fifty-two million cardholders by the end of 2012. (5)

Capital One

A relatively young credit card company, Capital One Financial Corporation was formed as a spinoff credit card unit in 1995 and is a bank holding company. The company was initially set up as a thrift operation, which enabled it to participate in the automobile installment loan and home loan industries. Credit cards are just one of its divisions today. Over the years, the company has targeted poor to above-average credit consumers.

Capital One has approximately 7 percent to 9 percent of the credit card market share. Interest rates range from 12.9 percent to 25 percent. Its annual fees depend on the type of credit card and can range from $0 to $60.

Discover Card

The Discover Card was a fairly radical introduction to the credit card market in 1986, because it was free and offered universally. Until then, free credit cards issued by older companies were rare. Discover also offered a cash-back incentive on purchases that was very attractive to customers. This and other perks greatly increased the level of competition among credit card companies.

In 2011, 58.7 million Discover Brand credit cards were issued. (6) The Discover Card has 5 to 6 percent of the credit card market.

Other Credit Cards

Visa, MasterCard, Discover, Capital One, and American Express are the five giants in the credit card industry. Other major issuers include store cards and oil company cards. These are credit cards issued directly by the companies that can only be used at designated businesses. There are an estimated ninety-six million store-card holders and fifty-six million oil-company cardholders.

There are literally thousands of different credit and charge cards available with varying interest rates, annual fees, rewards, and terms, making the credit card industry very complex. The interest rates and fees mentioned in this book are only meant to give you a general idea of how credit card accounts are structured. The rates can change at any time.

Factors to Consider When Choosing a Credit Card

The Right Reasons

The multiple credit card options, fee schedules, and perks make choosing a credit card a confusing process. However, several factors determine which credit card is best for your purposes and which credit card you are most likely to be eligible for based on your financial circumstances.

Purpose

You should first consider the reason you want to get a credit card. This is an important starting point, which should be considered very carefully. There are good and bad reasons for applying for a credit card. Debt is not bad in and of itself. The misuse of debt creates the problem. Millions of people responsibly manage debt by using credit only when necessary and never charging or borrowing money they cannot afford to repay.

Convenience and Safety

There are several good reasons to have a credit card. Many retailers and restaurants no longer take checks, and credit cards are necessary to make Internet purchases and electronic purchases. Sometimes, carrying cash just is not safe.

Build Credit History

One of the best reasons for getting a credit card is that a well-managed credit card account can help build or restore a good credit history. Paying a credit card payment on time each month, paying an amount above the minimum, and not charging up to the maximum amount will help a consumer establish or restore credit. The longer you manage your credit card account responsibly, the more your credit score improves.

Access to Emergency Funds

Another good reason to get a credit card is to have access to cash or credit during an emergency. For example, your car may break down. Even people with a savings account may not be able to access their money on nights and weekends, whereas a credit card is available anytime.

Manage a Monthly Budget

Consumers also use credit cards to manage expenses. Charging expenses on a credit card provides a detailed list of expenses that can be used for tax and budgeting purposes.

The Wrong Reasons

Credit cards can also wreak havoc on a consumer's credit rating. In fact, it is easy to go deep into debt using credit cards. The credit card debt per household will average anywhere from $5,000 to $7,500, depending on economic conditions and bank lending practices. The number also represents multiple credit card accounts, meaning multiple monthly payments must be met.

As a rule of thumb, expenses should not be charged unless you can afford to pay them off within a month or two. Making late payments will lower your credit score and make it difficult to get credit when you need it. A poorly managed credit card account also sends a signal to lenders that the account holder has financial problems or is unable to manage his or her finances.

Getting a credit card to buy items you do not need is seldom wise. "Keeping up with the Joneses" inevitably leads to excessive debt. Debt is not meant for splurging on nonessential items.

Application and Approval Process

Applying for a credit card is not difficult because most financial institutions rely on your credit score or credit history. You give the bank or credit card company your social security number and basic information like your name, birth date, place of employment, and address on an application. Many applications are now completed online. In some cases, you may get an invitation through the mail to apply or you might be offered a "guaranteed approval" if you just sign your name and return the form or enter an approval code online per the company's instructions.

Credit Check

The financial institution will use your credit information to approve or deny your credit card request and to determine the interest rate and fees you will be charged. People with excellent credit often get lower interest rates, no or minimal annual fees, and higher credit limits. Credit card companies will review the following information:

- Income level
- Whether you own a home or rent
- Employment history, including length of employment in each position held
- Credit score
- Negative credit information like judgments, liens, bankruptcies, delinquent accounts, and delinquent account collection activity
- Charge-offs where a prior credit card balance was written off due to lack of payment and creditor's belief that the account was uncollectible
- Active accounts and payment history
- Number of credit cards already active and their balances
- Number of credit inquiries indicating you have been searching for credit
- Age of credit accounts
- Account balance versus the maximum credit limit

The credit card company will consider the "big picture" by looking at how you have managed your debt up to this point. Since some people will not meet the minimum requirements for credit line approval, the credit card companies created the secured credit accounts. Some versions of secured credit cards can be converted to a non-secured credit card once you have developed a strong credit history. The prepaid cards purchased at retail stores do not appear on your credit history.

Anyone applying for a credit card for the first time may need to first obtain a store or gas-company card simply because those minimum requirements are lower than the ones for a Visa, MasterCard, or Discover Card. Capital One offers credit cards to people who have minimal or no credit experience. However, American Express is not a beginner's credit card.

Once you have established credit with a department store or gas card for at least six months, you can apply for a universal credit card. There will probably be an application fee, and you will only qualify for a higher interest card with an annual fee. However, once you prove you can use credit wisely, it is always possible to roll your balance to a lower interest credit card. Interest rates and fees reflect the creditor's assessment of your risk.

Credit Score

The annual costs associated with a credit card vary depending on the financial institution and the type of credit card. Today, there is a credit card for almost everyone because creditors use interest rates and fees to compensate for risk. If the company believes you are a higher risk due to a poor credit history, the terms of the credit card you are offered will not be as favorable as those offered to someone with a higher credit score. Creditors assume that someone with a fair credit score from 640 to 680 or higher is less likely to default than someone who has a poor credit score that is under 640. However, there is no magic cutoff score that determines whether you will be approved for a certain credit card.

Fair Isaac's FICO score is the credit score used most often to determine credit card terms. Terms include all of the annual costs associated with the credit card account.

- Rewards package
- Annual percentage rate (APR)
- Fixed or variable APR
- Secured versus non-secured status
- Variable rate periods
- Annual fees
- Payment grace period before late fee is charged
- Credit limit

The fees associated with credit cards can be considerable. They include the application fee, annual membership fee, over-the-limit fee, late-payment fee, and monthly service fee. Other one-time or routine fees include a set-up fee, cash-advance fee, balance-transfer fee, and credit-limit-increase fee. Many companies also offer insurance that will pay your monthly balance or pay off your credit card balance should you become unemployed or disabled. (7)

The type of credit card you qualify for will be determined by your FICO score and credit history. The credit cards issued to high-risk customers will have high interest rates and one or more fees. Most credit cards today have some kind of fee attached in response to the passage of the Credit CARD Act limiting the ability of credit card companies to change fees.

Security Features

Credit card security features protect consumers from loss. There are several types of security features that address specific issues.

- **Identity Theft insurance:** Optional identity theft insurance is sold by the credit card company and covers cardholders' losses due to identity theft. The insurance will pay for the cost of resolving the issues connected with the identity theft. These costs include legal fees, telephone expenses, and even lost wages.
- **Zero-liability protection:** If someone makes an unauthorized purchase on your credit card, the zero-liability protection ensures that you are reimbursed for stolen funds. Most credit card companies require that you report the fraudulent transaction within a certain period of time in order to dispute the transaction. The creditor may also limit the number of transactions it will cover.
- **Credit Protection Insurance:** Optional credit protection insurance will credit the credit card account for designated amounts in the event that you become involuntarily unemployed, are hospitalized, become disabled, take an unpaid family leave of absence, or die. These are usually offered as options when the cardholder is traveling.
- **Photo Security:** Some credit card companies also offer photo security in which you put your photo on your card for theft protection.
- **Temporary Card Number:** A fairly recent development in the credit card industry is a feature that allows you to create a temporary card number that is linked to

your permanent credit card account. The temporary number can then be used to safely shop online.

Promotional Programs

Promotional programs are designed to attract customers. These marketing tools can take many forms, including cash back, discounts on products and services, and airline points. Following are some of the most common types of rewards, incentives, and promotional programs:

- **Airline travel miles**: accumulated points that can be redeemed for savings on airline tickets or special perks with named airlines
- **Travel points**: accumulated points used toward hotels, restaurants, travel packages, concerts, sporting or athletic events, and more
- **Reward points**: accumulated points that can be used toward purchases of goods or services
- **Gas rebates (oil company cards)**: cash rebates credited to an account based on purchased gallons of gas
- **Cash back**: percentage of cash rebated to an account based on purchases, sometimes in the form of rebate checks
- **Membership benefits**: mixture of discounts on products and services, no or reduced card fees, cash rewards, and VIP status while traveling
- **Other Perks**: sign-up bonus, low introductory percentage rate, free sign-up gift, like a round-trip airline ticket, and others

Credit card companies mainly offer these promotions and incentives to encourage people to use their credit cards. The biggest difference between rewards programs and cash rebates is that rebates can be used to make any kind of purchase. Accumulated points can usually be used only with named vendors like particular airlines, hotels, or department stores.

When choosing a credit card, you have many features to take into account. Unfortunately, many people are lured into applying for a credit card based on an attractive introductory offer like a low interest rate and a waived annual fee the first year. Once the initial time period passes, the interest rate jumps, and you get a bill for an annual fee. Suddenly, the good deal is not so good. As the saying goes, if it looks too good to be true, it probably is not good for you.

Credit Card Pitfalls

Mismanaging credit cards can be costly. Credit cards make it easy to spend money you do not have, and that convenience is the downfall of many creditors. You can quickly accumulate crushing debt, lower your FICO credit score, and find yourself unable to make even minimum monthly payments. People fall into certain pitfalls or traps that can lead to excessive credit card debt.

- **Charging on a credit card just to earn cash rebates or rewards**: rebates and points represent only a percentage of the purchases, so you would have to charge a significant amount to get even a small rebate or to accumulate a small amount of points.
- **Making minimum payments**: a portion of the payment goes toward interest, so your payment is not paying down the balance as quickly as you think, leading to the slow increase in the balance as you continue to make new charges to the account.
- **Charging to the maximum credit limit**: carrying a maxed-out credit balance will lower your credit score and could force you into an over-limit situation when the monthly interest and fees are added, which leads to even more fees. High balances also raise your monthly minimum payment amount and will take longer to pay off.
- **Making late payments**: paying late will lower your FICO credit score. You will incur late payment fees that could possibly lead to a higher interest rate, depending the terms of your account.
- **Taking cash advances at ATMs or using credit card checks**: a cash advance is just like taking out an interest-bearing loan and can quickly lead to a maxed-out credit card because cash advances usually have high up-front fees and higher interest rates attached than credit purchases do.
- **Accepting multiple credit card accounts**: too much credit can harm your FICO credit score and lead to multiple maxed-out credit cards.

- **Lending out credit card**: letting other people "borrow" your credit card will run up your balance and cost you interest for items you do not even get to use.
- **Shopping online with unsecure vendors**: shopping with companies that do not have secure sites and do not protect your private information can leave you vulnerable to credit card theft and fraud; secure sites begin with "https" and display a picture of a locked padlock. You should only enter your credit card information on secure sites and remember to install security software on your computer.
- **Foreign currency purchases**: two issues that can develop into excess credit card charges include foreign currency transaction fees for currency conversions and changes in exchange rates that make your home currency drop in value, thus requiring you to spend more than you had intended to.
- **Accepting multiple credit cards with 0 percent introductory offers**: the interest rates will go up after the introductory period, leaving you with multiple credit card balances at high interest rates.

Recognizing credit card pitfalls can help you avoid these debt traps. Using a credit card and accumulating excessive debt is very easy to do. These pitfalls are all based on the same concept: spending money you do not have can lead to an unmanageable debt load.

Merchant Costs

Merchants that accept credit cards pay fees to the credit card companies or payment processors. These fees can be quite costly, so some vendors accept only certain cards. Just like consumers, merchants shop around for the best deal to minimize their costs. Merchant fees can include:

- **Statement fee**: general service charge, which is $10 or more per month
- **Monthly minimum**: fee charged if vendor does not meet an agreed upon charge amount total
- **Discount fee**: each sale is charged a percent that is retained by the credit card company and runs from 1 percent to over 2 percent
- **Transaction fee**: flat amount charged per transaction

The merchant usually pays a set-up fee when initiating the account. There may also be a monthly terminal fee, depending on the processing agreements that are in place.

Merchants earning a very small amount over the cost of a product may decide to refuse credit card payments because the fees consume too much of the profit.

Interchange fee

An interchange fee refers to the fee one bank pays another bank for accepting credit card transactions. The fee covers the bank's risk and cost of approving the transaction and then converting the customer's credit card transaction into cash for the merchant or vendor. This interchange fee amount is determined by the credit card companies and is passed on to the merchant as part of the discount fee.

When a customer pays with a credit card, the merchant's bank (acquiring bank) pays the cardholder's bank (issuing bank) a certain percentage based on the gross sale amount. Many different interchange categories account for transaction risk.

Debit Cards

A debit card is the equivalent of an electronic check issued by a financial institution. When a debit card is used, the transaction amount is immediately deducted directly from the consumer's checking account. Debit cards can be used for purchases and at ATM machines. They are convenient and add a level of security at the point of sale or the ATM because a personal identification number (PIN) must be entered before a transaction is authorized.

Most banks still do not charge a fee for making a purchase with a debit card, though that could change in the future. Most banks do, however, charge a transaction fee when debit cards are used to withdraw cash at an ATM. Some banks only charge the fee if you use an ATM operated by a bank other than the bank issuing the debit card. Those fees can be high. For example, you may pay $1 to $3 in fees on a $20 transaction. Some banks may also charge you a monthly fee to use their debit card service.

Debit cards can be used online just like a credit card. However, if your debit card number is stolen, the thief will have access to your bank account. It is better to use a credit card with a small credit limit for online purchases or to maintain a separate bank account just for online debit purchases.

One of the advantages of the debit card is that you pay as you go. The money is deducted from the checking account immediately. Using a debit card rather than a credit card limits the temptation to overspend. It is important to understand that if the bank allows an overdraft to go through, you will be charged a hefty non-sufficient funds fee. You can pay for overdraft protection, which may be less expensive in the event that you overspend your bank account. Merchants also pay discount rates and transaction fees on debit cards like those on credit cards.

Controversies Surrounding Credit Cards

The level of consumer credit card debt has been an issue in the United States for many years. An integral component of the economy, consumer revolving debt rose steadily between 1968 and 2009, according to the Federal Reserve. The recent 2008-2010 recession led to a reduction in consumer debt load that lasted between August, 2009, when debt was at $900 billion, and November, 2011, when it reached $798 billion. Consumer credit card debt is now rising again. In December, 2011, credit card debt was reported at $801 billion.

Today, credit cards are used for everything. Consumers charge clothing, food, hair salon visits, online purchases, and trips to the movies. Credit cards are used largely for discretionary spending during good economic times. During the recession, credit cards were used to cover house payments and to make up for lost income due to unemployment. Credit card debt has risen faster than disposable income, indicating that people are going into debt they cannot afford to repay in a reasonable amount of time.

As far as the economy is concerned, credit card debt is a catch-22. When people are charging on their credit cards, they are buying goods and services. Those purchases benefit the economy. When consumers accumulate credit card debt at a slower rate, it reflects slower spending trends. Yet consumers who accumulate more debt than they can manage on their household income will eventually find that they cannot pay their bills. The rate of delinquencies and bad debt will rise, and banks will be forced to charge off many of the accounts.

In other words, there is a fine line between debt that benefits the economy and debt that can slow the economy. During the recession, the credit card delinquency rates reached their highest levels in the history of the Unites States at 6.74 percent during the second quarter of 2009. By the end of 2011, the delinquency rate had fallen to 3.27 percent. (8) Yet 3 percent of $801 billion (about $24 billion) represents an enormous loss to financial institutions.

Almost two-thirds of the US economy relies on consumer spending, and credit cards create spending power. If people suddenly stopped charging en masse, the economy would grind to a near halt. Consumers must use credit responsibly, and creditors need to lend responsibly to maintain the balance. Two of the greatest concerns in relation to creditors are their aggressive marketing practices and deceptive practices.

Aggressive Marketing

Credit card companies are known for their aggressive marketing tactics. These practices include teaser interest rates, direct-mail credit card offers, and other special offers meant to lure consumers into accepting their offers. Many consumers accept the credit cards, only to discover they will need years to pay off the balances, hidden fees, and high interest. Prior to 2009, credit card bills did not have to state the account's annual percent rate (APR), and companies could raise interest rates and fees without giving the consumer advance notice. The credit card companies also used to post payments in a way that gave consumers the least amount of benefit by posting them first against the lowest interest rate balances. So even when a customer had transactions such as cash advances that typically carry a higher rate, the payment would not go to pay off the higher rate transaction balance, but rather to lower-rate transactions such as zero-rate balance transfers or regular purchases.

A good example of aggressive credit card marketing on college campuses recently came to light. As the competition between credit card companies increased, they began looking for new customers. And they found an eager group for their products. Approximately twenty years ago, financial institutions began to market credit cards on college campuses, despite the fact that most students had no credit history or reliable income. The result was nothing short of a disaster for many students' finances.

The credit card companies used enticements like free gifts to convince students to complete applications. After setting up tables with t-shirts, the salespeople would talk students into applying for credit cards without fully explaining the terms. Because they were considered adults, even jobless students did not need to get their parents' approval before assuming the debt.

These card issuers envisioned a long-term strategy for this new target market. The banks issuing the cards had hoped that the students would become loan customers after graduation.

Unfortunately, many of the students accepting one or more credit cards proceeded to max out the cards and ended up with large debts. This led to a public outcry, especially from the parents and credit-card-debt-burdened students.

Many blamed the colleges and universities, because they had formed partnerships with the credit card companies and allowed them to come to the campuses. Some education institutions even go as far as selling their students' names and addresses to credit card companies. Deceptive practices may have been curtailed, but marketing to students still continues.

Regulations to Protect Consumers

In response to consumer complaints about credit card company bad practices and spurred by the recession largely blamed on greedy bank practices of selling deceptive securities, the federal government passed a sweeping reform bill called the Credit Card Accountability Responsibility and Disclosure Act of 2009. This law, also referred to as the Credit CARD Act of 2009, put in place new rules concerning credit card practices that took effect on February 22, 2010. (9)

Credit CARD Act of 2009

Though the law does not limit the amount of interest a company can charge, it does make many new rules intended to protect consumers from deceptive practices. It instituted the following changes:

- Requires credit card companies to notify cardholders forty-five days before increasing interest rates or changing fees or terms. These rules not applicable if it is a case of expiring introductory rate or variable interest tied to an index or if you have not met the terms of an agreement.
- Requires more disclosure on credit card bills, including the amount of time it will take to pay off balance when making minimum payments and the total amount of interest you would pay.
- Prohibits increases in interest rates, fees, or limits the first year (exceptions include introductory rates less than six months old and variable interest tied to an index). Exemptions are made when your payment is sixty days late or if you do not meet the terms of the agreement.
- Requires that interest rate increases apply only to new charges.

- Requires the cardholder to notify the credit card company when transactions exceeding the account credit limit should be rejected. Credit limits are usually determined by what the cardholder can reasonably afford, and exceeding that credit limit can put undue financial burden on a cardholder and more fees in the pockets of the credit card companies.
- Sets fees at no more than 25 percent of the initial credit limit and no more than $125 during the first year.
- Requires that credit card statements be mailed or delivered at least twenty-one days before the payment is due.
- Specifies that payments must be posted to highest interest balances first.
- Forbids double-cycle billing.

The Credit CARD Act of 2009 also placed restrictions on credit card marketing to people under twenty-one years old. (10)

- People under the age of twenty-one must have a cosigner on credit card applications or else be able to prove ability to repay debt
- Free gifts are no longer allowed as enticements
- Credit-reporting agencies cannot provide the credit reports for people under the age of twenty-one to credit card companies without the consumer's permission
- Marketing agreements between universities and credit card companies must be disclosed annually

Dodd-Frank Wall Street Reform and Consumer Protection Act of 2010

On July 15, 2010, Congress passed the Dodd-Frank Wall Street Reform and Consumer Protection Act of 2010. The bill created a new office called the Consumer Financial Protection Bureau, which is responsible for enforcing the CARD Act. The new bureau centralized consumer protection responsibilities and was given wide regulatory authority. Its chief responsibilities include: (11)

- Enforcing federal consumer financial protection laws and making necessary rules
- Monitoring and restricting abusive or deceptive practices
- Investigating consumer complaints
- Promoting consumer financial education

- Researching consumer behavior
- Monitoring financial markets for consumer risks
- Enforcing consumer finance anti-discrimination laws
- Enforcing consumer finance laws barring unfair treatment

Using credit cards responsibly takes discipline. Too many consumers have come to rely on credit cards for paying routine expenses and do not pay off balances each month. It is much easier to incur too much debt than it is to pay off debt. If a household has multiple credit cards and high balances, then the first step to debt reduction is to make a payoff plan and stick with it. Once extra cards are paid off, they can be cancelled. Wisely used debt is beneficial. Carelessly used debt is a burden that can have a long-lasting negative impact on your finances.

CHAPTER 4

The Debate over Payday Loans

Chances are, people's opinion of the payday loan industry depend a lot on whether they have ever needed a small loan and needed it quickly. Opinions about the payday loan business tend to be very passionate for or against them, with very little support in the middle. This topic has been rife with controversy due to its many unorthodox policies, consumer targets, and lending practices. Many critics have said that these payday lenders are nothing more than legalized loan sharks preying on the less financially fortunate members of society. Clearly, critics and advocates get excited about this controversial, profitable, and growing industry for many reasons. In the following sections, I will review the history of payday loans, their regulatory status, typical loan terms, and alternatives.

What is a Payday Loan?

A payday loan is a type of loan that uses a future paycheck as collateral. It is quite possible to go to a credit union or bank and get a similar signature loan that relies on your future income as the source of repayment. However, several features of the payday loan set it apart from the typical loan.

Payday loans are usually a relatively small amount of money with a rather short repayment term compared to traditional loans. They also have very high interest rates exacerbated by fees added to the loan. Many advocates often argue that this type of loan is a better option than a credit card's cash advance if it is paid back within the allotted period. And acquitting these types of loans is fairly simple.

Quite simply, a borrower writes a lender a postdated personal check. The amount of the check equals the loan plus fees. In exchange, the lender gives the borrower cash for the check and deducts the fees from that amount. The lender agrees to hold the check until the due date of the loan. They are called payday loans because most people will ask for a loan due date that coincides with their payday. However, these types of loans are also referred to as cash advance loans and check advance loans.

Another common method of payday loan involves automatic funds transfers. A borrower may have the loan funds automatically deposited into a checking account in exchange for the postdated check. The loan repayment is then automatically debited from the borrower's account on the next payday or loan due date.

A payday loan amount is usually between $50 and $500. Qualifying for the loan is easy, and usually, the only requirements are that the borrower be at least eighteen years old, have income of some kind, be able to produce personal identification, and have a checking account. The amounts borrowed compared to the traditional bank loans are quite small, but millions of people request payday loans for a number of reasons. Here are some common reasons given for applying for payday loans:

- Pay for emergency car repairs
- Pay medical expenses
- Meet family needs
- Pay rent
- Buy groceries
- Pay delinquent utilities
- Cover unexpected travel expenses

Payday loans were created for three main reasons. First, many people cannot qualify for a traditional loan from a financial institution because of poor credit history, a poor credit score, or lack of adequate income. Second, sometimes, people need to borrow money quickly for an emergency, and the traditional loan process might take longer than the situation requires. Many proponents argue that banks and credit union loan processes do not provide for this emergency scenario and that this is why payday loans have proliferated in the lending industry. The third reason focuses on the fact that banks are not usually interested in making such small loans because they do not see them as profitable.

In general, payday loans:

- Do not require credit checks, so people with poor credit can qualify
- Involve a short process with money becoming available within twenty-four hours
- Are a simple process that is strictly between lender and borrower and does not require the involvement of cosigners
- Do not require cash up front for loan fees

Background and Regulation of Payday Loans

The roots of payday lending are found in the late 1800s and early 1900s in a practice called "wage buying." A wage buyer would lend a worker $5 one day and then require a payback of the loan plus $1 five days later. In the mid-1900s, interest rate caps were placed on these small loans with rates ranging from 24 to 42 percent. The first modern payday lender appeared in the late 1980s in Kansas City, and the industry grew rapidly during the 1990s. (1)

Prior to the 1990s, usury laws prohibited charging the exorbitantly high interest rates and fees that are commonly charged today. However, the banking industry began consolidating in the 1990s into the 2000s, significantly shrinking the number of banks in their pursuit of mergers and acquisitions. This closed a number of local bank branches, and accessing needed services became increasingly difficult for bank customers. Pressure was then put on state and federal legislators to allow these short-term, high-interest rate loans to be issued by non-financial lenders. Today's payday loan industry is the result of this lobbying.

Unfortunately, there is no national standard regarding this industry. There are fifty states in America and fifty different sets of regulations and laws concerning payday loans And believe it or not, they vary considerably from being illegal in some states to widely accepted in others. A lot of the differences are due to the states' attempts to protect consumers from predatory and other unscrupulous practices that some lenders were engaged in. Since there is no national standard, the states have enacted measures that they feel are appropriate in order for the payday industry to exist within their borders.

For example, in Georgia, payday lending is illegal if the loan is less than $3,000 and charges more than 16 percent APR. The Georgia Payday Lending Act of 2004 authorizes racketeering and felony charges against any violators, fines up to $25,000, and up to twenty-five years in prison for those convicted under the law. (2) Idaho takes a different approach and allows loans up to $1,000 at any interest rate the borrower is willing to pay. Missouri has another system that caps each new payday loan at $500 and limits the period to thirty-one days, but requires that interest on all authorized renewals may not exceed 75 percent. (3)

The range of minimum and maximum loan amounts also depends on the state where you obtain the loan. The amounts currently range from $50 to $1,000 per new loan. States allow a wide range of interest rates, which vary considerably from maximum flat rates on total loan amounts to fluctuating rates on unpaid balances. Some state regulations provide for fees, and others permit lenders to charge fees and lend without limits.

So why has the federal government not standardized the payday loan industry? The simple answer is that payday loans are treated as ordinary loans by the federal government. That means they are government regulated at the federal level according to the Truth in Lending Act (TILA), which requires full disclosure in writing of the annual percentage rate (APR) and the total finance charge as a dollar amount. (4) The TILA, which was passed in 1968, was intended to protect consumers by requiring lenders to disclose the APR so that borrowers could make loan term comparisons.

The annual percentage rate was also created by Congress as a standard simple interest rate measure calculated yearly. Most fees are included in the calculation. The calculation also takes into account the repayment term and the principal reduction as payments are made. The APR is used to compare interest rates on a variety of loans, including mortgages and auto loans. Payday loans are just another category of lending to the federal government.

The Federal Reserve Board finally required payday lenders to disclose the APR on payday loans in 2000. Payday loans could no longer be called cash advance loans and bypass TILA requirements. Until 2006, other than a few general loan provision requirements, payday loans were regulated by the individual states with very little involvement from the federal government. In 2006, the federal government felt it had no choice but to intervene, because the payday lenders' practices were starting to directly affect military personal, security clearance requirements, and military deployment schedules. Change had become necessary.

The Fiscal Year 2007 Military Authorization Act was enacted with provisions that limited lenders from giving military members payday loans that did not meet strict requirements. The law also prohibited lenders from charging more than 36 percent interest including all fees and charges on loans.

On February 26, 2009, Congress passed the Payday Loan Reform Act, which amended the Truth in Lending Act yet again. Due to payday lender lobbying, it does not limit the APR. It does establish a number of disclosure requirements that require clear descriptions of loan terms, a loan cost warning, and making credit counseling available as well as prohibiting threatening criminal prosecution for nonpayment. In addition, the consumer must receive a legible agreement copy and interest-free extended payment plans.

The 2010 Dodd-Frank Wall Street Reform and Consumer Protection Act created the Consumer Financial Protection Bureau (CFPB), which began its first supervision program to oversee non-bank financial services in January, 2012. Payday lenders are included in the non-bank designation and are now subject to federal oversight to ensure that all laws and regulations are met.

However, payday lenders still find ways to circumvent the restrictive state laws and the federal government's attempt to curb the industry. Some payday lenders engage in a practice known as "rate exportation" or "rent-a-bank" in order to get around states' restrictive usury laws. In these scenarios, a payday lender forms a business relationship with a nationally chartered financial institution with favorable APR limits or no limits at all in order to transact their lending. In such situations, the laws governing the chartered bank will generally take precedent over the state's usury laws. This precedent was set by the US Supreme Court case *Marquette National Bank v. First of Omaha Service Corp* case in 1978. The Supreme Court unanimously determined that nationally chartered banks were obligated to follow only the usury laws of the states in which they are founded, not the laws of each state in which they do business. This allowed nationally chartered banks to export their rates to any state. The credit card business was built on this strategy.

The Skyrocketing Annual Percentage Rate (APR)

To understand the payday loan controversy, you must first understand some details of the payday loan process and the APR.

Process

Payday loans are typically two-week loans. In Colorado, some payday loans can be extended up to six months. However, in most states, payday loans are to be repaid within a one- or two–week period, which coincides with most peoples' pay schedules. On the loan due date, the payday lender will cash the postdated check or complete the automatic withdrawal of loans and fees, which include the interest. The loan is paid off, and the transaction is complete. In many cases, the borrower will ask the lender to roll over the loan and extend the due date for another term equal to the original term, which may be one week, two weeks, a month, or any other term they agree upon. The simple interest and fees are charged again on the same principal.

The "rollover" or rolling forward the principal balance of the loan is where the controversy over payday loans usually begins. For example, if someone borrows $100 for two weeks at 17 percent interest, the lender will state that the interest rate is 17 percent for the two-week period, which is true. When the loan is rolled over, the 17 percent is now charged again on the new balance for the next two-week period. Each time the loan is rolled over, the balance generally increases, and the interest rate is charged again.

To make loans comparable for analysis, the APR is required to be stated. The loans' short-term interest rate will look quite different when viewed as an annual rate, and that is one reason that many payday lenders do not want to advertise the true annual rate.

Payday loan = interest rate of 17 percent for two weeks

Payday loan = 17 percent x twenty-six two-week periods for a year, which equals 442 percent

Stating an APR of 442 percent provides an entirely new perspective of the payday loan. The average payday borrower in the United States makes nine loan transactions per year that usually represent a single loan rolled nine times. It is estimated that over twelve million people are currently in a lending cycle that involves a 400 percent APR. This cycle of indebtedness supports the payday lending business. In fact, an average payday loan with a 300 percent APR that is rolled over for four months would accumulate interest that actually exceeds the principal, forcing the borrower into deeper debt. (5) If everyone paid his or her short-term loans on time without rolling over the loan, chances are, the industry would be much smaller.

However, the industry knows the difficult financial circumstances of some of its borrowers and has profited immensely because of those borrowers' financial misfortunes. Until recently, industry profit margins have been calculated in excess of 20 percent annually. That is quite a feat considering the lackluster returns in traditional business enterprises. In 1990, estimates suggested that fewer than fifty payday companies existed in the United States. Just ten years later, there were about fourteen thousand payday businesses. Less than a decade after that, twenty thousand were in operation. Some cities in certain parts of the country might seem to have more payday lenders than fast food restaurants. With remnants of a depressed economy still front and center in many areas, it is no wonder that payday loan industry growth has been on the uptick.

Benefits vs. Drawbacks at the Heart of the Controversy

As you can see, despite the controversy concerning that surrounds payday loan APR, the industry is thriving. According to the Consumer Federation of America in Washington, D.C., there are over twenty-two thousand payday lenders operating in the Unites States and making over $40 billion in loans each year. The loans still serve a purpose because they are easily accessible and serve clients who could not obtain an emergency loan anywhere else. Proponents of payday loans argue that people sometimes need money quickly, and payday lenders are their only source of help.

The main drawback to payday loans is the high interest rate and fees. The loans are also very easily rolled forward, thus accumulating more and more debt. A traditional bank loan would require the borrower to pay the loan and then take out a brand-new loan they still needed money. Since payday lenders let the same loan roll over from period to period while charging new fees each time, a person can end up with a loan they cannot afford to repay. In fact, opponents of payday loans believe that the industry drives many consumers into bankruptcy by charging fees that are difficult to repay and encouraging loan rollovers.

However, the debate really goes much deeper than just the APR. Payday lenders tend to target consumers who are less likely to be able to repay the loan. People who have many assets and an emergency savings account do not normally use payday lenders. Low-income individuals and families and senior citizens desperate for money frequent payday lenders. The very fact that the clients have limited financial resources means they will have a difficult time paying the loan and fees. To complicate matters, most payday loans are borrowed to pay monthly bills, not emergency expenses, which means these consumers use the service regularly. And in some cases, when payday arrives, the entire paycheck is needed for living expenses, and the borrower still does not have enough to pay back the loan. The borrower has no choice but roll it over again. From that perspective, it is easy to see why opponents of payday lending call the practice nothing more than a trap.

In addition, payday lender storefront businesses are located disproportionately in Latino and African American neighborhoods. Payday lenders are eight times as concentrated in Latino and African American neighborhoods in comparison to mostly white neighborhoods. This means the fees paid to payday lenders are not going back into the communities they serve. (6)

Though payday lenders say they do not target minorities, the numbers indicate that minorities compose the majority of payday lender business. For these reasons, payday lending is called predatory lending by its opponents.

Alternatives to Payday Loans

One of the first and best alternatives to payday loans is a loan through a bank or other financial institution. Recently, some financial institutions created small loan programs designed for those who need an emergency loan and have income that can be used as collateral. A number of credit unions, in particular, have set up small loan programs that are the equivalent of salary-advance loans.

Another alternative is to borrow cash on a credit card with the understanding that the full amount will be paid off with your next paycheck. In fact, many credit cards have a payment grace period. You can borrow the money and pay it back within twenty-one days without paying any interest. Even if you must pay interest, it will almost always be less than the payday loan interest charges.

A third possible option is to call the creditor and try to work out an agreement that gives you more time to catch up a delinquent payment. This alternative applies when you need the payday loan to pay a utility bill or to catch up a car payment.

Sometimes, it is possible to borrow a small amount of money from family or friends. Even if the loan includes interest, it is sure to be far less than interest paid on a payday loan. One other option is to talk to your employer about a paycheck advance or a small loan. Some employers and creditors are willing to work with you because your success and financial well-being will affect them.

There are also local government and nonprofit organizations within most communities that are willing to work with most people to improve their financial situation. These organizations might lend funds and provide the necessary financial counseling to break the cycle of payday loans and other debt dependencies.

Is it a Moral Debate?

Strong advocates for payday lending reform are working tirelessly to convince Congress to ban the payday lending businesses. However, many believe these lenders are filling the gap left by a financial industry is uninterested in serving the poor and in making small emergency loans. The Center for Responsible Lending has proposed a solution that would require federal legislation that caps the APR at 36 percent and limits the number of rollovers allowed annually. So far, the lobbyists for the payday lending industry have convinced Congress that such restrictions would restrict legitimate businesses that service the unmet needs of borrowers.

Sometimes, figuring out the right and wrong side of this debate is difficult, but one thing is clear: reforms need to be made in this industry, because if the financially unfortunate among us fail, then taxpayers will have to step in to support them. Therefore, it is in all of our best interests to ensure that the right reforms are enacted obliging payday lenders to be accountable and responsible lenders. The message has to be clear that if they are preying on the less fortunate, then they are, in reality, preying on taxpayers, and that will not be permitted.

SECTION 2

Personal Finance

CHAPTER 5

A Budget for All Your Needs

Say the word "budget," and people tend to cringe a bit, even if they believe budgeting is a good idea. They cringe because the word implies discipline, patience, and sacrifice. However, thinking of budgeting in only those terms is unfair, because budgeting is not about sacrifice. It is about prioritizing needs and wants, learning to live within available financial resources, and achieving financial goals. Viewed from that perspective, personal and family budgets are important tools for financial success.

Many people discover they have no idea how they have spent their paychecks once the money is gone. After you get paid, the relief at having money in the bank can lead to careless spending. For some, even buying a few "little extras" can leave them short on funds for days or weeks. Though budgeting may seem tedious, it is a plan for allocating income so that essential expenses are paid while also creating a plan for debt repayment and savings.

Frankly, budgets are good for everyone from the wealthy to the low income. Anyone can overspend, fail to save, miss financial goals, and live beyond their means. It is all a matter of scale. It is true that middle-class and low-income persons may have a tighter budgeting plan; nonetheless, budgets can help everyone keep their spending on target and enable people to manage their incomes and expenses in a way that benefits their financial futures.

Budgeting is a good strategy for all age groups, whether someone is just starting out, is accumulating assets, or has retired. The specific expenses on your budget may change throughout your life, but the need for long-term financial planning does not change. In the following sections, I will review the types of personal and family budgets and discuss the various factors that can lead to budgeting success or failure.

Individual Budgets for Individual Needs

In general, a budget is a financial plan that schedules income and expenses. It should reflect honest and reasonable goals for spending or saving, depending on the purpose of the budget. So in that regard, it is a strategic plan for future success. You can prepare one or multiple budgets that serve different purposes, and each budget should be equally honest about the income, expenses, and goals.

A budget can be created for any purpose, including managing monthly or annual income and expenses, managing investments, purchasing large or expensive assets, emergency spending, or vacations. In general, you should start with your monthly budget, and that budget can be supported by other detailed budgets.

For example, you may develop a household budget and include the amount you will save toward the purchase of a new vehicle or to make investments. The supporting budgets would then show details for just those goals. The vehicle-purchase budget would indicate the monthly savings amount that would be set aside for purchase of the vehicle, while the listed expenses would include the purchase of the vehicle, the cost of a vehicle license, required up-front insurance amounts, and so on. The common types of major personal budgets include the following:

Line Item Budget

Most people use a spreadsheet format and identify all planned income listed with each expense item. Each month, they compare their actual income and expenses to the budgeted items. Some people like to budget weekly when developing the discipline to stick with a budget. Whichever you choose, the important thing is to monitor it according to schedule.

A typical line item budget may look like the following. (1)

Category	Annual Budget	Monthly Budget
Income		
Earned Income		
Taxes		
Net Take Home Pay		
Other Income		
Total Income		
Expenses		
House Payment or Rent		
Insurance (House or Rental)		
Food		
Gas		
Loan Payment (vehicle)		
Vehicle Insurance Vehicle Maintenance		
Insurance (health, life)		
Medical and Dental Expenses		
Loans (Secured/Unsecured)		
Credit Card Payments		
Clothing		
Personal (Hygiene, gifts etc.)		
Utilities (Electric, Gas, Heating Oil, Garbage Sewer)		
Telephone and Internet Expenses		
Entertainment		
Emergencies		
Other		
Savings		
Investments		
Total Expenses		
Net Income (= zero)		

Realistically assessing your income and expenses and then establishing financial goals is necessary for financial planning. You may want to buy a house, start a family, or save for retirement. That would be built into your budget as a savings plan. The sample budget sheet obviously does not include every expense item like child support or expenses particular to your life. You should add separate expense lines for every significant expense item in your life.

Percentage Budget

The percentage budget develops major expense categories based on a percentage of income. For example, living expenses should not exceed 26 percent of your income, and the mortgage payment including house insurance and property taxes should not exceed 30 percent of your income.

First, you calculate monthly income:

Earned Net Income
Investment Income
Other
Total Income

Then, you determine the categories you want to budget and assign a percentage to each. The expense category total should equal 100 percent. Following is an example of this type of budget.

Category	Budgeted % of Income	Budgeted Amount	Actual % of Income	Actual Amount
House Payment	30%			
Living Expenses	48%			
Unplanned Expenses	2%			
Savings	10%			
Investments	10%			
Total Expenses	100%			

Major Event or Asset Budget

A major event or asset budget represents financial planning for a major purchase, which could include:

- Down payment on a house
- Vehicle purchase
- Vacation
- Moving
- Furniture
- Medical or dental expenses (new baby or major dental work)

- College tuition and expenses
- Wedding

The total amount you choose to save for these events based on the budgeted expenses will become a separate amount in the line-item budget, similar to a savings target amount, or it can be included in the general savings amount.

Emergency Fund Budget

Everyone should budget for an emergency fund, because everyone has emergencies. An emergency fund should be easily and quickly accessible, because by its very definition, an emergency gives little warning. A reasonable goal is to save at least three months' of living expenses, and six months' is even better. This money is above and beyond any savings or investment funds you have in other accounts.

If accumulating three full months' of living expenses seems impossible at the moment, it is still important to set a goal of some reasonable amount that could be used for emergencies like the following:

- Medical expenses
- Vehicle repairs
- House repairs (e.g., new roof, remodel)
- Job loss
- Family needs
- Household expenses (like appliance replacements)

It is simple to bypass saving for an emergency because you do not think about these types of expenses on a day-to-day basis. You cross your fingers that the car will keep running or that your employer will not have to scale back its workforce. However, you have to ask yourself, "*What would?*" *What would* you do if the car needed a new transmission? *What would* you do if you broke your arm and could not work for a month? *What would* you do if your elderly parents could not pay their utilities bills?

To develop an emergency budget, you must list possible emergencies that could happen within the current year. Let the ideas flow freely, make a list of the ideas, and then attach an amount to each. It is difficult to estimate expenses related to a medical emergency, but consider your health insurance copays; or if you have no insurance, remember that the emergency room visit still needs to be paid for. Assume the emergency will prevent you from working for a week or two. This is the type of thought process that will lead to a better understanding of how large the emergency budget needs to be to give you some financial cushion.

An emergency budget can be funded with an amount set aside each payday, and that amount is treated like a line-item expense. It is also possible to commit to funding the emergency account using unexpected refunds such as money from a raise you get at work and money once used to pay a debt, like a credit card that is now paid off.

The money you save should be deposited in an account you can access within a week, at the most. These types of accounts include:

- Local bank savings account
- Online savings account with checking privileges or local office withdrawal option
- Money market accounts with no penalty for withdrawals
- Checking account

Investment Budget

Similar to the event budget, the goal of an investment budget is to establish a budget that enables you to meet investment goals. The investment budget is based on your long-term financial goals. Unfortunately, people often put off developing investment budgets until they are older and realize the available time for retirement planning is getting short. The sooner you develop an investment budget, the better. It is estimated that approximately seventy-five million people do not save anything for retirement and that 30 percent of adults do not have a savings account. (2)

An investment budget can begin with a simple savings account or a pre-tax retirement plan available through an employer. Any account that earns interest or dividends that can be reinvested or will experience earnings growth (or capital loss) qualifies as an investment. Though some would not classify a savings account as an investment, it is an account that earns interest, and once you have enough money in savings to cover at least three months of living expenses, you can begin to invest in other types of accounts like mutual funds, Roth IRAs, and retirement accounts.

The investment budget is a moving target because the more money you have available to invest, the broader your investment choices become. For example, you may start with a savings account budget earning 2 percent interest. After you have accumulated three months' of living expenses, the budget can expand to include contributions to the employer's retirement savings plan. Eventually, you will enter the stock market and buy growth stocks or start a 401(k). At some point, you will want to diversify your portfolio for security. Diversifying enables you to manage economic upturns and downturns if you invest regularly. For example, at some point, you may balance out your portfolio by investing in bond funds, EFTs, or precious metals, but will eventually change from growth to income stocks for less risky investments as you get closer to retirement.

Your goal is to eventually invest 15 percent of your income in an investment portfolio. The sample worksheet shows 10 percent for investments. That percent can periodically increase as you pay off loans and credit cards.

Family Budgets

The more people you have in your household, the more expenses you are going to have. However, a budget for a group of people like a family will have to consider all of the family's needs, not just your own. The previous budget discussion applies to everyone, but there are more things to consider when the budget is for a family.

Line Item Budget

The line item budget for a family may include expense items for additional family needs like college expenses and braces for the children. Budgeted income early in life as a single person usually consists primarily of earned income. As people grow older, invest, and go through the cycles of life, other sources of income are generated. When developing a budget, you should include these sources:

- Employment income
- Investment income
- Child support
- Disability income
- Social Security payments
- Rental income
- Pensions
- Other including royalties, gifts, bonuses, legal awards, and so on
- Daycare fees
- School activity fees and supplies
- Cultural or athletic fees (e.g., music lessons, sports team fees, etc.)
- Tuition and fees
- Student loan payments

Only certain income(s) should be included in the budget. If you expect to receive a one-time income, it is a good idea to use it to either pay off debt or put it into a savings, emergency, or investment account. Income should also include only net amounts, so it is important to deduct all taxes and count only on net income. If money will be paid to you as a lump sum, then deduct the taxes on a separate budget line and figure the net income yourself.

Reviewing a full year of bank account statements and cash receipts is an excellent way to make sure you budget realistically and do not exclude expenses. To those amounts, you would add new items of which you are aware, such as daycare fees.

Envelope Budget

Some individuals and families have trouble maintaining a detailed line-item budget. A visual type of budgeting is more to their liking and can be a simple way to start a budget.

The envelope budget involves identifying individual envelopes for each major category of discretionary spending items. Discretionary spending refers to any spending that is not fixed, meaning you have control over the amount you spend on these things. A mortgage payment is not discretionary, whereas the food and entertainment budgets can be managed.

You would place the amount of cash you budgeted for that item for the budget period in the corresponding envelope. If you get paid twice a month, then you might set up an envelope with a two-week budget amount. If you budget monthly, then a month's worth of grocery money, gas money, or entertainment money should be placed in the envelope. When the money is spent, you cannot "borrow" from a different envelope.

In fact, the envelope budget will only be successful if you are diligent and adhere to your budget. This method can accommodate debit card purchases for items like gas if you substitute written chits for cash. Remove a chit each time you use your debit card. It will take sincere effort, though, to adhere to the envelope budget style if you accommodate debit card purchases. At the end of the budget period, unspent money should be used to pay debt like credit cards or added to savings or retirement accounts.

Family Emergency Fund Budget

Following the same guidelines as discussed for individual budgets to accumulate an emergency account will also work for a family emergency fund. There are a few differences, though. For one thing, the budget will need to be larger to cover particular family needs beyond what you need for yourself. For example, you may want to budget for:

- New baby expenses
- Six months' of income or more should you lose your job
- Children's emergency expenses
- Possible special medical needs of family members
- Weather emergencies causing house damage

The money should be easily accessible, but you must resist the temptation to withdraw on a moment's notice. Though some people open a checking or savings account in a bank that is different from their main bank, the money is still quite easy to withdraw. It is a good idea to keep the money in an account that may take you at least a few days to access so it cannot easily be used for everyday living expenses.

Investment Budget

The investment budget may not be one of the first budgets you set up. Instead, you may need to pay off credit cards or establish a savings accounts and emergency account before budgeting for investments. You can begin budgeting for investments long before you can commit significant funds by contributing a small amount every payday or once a month to an investment account. The power of regular investing and compounding cannot be overstated.

For example, if you began investing only $10 per month in a Roth IRA starting at age twenty-five and were faithful in your contributions, by the age of sixty-five, you could be earning approximately $125 to $150 each month as tax-free income. That may not sound like a lot, but even someone earning minimum wage could be investing over the years.

Following are some guidelines for budgeting investment funds:

- Save regularly, even if you contribute only a small amount to an investment account
- Have an amount automatically deducted from your paycheck and put into an account that earns compound interest
- Always participate in a retirement account that allows employers to contribute matching funds like the SEP-IRA or SIMPLE-IRA
- Begin with an IRA if you are just starting to save and worry about expanding into other investments like a 401(k) as your income grows

- Select an investment account that fits your particular situation and retirement goals (There are different types of IRAs)
- Choose investments that have an acceptable risk level

Investing regularly even when you cannot afford to invest very much will help you develop the budgeting discipline needed to improve your financial status over the years. Also, developing an investment diversification plan gives you protection no matter which way the economy turns.

College Budget

A college budget may be tied closely to an investment budget. First, you need to estimate how much you will need for college tuition, fees, and books by the time your child is ready to attend. The amount you will need to save is sizable, because college expenses are expected to increase approximately 6 percent every year. A child who is currently five years old and will attend a college *currently* costing $40,000 for a four-year education will cost approximately $95,000 by the time that child is eighteen due to inflation and other factors.

Obviously, the sooner you start saving for college, the easier it will be to save monthly. In the example given, if you are able to earn an average of 7 percent in an after-tax college savings fund each year, it will be necessary to save about $290 each month to reach the goal of $95,000. The lower the interest rate on savings, the more you will need to save each month.

There are college savings plans available called the 529 Savings Plan and the Education Savings Account (ESA). The 529 Savings Plan is offered and managed by either an educational institution or the state. This plan offers federal tax benefits that allow the tax-deferred investment to grow and be withdrawn for college costs tax-free. (3)

The Coverdell Education Savings Account, once called an Education IRA, is another way to save for college. Earnings grow tax-free. Distributions, where they are used for IRS-qualified expenses, are not taxed as long as they are less than the education expenses at the eligible educational institution where the student is enrolled. However, total contributions are limited to $2,000 annually.

Successful Budgeting and Saving

Budgeting is an ongoing process. That is one of the most important points to learn from this discussion. Most people understand identifying sources of income and listing expenses. What they lack is an understanding of the fact that establishing a budget promotes financial discipline and that a budget must be constantly monitored and then revised as life circumstances change. In other words, a budget is a moving target designed to fit current and long-term goals.

Successful budgeting requires more than simply putting numbers on paper or in a spreadsheet. To be successful, you must evaluate the information you glean from your bank statements and cash receipts. The first step is to determine if any particular expense is out of line. Do you spend too much on groceries or clothes? Did you fail to save any money last year? Are you still paying for last year's vacation on your credit card?

Asking yourself these kinds of questions can give you a perspective and guide your current year's budget. For example, you may decide to reduce the amount spent on groceries by 10 percent by cooking more foods from scratch and then move the 10 percent saved to the emergency budget.

Budgets can be written on paper, entered in a spreadsheet software program, or prepared using budgeting software purchased online or at the local office supply store. As you begin to get into the habit of budgeting, one of the first things you have to decide is whether you will budget daily, weekly, or monthly. The monthly budget will give you the most realistic guidance for future periods. Ideally, the expenses should be recorded on a daily basis, but weekly, at a minimum. Waiting until the end of the month to record expenses makes it more likely you will miss recording some of them.

At the end of each month, evaluate whether you are over or under budget. If you have gone over budget, then identify the specific reason and begin a new month ready to start again. Repeat this process each month and then annually. Sometimes, you will need to adjust the monthly budgets. For example, the electric company may raise rates. If you paid off a credit card, the budgeted payment can be distributed to cover a higher budgeted utility line item and the balance into savings. If you end up overspending your monthly budget, try to make up some of the overspending in the next month.

There are a couple of caveats to modifying budgets:

- Only modify the budget for legitimate reasons out of your control
- Do not modify the budget because you are having trouble adhering to it

In other words, it is important to rework the budget, but only in a way that keeps you on budget. The reality is that the utility company may raise rates, but your income will probably stay the same. In the future, as your income goes up, you can possibly invest more money while continuing to live within your old income.

"Cookie jar" accounting may help those who need to ensure that unspent money that has been budgeted is saved. The cookie jar concept could include an actual clear jar to hold surplus cash, but a better choice is to open a special interest-bearing bank account and deposit the surplus cash at the end of each month. This reward system reinforces budgeting.

One of your first main goals is to pay off credit card debt and high interest rate loans to free up money for savings and investments.

Avoiding Budgeting Failure

Budgets fail for a lot of reasons, and you should be aware of those reasons before you begin budgeting. A budget failure means you overspent the monthly budget or did not meet a savings goal. Most people prepare a budget with a sense of hope. A budget represents taking control of your current finances and future financial security.

When efforts to live within a budget go awry, it is human nature to throw caution to the wind. You agree to go out to dinner with friends and spend three days' worth of food budget on one meal. Perhaps you could not resist the new smartphone upgrade, or the car broke down before you could establish an emergency fund. There are hundreds of reasons why people go over budget despite good intentions. Here are a few:

- Budget was not realistic and was impossible to adhere to
- You did not record expenditures daily or weekly, so you do not know how much budget remains unexpended or how much is already over-expended
- Budget left out periodic expenses like a six-month insurance premium
- Emergencies cost more than the emergency fund allowed
- Budget is too complex and takes too much time to track
- You get frustrated and tired of worrying about spending details
- Family members will not cooperate

When you do not follow your budget or fail to spend the time needed to keep appropriate track of expenses, it is tempting to just go back to your old ways. A better approach is to determine exactly why you failed to meet your budget and then take steps to correct what went wrong. The one thing you should not do is stop budgeting. Do not begin spending with abandon; just get back on track and do better the next month.

Why Budgeting Succeeds

Budgeting fails for many reasons, but millions of people find budgeting success for just as many reasons. Certain actions will significantly improve your chances of reaching financial goals:

- Develop an honest and realistic budget
- Faithfully track your expenses
- Use budgeting tactics that work for you
- Include the whole family in the budgeting process
- Regularly assess your progress toward long-term financial goals
- Welcome opportunities to save money, like buying a used car instead of a new car
- Learn delayed gratification
- Plan for future purchases of items you can live without now
- Take pride in saving money and paying down debt

The process of identifying financial goals, budgeting monthly expenses, and saving money for a variety of purposes requires discipline and persistence. Budgeting can help you enjoy the freedom of knowing you have financial goals, have a plan to reach those goals, and that you are prepared for financial emergencies. The really good news is that budgeting works for everyone, regardless of age or income level.

CHAPTER 6

Learning to Respect Debt: The Reduction Plan

Debt is one of those topics that can either make you smile, if you have little or none, or make you hide, if your obligations are excessive. Very few people are debt free, but that is because some debt is acceptable. However, even acceptable debt, like a mortgage payment, can become unacceptable when the payment is too high. The question is: What is too high? The answer is: it depends on a variety of factors, including age, income, lifestyle, and financial goals.

The topic of debt is complex since each person's circumstance is different. According to the Federal Reserve, as of November, 2011, the total outstanding revolving credit stood at $793 billion and non-revolving credit was at $1.6 trillion. This represents a total of over $2.4 trillion in credit debt. By anyone's standards, that is a lot of debt. During the 2008 recession, consumer credit declined as financial institutions tightened credit availability, but lending is on the rise again. Major credit issuers include commercial banks, finance companies, credit unions, the federal government, savings and loans institutions, nonfinancial businesses, and other types of lenders using securitized assets as collateral. (1)

The most telling number is the fact that the third quarter of 2011saw $5.63 billion in credit card charge-offs, $1.26 billion in write-offs on other consumer loans, and $1.52 billion in charge-offs on residential property. (2) Charge-offs represent debt that had to be written off because it could not be collected by the lender. In other words, it is the equivalent of bad debt.

As Americans begin to increase their debt load post-recession, it is time to realize that debt can be managed in a responsible manner. Responsible debt management means only assuming essential debt, keeping the debt-to-income ratio within reasonable levels, and establishing a financial plan that includes scheduled debt reduction. The only way to achieve these goals is to understand how to analyze your debt, deal with problem debt, and develop a reasonable debt-reduction plan based on available resources.

Learning to Analyze Debt

The first step in the debt-reduction process is learning to analyze your current debt position, which includes identification, prioritizing, and dealing with delinquencies. Once you understand your debt status, the next natural step is to analyze the financial resources available to reduce your debt.

The best place to begin analyzing debt is by obtaining a copy of your credit report. Some state agencies have a mechanism in place where you might be able to get a free copy of your credit report from the national credit-reporting agencies. The three major agencies are:

- Equifax (www.equifax.com) at 1-800-685-1111
- Experian (www.experian.com) at -200-397-3742
- Trans Union (www.transunion.com) at 1-800-916-8800

The credit reports list only debts reported to the agencies and credit scores that are used by lenders who need to decide whether to approve your loan or credit. Credit scoring is based on a complex formula and scoring system that includes a lot of factors, including your current debt status, credit history, and even recent changes that might show signs of improvement or financial problems. The higher your score is, the less financially risky you are considered to be.

Each of the credit-reporting agencies uses a different scale, but in general, the following applies:

- 499 and below: bad (no) credit
- 500-549: bad credit (but may still get some credit like high fee credit cards)
- 550-599: poor credit
- 600-649: below average
- 650-699: average credit
- 700-749: good credit
- 750-799: very good credit
- 800 and above: excellent credit

The debt listing on the credit report probably accounts for the majority of your loans and all of your credit card debt. However, you need to remember that the credit report will not include debt incurred by borrowing from friends, family members, payday lenders, or others who do not report to the credit-reporting agencies. When making a list of debts, you will have to include those loans also.

The credit report contains a lot of information including:

Personal Info

- Address
- Place of employment
- Criminal public records
- Civil judgments
- Bankruptcies

Debt Data

- Home mortgage
- Credit cards
- Bank and credit card loans
- Vehicle loans

Debt Status

- Accounts in collection
- Accounts with negative information
- Individual accounts with terms, credit limits, balances and payment histories
- Inquiries by companies and lenders

Following are the first steps to take to analyze your debt in preparation for developing a debt-reduction plan to deal with existing debt problems.

Prioritizing Debt

1. Make a comprehensive list of all your debts. Using a spreadsheet program is ideal, because it can be reordered based on chosen criteria like balance and interest rates. On the spreadsheet or a piece of paper, enter or write down:

    - Account name
    - Balance
    - Interest rate
    - Monthly payment amount
    - Annual fees
    - Totals for debt and for monthly payments

2. Consider a monthly budget that identifies monthly income sources and current expenses. The difference between income and expenses tells you how much

money is available each month to pay off debt faster and create a savings account. All the expenses incurred should be listed, including the mortgage payment, groceries, credit card payments, loan payments, and entertainment.

This is where people quickly discover they do not have any money remaining after paying bills and supporting their current lifestyle. If you spend all of your income plus some, the next step is to free up some money by making changes in your lifestyle. For example, you should reduce weekend entertainment expenses and commit to eating out less. You may be able to drive less and save gas money, commit to buying only necessities, or switch to a cheaper cell phone plan, and so on.

3. The third step is to prioritize the list of debts. There are no hard-and-fast rules for prioritizing debts, but factors to consider include:

   - Interest rate
   - Balance over credit limit
   - Delinquent accounts
   - Accounts with balances over half the credit limit
   - Accounts close to being paid off
   - Accounts with high fees

   Based on these criteria, you would put delinquent accounts at the top of the list, followed by those with balances over the credit limit. Next on the list would be accounts you can pay off quickly, because the payments that were going to those accounts can then be applied to the high interest rate and fee accounts and then the remaining accounts.

   If you are not delinquent on accounts, the high-interest credit card accounts and payday loans will be first on the list. The mortgage is last on the list because of the loan size and because mortgages usually have the lowest interest rates compared to other loans.

4. Finally, you want to put all this information into a single debt-reduction plan. There are two things going on at the same time. First, you use any remaining amount after paying monthly obligations to begin catching up and paying off debts on your prioritized list. Second, you work on a reduction plan that resolves serious debt issues and leads to a long-term healthy financial status.

Delinquencies

Resolving delinquent debt is important. Delinquencies on your credit report hurt in many ways and not just when you are trying to buy a house or vehicle. More businesses are doing credit checks for a number of reasons, including for life insurance and employment. The status of your debt indicates your ability to live responsibility and within your financial means and your seriousness about meeting contractual obligations. Therefore, your debt status reflects your personal qualities.

Getting into debt is easy, but getting out of debt is much more difficult. Yet anyone can do it with some perseverance, determination, and the right approach. When accounts like credit card debts become delinquent, the late fees, penalties, and interest can quickly turn a delinquent account into an unmanageable one. Like a snowball that gets bigger and bigger as it rolls down the mountain, a delinquent account will sink deeper into delinquency, especially if the payments you are making are mostly for late payment fees, other account fees, and interest on the account's growing balance. Eventually, some people just give up trying to pay, and the account goes to a collection agency.

Delinquencies and collection activity reported is very damaging to a credit report. Despite the large number of charge-offs I noted earlier, lenders go to great lengths to collect on accounts before charging them off. They are not in the business of lending so that they can later write-off the money, and they will take account holders to court to obtain judgments, which add another black mark to your credit report. Many of the charge-offs are also due to consumer bankruptcies, which can remain on credit reports for ten years.

Therefore, one of the best approaches to getting an account back under control is to contact the lenders directly. Since the fees and interest rates make paying off the accounts extremely difficult, start negotiations with the lenders by seeing if they are willing to lower or modify the interest rates and other fees on the account. You might be surprised how many credit cards issuers will consider:

- Writing off or lowering delinquency fees
- Lowering interest rates
- Moving high interest rate amounts to lower interest rate credit cards

If the lender refuses to lower fees and interest rates, you can then consider other resources to pay off delinquent amounts, catch up payments, or pay off balances. For example, you may be able to use home equity line of credit funds with a lower interest rate to pay off credit cards if the loan is already in place. It is difficult to borrow money to improve your financial position if you have accounts with delinquent status. But it is worth a try.

You should also investigate whether consolidating debts into one account makes sense. One or more delinquent credit card balances can be moved to credit cards with available credit in good standing. The delinquent accounts can then be closed.

Delinquent loan payments also harm your credit. Sometimes, you can negotiate an agreement that allows you to catch up past due payments by paying a current payment plus a portion of the delinquent amount. The lender may also be willing to renegotiate the loan so you can start fresh. When dealing with delinquent accounts, the most important step is to contact the lender.

Deciding Which Financial Resources to Access

In the previous discussion, I mentioned using net income as the primary source of debt repayment, but there are other sources that can also be accessible depending on your financial situation. They include:

- Savings accounts
- Emergency funds
- 401(k) funds
- Investments
- Consolidation loans
- Equity loans

There are several points to keep in mind before withdrawing or borrowing certain funds, but, clearly, interest rates and tax penalties should be two of the most important. Each source of income must also be evaluated based on its own merits. For example, if you have an investment account earning 10 percent annually and a loan that costs you 8 percent per year, it would not make sense to withdraw money invested at a higher return rate or sell assets like stocks to pay off the loan just to get out of debt if other options are available.

It would also be shortsighted to drain a savings account and emergency funds to pay off debt if there are better alternatives, because that leaves you with no financial fallback for other potential emergencies. Though you could re-borrow money on the credit cards later should you pay them off now and not close the accounts, the net result would still leave you deeper in debt with high-interest-rate debt. You can consider using some savings, especially in circumstances where earnings on your savings account is far lower than the interest rate you are paying on the debt. Also, if you take into consideration that you will owe taxes on interest earnings and are actually earning a low or even negative interest rate because of those taxes, paying off debt might make more sense. This way, you save the cash outflow servicing interest payments. This strategy might reduce how much you can save in the short term, but over the long term, you are actually creating a situation where your savings can grow at a higher rate, because you are not making unnecessary interest payments on debt.

For example, assume you are earning 10 percent on savings or investments but paying 20 percent on credit card debt. The 10 percent in earnings is reduced by federal and state taxes, and in this case, we will assume these total taxes result in a 3 percent net reduction. By using the money in savings, you eliminate the expense associated with the 20 percent interest rate while losing the 7 percent net after-tax earnings on the saved dollars. As you can see, you still come out ahead by about 13 percent. If the credit card debt has a low or zero interest rate (some creditors offer 0 percent or low promo rates often for six to twelve months), depleting your savings would not make sense, especially if that is your only financial safety net.

Investors in search of potential financial resources might ask whether it makes sense to borrow against a 401(k) retirement plan or whether to take a distribution for the purpose of paying off debt. It simply depends. In general, your 401(k) does offer tax benefits, but it also has a mechanism in place so you can borrow against your account. Some 401(k) administrators have strict borrowing rules, so be sure to read the terms carefully. And the attractive part of that setup is that you will usually be paying competitive market rates of interest not to a bank or other lender, but to yourself!

However, to be clear, the net benefits of borrowing against your account are only realized when you pay back the borrowed funds. Also, if the rate on the loan you are paying back to your 401(k) is higher than the returns that the securities are generating, then you are actually coming out ahead. However, this is the upside.

One downside to borrowing against your 401(k) account is that the balance of funds working for you is then reduced by the borrowed monies. So if your 401(k) is doing really well, you are actually losing out on the gains you could be making with the money you borrowed. And even if your 401(k) does not have jaw-dropping returns, you can still lose out on the power of compounding factor. The time factor becomes evident when you borrow large amounts against your account for lengthy periods of time. Therefore, the amount of potential growth you missed out on due to the compounding power of time should be a critical part of the borrowing analysis.

Another downside is the potential for double taxation. This occurs because the 401(k) is generally set up as a tax-deferred retirement vehicle that also allows for contributions that do not get taxed until they are distributed at retirement, when your tax bracket is usually significantly lower. So, when does the problem of double taxation begin? When you start to pay back the money borrowed against the account, you are more than likely doing so with after-tax dollars. You pay the money owed back to your 401(k) when it continues its preferential tax-deferred status. When retirement comes around, you start withdrawing monies *and* possibly paying taxes on that same dollar you paid taxes on already. So tax implications must be considered in your borrowing analysis.

Another unfortunate downside scenario involves borrowing money and then losing your job. In this case, the loan must be paid back within sixty days, because it will be reclassified as a distribution. If you cannot pay it off within that tax period, the loan is then treated as a taxable distribution. You will have to pay income taxes and a penalty for early withdrawal if you are fifty-nine or younger.

Even if you choose to take a distribution instead of a loan to pay off your credit card or other debt, you now have less available for retirement. However, if you are delinquent on loans and are paying exorbitant fees and interest rates, using 401(k) funds may make sense to get on an even financial keel. It only makes sense, though, if you are fairly certain you will not lose your job. Debt collectors normally cannot touch 401(k) retirement money.

Another questionable financial resource concerns the use of mortgage funds or home equity funds. It seldom makes sense to refinance a house to pay off credit cards and loans that have terms than the house loan terms would be. And this option becomes even less attractive given the significant costs and sometimes hidden fees of refinancing. Even when mortgage rates are low, you are still talking about borrowing money for twenty to thirty years to pay off a credit card balance that could be paid off in less than ten years with minimum payments. You cannot possibly get ahead financially by making such a decision, unless you pay off your mortgage early, which is something that most people do not do!

A home equity loan, on the other hand, is sometimes a good way to consolidate debt. The equity loan interest is tax-deductible if you itemize deductions, and the loan's payback period is usually shorter than a mortgage's. Using a lower interest equity loan to pay off high interest debt can also get you out of debt at a faster pace. And since the equity loan is tax-deductible, the effective interest rate is lower than the actual interest rate by approximately 1.5 percent. For example, the equity loan may have an actual interest rate of 5 percent, but an effective rate of 3.5 percent due to the tax-deductible benefits. Compared to 18 percent on credit cards, 7 percent on student loans, or 7 to 10 percent on signature loans, the equity loan is definitely more appealing.

Once your credit cards are paid off, it is important to close the accounts and destroy those plastic cards, except maybe one for emergency purposes. The last things you want to do are borrow on an equity credit line, pay off the credit cards, and then charge them right back to their limits. Unfortunately, this happens more than it should and highlights the fact that some people are living above their means.

Deciding which financial resources to use to get out of debt is not always clear-cut. However, it is important to have analyzed your options and have a plan of attack against debt. The options open to debtors are to manage expenses to free up net income and then use the net income to begin paying more than minimum monthly payments. Paying off loans and credit card balances based on the prioritized debt list and negotiating better debt terms when possible are also important.

Getting Outside Help with Debt

By visiting www.usa.gov ("the US government's official web portal") and typing in "debt relief" in the search box, you will discover a wealth of information about debt relief for individuals, seniors, students, and credit cardholders. However, most of the resources are just that—information. The site has information about filing bankruptcy, debt collection laws, fair credit billing, choosing a credit counselor, settling debt, and so on. Information on public assistance programs for personal debt payments is noticeably missing.

The government does not directly help people pay off credit cards or personal loans. All the advertisements on the Internet and television offering to help consumers get personal debt relief are not telling the full story. You can get help with student loans and mortgage foreclosures, but unfortunately, that help is available only under certain circumstances and in very limited ways. The US government does, however, award grants to nonprofit debt counseling programs so that consumers have easier access to good debt advice and help negotiating with creditors.

- Foreclosure Avoidance Counselors: Free foreclosure prevention services funded by the US Government Home owner Affordability and Stability Plan and operated through the US Department of Housing and Urban Development (HUD).
- Making Home Affordable programs: These government-funded programs help home owners struggling to make mortgage payments negotiate mortgage and interest rate modifications, refinance loans, defer payment plans, or plan for an orderly transition out of the home without foreclosure; the program also offers help with refinancing homes that have a market value below the mortgage balance (negative equity).
- Student Loan Forgiveness or Relief: Several programs offer educational loan forgiveness if you do volunteer work with Volunteers in Service to America (VISTA), AmeriCorps, or Peace Corps or if you do serve in the military (including the Army National Guard), teach in low-income schools, or serve in a public interest or nonprofit position. In addition, if you fall on economic hardship like losing your job, the government may agree to a deferment or forbearance that would either reduce your payments or suspend them for a particular period of time. (3)

Except for the student loan forgiveness programs, the main drawback to the government programs is that debt is not erased. The debt is either refinanced or restructured. The student loan relief programs also may suspend or reduce payments or modify the payback period, but the interest will continue to accrue. With the high rate of foreclosures occurring due to the 2008 housing market collapse, a lot of people have wondered why the government does not step in and help home owners more with their loans. The US government operates on the principle that it does not have the right to interfere in a private contract. It can forgive student loans only because the contracts were made between the student and the government.

In the private world, you will find for-profit and nonprofit credit counseling organizations. Unfortunately, the term "nonprofit" implies that there is no fee attached to the service, but that is not true in all cases. Legally, the nonprofit designation means that profits are not distributed to shareholders, but are reinvested in the business. There are, however, some nonprofits that are truly service-fee free, and those usually operate on government grants or funding from the nonprofit organization.

Debt counseling agencies and organizations work with consumers to find ways to address unmanageable debt. The laws have been changed so that a business charging a fee cannot collect that fee before completing services like creating a restructured account payment plan or a consolidated debt payment is in place.

Debt assistance from outside organizations includes:

- Credit counseling: The counselor evaluates your debt position and helps you develop a workable plan for systematic debt reduction. Some lenders will lower your interest rate if you participate in a credit counseling program. You will have to ask the lenders, though, because they will not volunteer this information.

- Debt Consolidation: Debt consolidations sounds just like what it is—combining all your debt into one loan. Usually, the mortgage is excluded due to its size. The vehicle loan may or may not be included, depending on the type of loan you obtained. Mortgage and auto loans sometimes have penalties for early payment or the interest rates are so low that consolidation would not make sense unless you could not afford to make the payments. For debt consolidation to be a truly successful debt-reduction plan, it must be structured so that you pay less interest, are able to pay off debt quicker, or make a single payment that is lower than the sum total of the payments you were making. Otherwise, debt consolidation is simply a convenience that allows you to make only one monthly payment.

- Debt Management Plan (DMP): Using a reputable credit counseling organization, a credit counselor works with your creditors to obtain lower interest rates, waive fees, or lower monthly payment amounts only on unsecured debt. Once the debt management plan is in place and monthly payments are agreed upon, you are given a single payment amount to send to the credit counseling organization each month. The DMP then forwards payment to each creditor by the due dates. A fee for service is included in the total amount you pay to the DMP. The DMP cannot remove negative account information from your credit report.

- Debt Settlement Programs (DSP): In this type of plan, you work with a debt settlement company that acts as a mediator and negotiator with your unsecured debt lenders. The DSP tries to negotiate a lower debt amount, meaning the lender agrees to write off part of your debt. In some cases, you can continue to make payments, while in other situations, you must pay the lower amount in full to take advantage of the offer.

In the past, many DSPs were not legitimate. They charged a fee up front and then never attempted to settle debt obligations while telling consumers to stop making debt payments. Since the consumer stopped making payments, the accounts were reported as delinquent to credit-reporting agencies. As a result, new federal laws were passed and amendments were made to the Federal Trade Telemarketing Sales Rule that prohibit up-front fee collection before debt settlement or reduction occurs.

- Bankruptcy: Bankruptcy is a last resort to eliminate unmanageable debt that you have no hope of being able to pay in a reasonable amount of time. Additional discussion on bankruptcy follows in the next sections.
- Family and Friends: This is added as an option because, sometimes, it is possible to borrow money from family and friends. However, such a move is fraught with emotional risks if you fail to repay them as agreed. This is also a truly last resort. It is difficult enough to be in debt without alienating family members and friends by not repaying a loan. Also, it is fair to pay your family and friends interest because they are foregoing interest earnings by lending you money.

Any organization that you use for debt management, settlement, or restructuring should have certified credit counselors. The companies should also have a good reputation that can be verified through the Better Business Bureau, the Federal Trade Commission, or your state's attorney general's office. Unfortunately, there are a lot of people pulling scams on desperate consumers looking for debt relief. That is why it is important to exercise due diligence before relying on any organization. Remember, you should care more about your interest than anyone else does. Therefore, it makes the most sense to be actively involved and even proactive if you are serious about debt management.

Setting a Plan

A good debt reduction plan will be simple. Like personal or household budgeting, the more complex you make the plan, the more difficult it will be to adhere to it each month. In many cases, the best debt-reduction plan is intended to:

- Eliminate all non-essential spending
- Develop a realistic budget
- Monitor spending
- Negotiate with creditors if debt relief or more payment time is needed

- Borrow lower interest money to pay off unsecured debt
- Eliminate or lower debt by selling or exchanging assets like a new vehicle for a used one
- Aggressively pay on accounts

The debt-reduction plan must be incorporated into your current budget. Income and spending directly impact your ability to reduce and manage debt. Trying to look at a piece of the puzzle without looking at the whole picture can lead to poor decisions. For example, you may need to reduce certain expenses so that you can make more than minimum payments. Only by budgeting the revised payments that make up your debt-reduction plan can you keep track of your total monthly spending and know when adjustments need to be made.

Once you have analyzed your debt, it is time to develop a specific plan. The plan should be in writing or entered in a spreadsheet, and then you should:

- Create an account payment schedule with due dates
- Sign up for automatic bill payments to ensure that you stay on schedule and pay on time
- Review your debt-reduction plan each month to compare actual progress to planned progress
- Modify the plan as accounts are paid off or circumstances change
- Sign up for credit monitoring so you can regularly verify your improving credit status and ensure that no errors are made

A debt-reduction plan has many similarities to a household budget in that you determine what income is available to cover expenses and then budget actual payments. Budgets are not static and need to be reviewed periodically to make sure you are doing everything possible to reduce debt as quickly as possible.

As you pay off your credit cards and other loans, the final debt to review is your mortgage. Paying off your mortgage early or refinancing to lower the interest rate may seem to make sense, but, of course, it is not that simple. Home mortgage interest is a tax-deductible expense if you itemize on your tax return, and that, in effect, reduces your interest rate. If you are debt free other than a mortgage, you may decide to keep the interest deduction.

However, there are other factors to consider. You may want to pay off your house in order to eliminate debt before retirement. Even if you decide to sell your home when you retire, having no mortgage means you get to keep all of the after-tax sales money. You might want to free up the money you put into a mortgage payment and divert it to investment accounts. There are several ways to pay off a mortgage at a faster pace: (4)

- Make one extra payment each year on a thirty-year fixed-interest mortgage to take off seven years on the mortgage term
- Using money once paid for credit card or loan debt, add an additional amount to each payment, but make sure the mortgage company knows to apply it to principal
- Refinance your loan for a shorter term or lower interest rate
- Apply new income to your mortgage payment

The main disadvantage of funneling cash into an earlier mortgage payoff is that the cash could be used elsewhere. For example, you could increase your savings or investment accounts or increase the emergency account balance.

Throughout this discussion, I have talked about a variety of ways to pay down or eliminate current debt:

- Use net income to pay more than the minimum payment on accounts using the prioritized debt list
- Pay down the prioritized debt list from top to bottom, even if you can only make minimum payments
- Consolidate credit cards with balance transfers or by obtaining a debt consolidation loan
- Consolidate other loans via a consolidation loan
- Sell assets securitizing loans and use net cash to replace asset with one that costs less or does not require a loan (replace a new vehicle with a used vehicle)

It is also possible to use a strategy called "snowballing" to pay down credit card debt. You will make a minimum payment on all credit cards except the one with the highest interest rate or the lowest balance and then pay as much as possible on the last card. The goal is to pay off the last card as quickly as possible.

Once that card is paid off, do the same thing to another credit card, but increase the payment by the amount of the payment you were making on the paid-off credit card. You would then continue this procedure until all your credit card debt is paid.

As you can see, a debt-reduction plan requires a variety of steps and is not simply a matter of creating a schedule. You have to consider interest rates, taxes, available income, financial goals, and the type of debt. A lot of thought needs to be put into the plan to ensure you are paying off the debt in a way that is the most beneficial to your long-term financial health. Simply replacing one debt with another is not a good plan.

Life After the Debt-Reduction Plan

Once the debt-reduction plan is in place, the final step is to plan for a managed debt future. One of the first points I made in this discussion is that not all debt is bad. Sometimes, you will need to borrow money for major purchases or to pay for emergencies if you do not have an emergency fund. As you pay off credit card debt and loans, some money should go into a savings account and emergency fund. The amount you save will depend on the budget you develop.

Maintaining a good financial status requires managing debt rather than letting debt manage you. Debt should only be incurred for essential purposes that will provide you a distinct long-term benefit. Borrowing money to go on a weeklong vacation is not good debt management. Buying an iPad you cannot afford on a credit card when you have a laptop that works well is not good debt management, either. Good debt has certain characteristics:

- Enables you to come out ahead financially in the long run – investing that earns more than interest on debt, starting a business, paying off debt at a lower interest rate
- Is essential to your life – buying a car or house
- Improves your life – covering college expenses, dental work, etc.
- Covers an emergency – paying for medical expenses, repair roof, etc.

Instead of reaching for the credit card or agreeing to take out a loan, you need to consider other payment options first. For example, you need to think about the cost of borrowing money in view of your earnings and cash you will or currently have access to. If your cash is in a savings account that earns low interest and the debt will cost you a high interest rate, paying cash or making a large down payment to keep debt as low as possible might make more sense.

Many purchases people put on credit cards are not essential. Debt is incurred for clothes, entertainment, vacations, toys, and items on sale you think you just cannot live without. In many cases, you can defer the purchase and wait until you are able to free up the cash. Reviewing your current budget and finding ways to reduce expenses to create net income are good places to start. For example, you can learn to use discounts and coupons regularly, which can generate significant savings. The cash you save should then be moved to a separate savings account.

Before significant purchases, some misers like to close their eyes and think of the number of long, hard hours they toiled to earn the amount of money they are about to spend. In these moments, they become a little bit more connected between the hard work and its impact on the justification of these significant purchases. They look at how that purchase will change their life. They then take another step back and ask what ongoing costs and additional labor will be necessary to support this purchase. Only after coming to terms with the labor aspect, the impact of the purchase on their life, and the cost to maintain the purchase do they make a decision to buy or not to buy. We all might not go through this process, but we can clearly benefit from looking at the buying process beyond just the point of purchase.

Small purchases are one thing, but when you are obtaining a loan, especially a significant one, reading the fine print is really important. It may be difficult to believe, but once a financial institution or auto dealer approves a loan, the borrower does not usually even take time to fully understand the terms of the loan. This is common practice for many, but hopefully after reading this, you will aim to be among the ones who do read the fine print, if you do not already. It is imperative that you:

- Shop for the best terms on loans
- Negotiate terms with the lender. You can negotiate the down payment, interest rate, type of interest (variable or fixed), loan fees, payback period, and payment due dates.

If you do not ask the right questions, you will never know what options are available to you. So do some research before you shop for loans or a mortgage or do any kind of shopping, for that matter. That way, you are armed with the necessary knowledge to fight a little better with those who spend countless hours training on how to best remove the hard-earned cash from your pocket.

Unless you are borrowing to buy something that truly improves your personal and financial life and has future value, you probably do not need to buy it right now. Staying out of debt means learning to enjoy life now while living within the financial means you have available and by developing a plan for accumulating future resources.

Another important step is to periodically monitor your credit score. If your score is not where you want it to be, then work on increasing it. To improve your credit score, you will need to pay your bills on time and pay off most of your debts. Checking your credit report often to make sure it is accurate and to safeguard against identity theft is critical. Read your monthly statements closely and verify that nothing has changed, including interest rates or other terms. That fine print you did not read when you accepted the credit card may have included variable events like a low introductory interest rate that has now increased significantly. These types of changes alter your current debt picture and at the very least, mean that you need to review your debt-reduction and budgetary plans.

At the end of each month, make a point to review your household budget and debt-reduction plan and assess progress, problems, successes, and goals. You might find it helpful to circle a day on the calendar or add a reminder in your electronic planner. Do whatever it takes to keep yourself on track. Benjamin Franklin and others before him realized that most people do not "plan to fail, but rather fail to plan." Well, you are ahead of the pack in making your plan. Now you just have to follow it. Stick to your plan. Yearn to be free of bad debt.

Bankruptcy as a Final Option

According to the US courts, there were 1.5 million bankruptcy filings in 2010, and 1.4 million consumer bankruptcy cases were completed. Approximately 85 percent of the cases were filed as Chapter 7 bankruptcies, while 15 percent were Chapter 13. (5) Sometimes, consumers find themselves in a situation where they will never be able to catch up on delinquent accounts. This is compounded further by their quality of life also being changed by collection calls, collection letters, and lack of income to even pay for essential items due to high debt. This has been the reality for many since the outset of the 2008 recession, when millions of people lost their jobs and found they were unable to stay current on their debt payments.

Bankruptcy is a legal action in which the US Bankruptcy Court allows certain debts to be discharged (written off) or paid according to a court-ordered schedule. Bankruptcy is often called a "fresh start," but it also has consequences.

- Might require the sale of some assets
- Stays on your credit report for ten years
- Can increase the cost of future debt or make it difficult to obtain new loans
- Can negatively impact employment opportunities
- Can negatively impact rental opportunities

Fortunately, many courts will now allow a person to keep one credit card so that they can continue functioning in a credit-based society. The bankruptcy court's goal is to help you get into a workable financial situation and not to leave you destitute. In many cases, those who go through this process are allowed to keep their home and are able to negotiate a new agreement for their vehicle loans, as well.

Lately, many high profile businesses have filed for Chapter 7 or Chapter 11 bankruptcy. A Chapter 7 filing usually means that the business's future is so bleak that it probably does not even make sense to restructure the business. Therefore, its assets must be liquidated. To contrast, in a Chapter 11 bankruptcy, filers usually go through a scrutinizing and laborious process with creditors, vendors, the government, lawyers, and a host of others who are financially vested in the business. When the business is deemed salvageable, reorganization will be done to fix the various problems that the business may have. The ultimate goal of the reorganization is to have a financially stronger company emerge from bankruptcy ready to compete successfully in the marketplace.

The latter filing goals should also be the goals of consumers who are thinking of filing for bankruptcy. At their low points, businesses have many ways they can legally reorganize themselves, and consumers also have options. Currently, there are two main types of consumer bankruptcy filing options: Chapter 7 and Chapter 13.

Chapter 7 (Liquidation)

Chapter 7 bankruptcy requires the liquidation of non-exempt assets to raise funds to pay off debts. Upon filing for Chapter 7, an automatic stay is put into effect so that creditors and other collectors must go through the court process to get to debtors' assets. The court will also appoint a trustee to act as the debtor's representative. The trustee will have power to make decisions about debts and asset liquidations involved in the bankruptcy process. The trustee will also make a recommendation to the court about the final discharge or outcome of the bankruptcy.

Assets are also classified into exempt and non-exempt groups for the proceedings. Non-exempt assets vary from state to state, but include items like furniture and jewelry. Exempt debts that cannot be discharged include child support. A house is usually exempt, but mortgage payments are usually delinquent by the time a Chapter 7 is filed. In that case, it may not make sense to try to keep the house and thus the debt. A collateralized loan has an underlying asset like real estate or a vehicle that the lender can foreclose on or repossess and sell to settle the debt. It is also possible to negotiate a new agreement called a reaffirmation agreement with the lender.

Chapter 13 (Debt Consolidation and Modification)

Chapter 13 bankruptcy gives a debtor a little bit more breathing room, so to speak. Filers are allowed to repay some or all of their debts if that can be done within a three- to five-year period. The mortgage is usually exempt, but delinquent amounts usually must be caught up during that time period according to an agreed-upon schedule. If the house (or any other asset) is valued too low in the bankruptcy filing, the trustee does have the right to object to the asset being exempted and sell it. The approval of the debt-repayment plan depends on the availability of proven adequate income. Assets are not taken by the court, but the court trustee will administer creditor payments. Debts are discharged once the debt-payment plan is fulfilled. For this reason, a Chapter 13 is called reorganization rather than liquidation.

Regardless of the option you might be faced with choosing, bear in mind that filing for bankruptcy should always be taken seriously. It is a decision you will live with for many years. The bankruptcy will remain on your credit report for up to ten years after it is settled. Federal law does entitle you to report discharged accounts as zero balances on the credit report. Some lenders will consider you to be more creditworthy since you do not have as much debt as you did before filing, but the some will be wary even if your earnings increase.

A bankruptcy does negatively impact your credit score. As long as the bankruptcy is on your file, it will continue to lower your total score. Due to lobbying efforts from the consumer credit industry, in 2005, the Bankruptcy Abuse Prevention and Consumer Protection Act was enacted with new requirements that make filing for bankruptcy a little more difficult. The lobbyists told Congress that their goals are to stop the abusive and unnecessary filings by consumers. The consumer credit industry cannot claim a complete victory, however, because the number of filers has outpaced what they imagined under the new law. According to the more vocal critics in the consumer credit industry, this is because the new requirements, like credit counseling and a prescreening battery of tests, makes the process much longer and more expensive, but these requirements do not stop people from filing. The credit industry sympathizers should not be too upset at the debtors' tactics since these debtors are using lawyers to gain some financial relief just as the credit industry uses the lobbyists to petition the government for financial relief. Overall, the process has become more difficult, which might dissuade a few, but for the majority, a well-paid, competent attorney can easily outmaneuver the bankruptcy laws for those who are willing to pay.

Treating Debt with Respect

Debt reduction and management is certainly a complicated topic, but it is also one of the most important. Debt can take the joy out of life in so many ways. Fortunately, you have many options to get out of debt and stay out of debt. Debt should always be treated with respect and only incurred for essential items. Let us face it, you have better things to do with your money, like investing for your future. Do not be a slave to debt. Keep your money working for you.

CHAPTER 7

Fear of Generic Products

Generic products are equivalent to brand-name products in the sense they are meant to provide the same form, benefits, and safety. They are sold under a general name rather than being sold as a specific brand. Most categories of consumer products have generic versions, which include food, drugs, clothes, cleaning products, and cosmetics.

These products are actually produced in two ways. Sometimes, they are manufactured by companies that have nothing to do with the production of the brand-name products. However, some generic products are actually made by the same manufacturers that produce the brand-name products. In that case, the only difference between the brand-name product and the generic product is the label.

The purpose of generic products is to provide consumer items at lower prices. Sometimes, the quality of generic products is equal to the quality of brand-name products, but that is not always the case. There are plenty of generic products on the market that have inferior quality compared to brand-name products.

Most savvy consumers will try a recommended generic brand if they can get the same quality and benefits as the brand-name labels. After calculating the cost savings for a relatively similar product, the astute consumer will more than likely switch to using the generic brand. However, some consumers cannot overcome the psychological aspect associated with the purchase of generic brands, regardless of the quality.

The Powerful Association of Branding and Feelings

Branding is a marketing strategy that creates an association between the product brand and consumer satisfaction. For example, a product is advertised over and over again by showing a happy family, friends having fun, or a problem being solved by using the product. The brand name becomes associated with warm thoughts and feelings that make people feel good. When you see the product in the store, these feelings are evoked, leading you to buy the product. Companies spend millions on marketing and building brand recognition because they want you to spend money on their products instead of similar competing products.

In the stores, you will find brand-name products sold alongside generic products. When standing in a grocery store aisle looking at the brand-name and generic name products sitting side by side, you can fully appreciate the impact of effective marketing. The brand-name will generate an emotional response, even if it is on an unconscious level. The generic product does not create any feelings or response because there has been no marketing to create an association of some kind. An emotional response has you reaching for the brand-name product even though the generic brand is just as high quality and offered at a lower price.

Consumerism is rooted in marketing brands and creating those emotional responses. We live in a culture that promotes instant gratification and the idea that products can make us feel good about ourselves. This leads to buying decisions based on emotions rather than unbiased assessments of the product's performance, price, and quality. When emotions influence product decisions, consumers tend to pay more than necessary for products, and the accumulation of these kinds of decisions can lead to excessive and unnecessary debt. In addition, some consumers tend to purchase more goods at sometimes at higher prices due to the accessibility of store charge cards. So the stores can be seen as enabling bad purchasing decisions by providing these consumers the means to complete transactions they might not otherwise be able to afford.

In general, wise buying decisions should be based on actual facts and not emotional sentiments. At times, the brand-name product will have the best quality and deliver the best performance when compared to its generic versions. However, the analysis should not stop there. Even in that case, a good buying decision will also consider if the price difference between a brand-name and a generic product is justified by the brand-name's quality and performance and if the higher quality is significant enough to warrant the higher price point.

Categories of Generic Products

Let us now turn to the discussion of some typical generic products relating to food, cleaning, clothing, and pharmaceuticals.

Food Products: Generic food brands are typically store brands, but many stores also carry second-tier generic products. The generic products are less expensive than brand-name products, costing as much as 20 percent less. They include canned, frozen, and packaged foods. Consumer reports and the American Dietetic Association studies have found that many generic food products have the same nutritional quality as brand names. This is especially true for store brands. The second-tier generic products usually cost the least of all types of products, but some of them were found to be lacking in taste and nutritional quality. Consumers can save as much as 30 percent on their food bills by purchasing generic food products. (1)

Cleaning Products: Brand-name cleaning products are more expensive than generic brands, largely due to marketing costs. Some brand-name and generic products like bleach, which is normally diluted during use anyway, are identical. To determine if a generic product has similar quality to the brand-name product, you can read labels to check for ingredients like antibacterial agents. You can also simply try the generic brands. Generally speaking, generic cleaning products are as good as brand-name cleaning products. Brand names attempt to differentiate their products and justify higher prices by claiming additions to the product, such as color-safe bleach for detergent or lotion in soap.

Clothes: Like food products, most generic clothes are store brands. One study on consumer responses to store brands determined that perceived quality and value of store brand are the main drivers of buying decisions. The store image also contributes to the buying decision. Approximately 20 percent of clothing in the United States is sold as private label or store brands. (2) Private labels are clothes that are not identified by manufacturer, making them generic, but are differentiated by retailer. Many of the generic clothing brands have the same quality as brand-names, and some are made by the same manufacturers. Consumers can save much money buying private label clothing.

Drugs: Generic prescription and over-the-counter drugs get the most attention in the world of generic products. The Food and Drug Administration (FDA) defines generic drugs as, "identical—or bioequivalent—to a brand-name drug in dosage form, safety, strength, route of administration, quality, performance characteristics, and intended use." (3) Generic drugs are almost always much cheaper than brand-name drugs. Consumers save billions of dollars each year by buying generic drugs. Generic drugs are manufactured after a patent on a brand-name drug has expired. The generic drugs are chemically identical to brand-name drugs and are controlled by the FDA, just like brand-name drugs.

Facts and Not Emotions

There are many other generic products sold on the market, including paper products, gasoline, electronic accessories, and hygiene products. In many cases, consumers can significantly reduce household expenses by purchasing generic products rather than brand-name products. At one time, stigmas were attached to the purchase of generic products, because it implied a lack of wealth. That is no longer true, especially since the recent recession eroded so much consumer wealth. The key to saving on quality product purchases is realized when you make informed buying decisions based on facts rather than emotions.

CHAPTER 8

Why Banks Nickel and Dime You

Some Reasons for Fee Changes

Back in the good old days, way before your time or mine, banks were revered institutions. Banks were pillars of the community that encouraged economic activity among its small businesses, participated in community improvements, and even provided a safe place for you to keep your hard-earned money. However, times have changed, and some banks no longer pretend that they are there to serve you. These new callous banks act as though you are there to serve them. And unfortunately, their ethics and behavior have even affected institutions that were once well respected. They are getting away with this behavior because they know that you need them now more than ever and because, sometimes, the bad apples at these financial institutions are the top producers or revenue generators. And while their tactics may be crude or borderline unethical, they have transformed some underperforming business lines into profit centers. These individuals may be in the minority in terms of their indifferent views toward the customer, but they are unfortunately representative of the company, and their business practice is what the customer sees every day.

Banks have unleashed a more aggressive campaign against the consumer in the last couple of years. These places are now charging for services they have not charged for before or they are increasing the fees on services that people commonly use. There are a lot of reasons for these practices, but the primary reason is profit. Banks are in the business to make money, and there are a lot of pressures from Wall Street, investors, and executives to squeeze as much as they can from their customers.

The various banks' campaigns to generate more revenue and hopefully profits are their response to the changing banking climate and financial laws (Credit Card Act of 2009, Dodd–Frank Wall Street Reform, and Consumer Protection Act of 2010, etc.) that have been passed in recent years. When was the last time that you went into your local branch of your bank? For most people, that has become a rarity. Technology has made it possible for you to no longer have to visit your local bank's branches or even set foot inside a bank. Banks now have ATMs, online banking, smartphone access, and other technologically savvy ways to do your banking. And unfortunately, all this has been at a high cost to the banks.

If you are doing your banking without reliance on local branches, then you are saving the bank money in the long run, but costing them money in the short run. Whether you use the banking facilities or not, most reputable banks must still maintain a community presence.

That physical presence is still necessary to deter competition as well as to provide traditional banking services to its more traditional customers. Some of these services are directed at businesses, but deposit boxes and loan services are directed at consumers who have traditionally walked into the banks to secure these services.

Some might suggest that banks can downsize, much like seniors downsizing to smaller homes after their children have grown up and moved out. While that cost-saving measure will be ideal in the long run, in the short term, banks are still faced with larger-than-life physical establishments that they still need to maintain whether they have five customers coming in a day or hundreds each day. So much like a car dealership, when you walk into a bank, do not be surprised if you are ambushed by banking representatives. Even at the ATM, I have seen some customers accosted by these representatives.

These walk-in customers are very important to banks. When you walk into a branch, the tellers or bankers are able to look through your account. They are trained to figure out what types of other services they can offer you depending on your account balances, types of accounts you have, and types of activity in your accounts. Bank employees are also trained to bring certain accounts to the attention of investment representatives depending on your account balances and personal information. This was one of the primary benefits to banks for the merging of consumer and investment banking. There is no more firewall. They now have access to your personal and investment information. Why do you think your teller or other banking representative take so long just to tell you your balance after making a deposit? Trust me; I used to be a banking representative.

So as you can imagine, the decline in foot traffic into banking establishments coupled with new restricted laws has essentially put banks up against the wall. So banks have become creative and, in some cases, callous in aggressively generating revenues for its owners, which are not you, unless you are a shareholder. Banks feel that they have no choice but to rely on other means to increase banking revenues and profits.

This piece will briefly introduce some common ways in which banks are aiming to gain additional revenues from you. This list is a mere introduction to some of the tactics and current changes or changes on the horizon as some of these financial institutions get more desperate in their attempts to generate more revenues than they did in previous reporting periods. I would advise you to review your current accounts and make a list of the services your bank offers. Then take a look at what changes have been or are planning on being implemented for your current services. Do not get blindsided. Most banks would have sent some type of notification already if changes were taking place. Do not just discard these mailings without examining their content.

Educate Yourself on New Practices

Read the correspondence that your banks or other financial institutions send you. Most banks send customers notices regarding changing fees as well as other bank policies and new practices. If you do not have documentation, then go online, call, write, or visit your financial institution in person (if that option is available) to ask for updates. You are probably aware that some banks charge up to $24 or more for a box of checks, but this was probably explained to you when you first opened your account.

Most people pay little attention to the number of other charges or fees that were part of the list they received when they first opened the account. And to make matters worse, you probably do not pay much attention to your monthly statement or look for the new charges that are placed against your account. Of course, I am hoping that the last sentence does not apply to you. I am sure you are keeping a watchful eye on all your financial statements, especially at a time when financial institutions are looking for ways to charge for anything. So go ahead and get that statement out or go on your computer and open that electronic "paperless" statement, because I am about to review some banking fees.

Inquire About Ways to Avoid Fees

Always speak with your bank to see if they will reverse any of the charges. If you are getting more problematic fees like bounced checks or overdraft charges, then it might be in your best interest to seek financial management counseling or read some books that help you see why it is important to have good financial health.

A simple phone call or meeting with a knowledgeable representative can provide you with some viable alternatives to current fees that you may be paying. Financial institutions and businesses in general need to make a profit. Therefore, the representative or bank mailings might alert you to different ways to avoid certain fees. The most common options available are paperless statements, linking accounts for balances, adding new accounts or services, changing account activity, online banking, and direct deposits. They might even offer incentives to become a shareholder of the financial institution. Some financial institutions give discounts and other perks to their shareholders. So it might be wise to find out the minimum level of ownership and invest in a few shares. Go online or give your bank a call today for fee-saving options if you are still paying bank fees or think you will be in the future.

Look for Alternatives to Fee-Based Services

Electronic Services

As technology permeates every facet of our lives, it brings new options to the average consumer that used to be a perk only for the wealthy. The Internet is a plethora of new online retailers and financial service providers as well as an online presence for traditional brick-and-mortar stores and financial institutions. By using the Internet, a consumer can compare options for just about any kind of purchase. Of course, due diligence and exceptional alertness to website authenticity and your financial information should be the rule, not the exception, when performing any online transaction.

Community Banks and Credit Unions

Of course, do not forget the options that community banks and credit unions offer. Many small community banks and credit unions have similar products for consumer savings and checking needs that larger banks provide. However, they generally have lower fees and often more personalized service compared to some of the big commercial banks. In October 2011, an estimated 650 thousand customers opened new credit union accounts. This was done mostly in protest to Bank of America's barrage of new bank charges, including the proposed $5 debit card fee and an $8.95 fee for online banking customers if they want to use paper statements, a teller, or other bank services not covered by the online banking account. The last two arguably appeared to be the tipping point for many customers who did not even turn back after Bank of America decided to change some of its fees amid the public outcry.

This mass exodus will add to the more than ninety million credit union members across the country. Although some of the bigger banks say that some of those customers were unprofitable to them, it still is unsettling that many consumers are not keen on some of the bigger financial intuitions' fee practices. Credit unions also seem to have such a large following because of their ties to the community through churches, organizations, or employers. So check online to compare the various financial institutions in your area and even visit your local community financial centers to see what they offer. If you have an investment account, you should also compare the checking and savings options that they have to what you are currently getting. It might make sense to switch to their services, depending on what they are offering and for how long.

And remember, banks and other financial institutions will always be looking for ways to boost their earnings. It is their job to grow their business. If old strategies and products are not working, then new ones will be tested. If those new ideas are met with little resistance, they will be deployed into the markets. And you better believe that if there are profits to be made, then other competitors will also join in raising the "fee du jour." But it is almost guaranteed that once those fees are established, they will be anything but fleeting.

ATM Fees

What it is: Many banks charge a fee for using your debit card at their automatic teller machines (ATM). Some even charge a surcharge to cardholders who are not their customers.

Estimated Annual Revenue to Industry: According to a study done by Bankrate.com in 2007, ATM fees generated almost $4.5 billion annually.

Source: Bankrate.com, "Annualized cost ($ billions) of ATM fees"

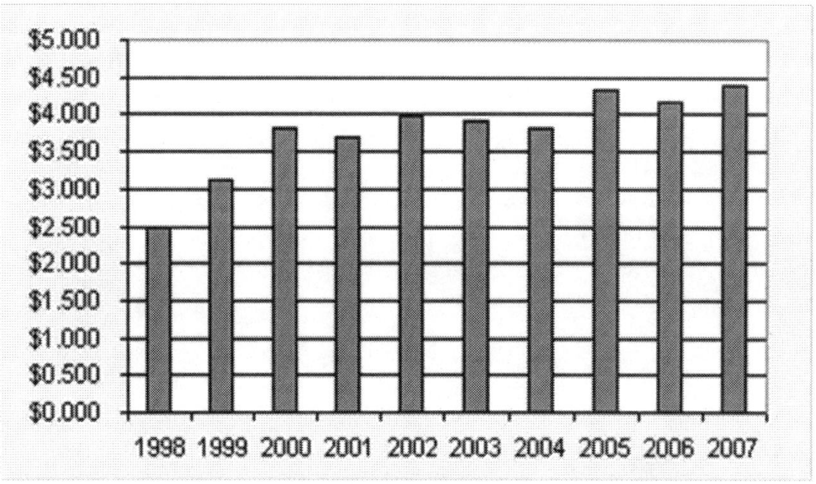

New Fees/Annual Cost: Average is less than $1.50 a month, but there are also additional fees of $2.33 on average per incident if you use another financial institution's ATM. Depending on your location, that ATM fee or surcharge fee can be very hefty.

There are also fees charged at the ATM by some financial institutions for certain types of transactions such as printing balances. These fees can be $3 or more per transaction.

Source: Bankrate.com, "Average ATM surcharge fee"

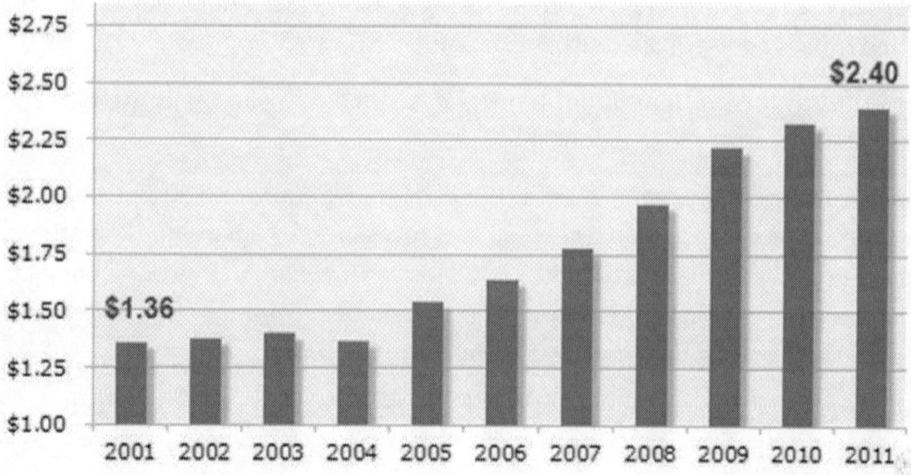

Rumored Fee Increases: Increases if there is no customer push back or regulator intervention

Bottom Line to Customer: Check into options available from other financial institutions for free or rebated ATM fees. Some online alternatives do provide refunds for ATM charges, but you must weigh all the cost of services you use to determine if switching banks makes sense.

Also, if you have exceeded your monthly allotted ATM transactions or in an area where you do not have access to your bank ATM, then you should consider using your debit card to make a purchase and getting cash back. There usually is no fee for requesting cash back, but check with your financial institution for details.

Debit Card Fees

What it is: This fee is a monthly charge for using a debit card. Some banks charge this fee monthly, and others charge a fee per transaction.

New Fees/Annual Cost: A handful of banks have started to charge up to $1.50 per debit transaction. Steer clear of those if you can.

Bank of America has proposed a charge of $5 per month or $60 per year. However, due to customer push back and the resulting pressures from regulators, the planned charge has been put on temporary hold. In the meantime, lobbying groups have been sent to Washington to petition Congress and the members of new Consumer Protection Bureau. So it is just a matter of time before this is implemented.

Rumored Fee Increases: Increase to $5 if there is no customer push back or regulator intervention

Bottom Line to Customer: Compare the cost of owning a debit card to that of a credit card. It might be worth taking a look at the different credit cards with various perks such as air miles, cash-back bonuses, and other rewards incentives. The good news is that some of these cards do not charge an annual fee while those that do charge give you a reason for paying an annual fee. Always do comparison shopping in this area, as you should naturally do in all your transactions. Remember that as a consumer, you should always look out for yourself rather than expecting a business to have your best interests in mind. A business's goal is to make a profit, or else they will more than likely cease to exist, at least in a true free-market society.

Minimum Balance Fees

What it is: Some banks require their customers to have a minimum amount of funds available in their various accounts, but the checking account is usually the target. Banks rely on these accounts balances to generate revenue for their financial institutions. The money deposited into accounts by customers is used to make loans, invest in various business ventures, and earn interest for the bank. Therefore, banks want to make sure that you are keeping at least a minimum balance in your accounts.

These balances are also calculated differently, depending on your financial institution. Some calculations require minimum average daily balances while some may require monthly balances or use other calculation methods. Some banks also allow you to combine account balances in order to reach the minimum balance requirements. Check with your financial institution to see how they determine minimum balance requirements. Banks might also encourage you to make direct deposits to satisfy your minimum balance requirements. Financial institutions use this strategy because when you direct deposit, the bank is guaranteed that you will have money flowing into the account at somewhat regular intervals each month. There is also a lag, usually a day or less, between when the money is deposited into your account and when it is available for your use. Banks also know that if you have a check to cash, you might deposit only some of the money or none of it. However, if you directly deposit your paycheck or other funds into your account, you are more likely to keep it there longer, which is not necessarily a bad thing. This means that the bank will be able to earn interest, which can be very substantial considering all the direct-deposit accounts that the bank may have.

New Fees/Annual Cost: Fee waived if get direct deposit, complete required number of transactions, combining accounts.

Not maintaining a minimum balance per your financial institution's requirements can mean that you will be paying the full monthly charge for the particular account or accounts that you have with them.

Most banks charge from about $6 per account to over $25 per account on a monthly basis. This means an annual cost of $72 to over $300 just for the privilege of keeping your money at the bank.

Rumored Fee Increases: Increases in cost if there is no customer push back or regulator intervention

Bottom Line to Customer: The first line of defense is to ensure that your accounts are appropriate for your daily and monthly activities. The best way to do that is to communicate with your bank and find out whether there are more affordable accounts given your level of activity in your account. Why spend over $20 a month for a high-activity account when you only have about five transactions a month? If you do not meet the minimum balance requirement, it would seem that a more basic account with lower fees would suffice.

Once you have the correct accounts, ensure that you are taking advantage of useful services that the bank offers to lower your monthly costs. Linking accounts and adding e-mail or text alerts when your account balances go below a certain amount are just a couple of ways to stay ahead of the game. Also, look for alternative banking online or elsewhere in your community if your banking needs and costs requirements are not being met by your current financial institution.

Non-sufficient Funds (NSF) and Overdraft Protection

What it is: In the past, banks would simply reject transactions that were made to accounts that did not currently have the sufficient funds to cover that transaction. The check or transaction would simply "bounce" or be returned to whoever had made the request. However, through industry studies and live testing in the 1990s, banks began to realize that they could benefit substantially if they charged customer for overdraft protection. They were correct.

Records show that by as early as 2004, overdraft fees were generating over $10 billion in fees for banks and that amount more than doubled to over $20 billion about four years later. By early 2011, this fee was still seeing revenues of almost $30 billion. The new Consumer Financial Protection Bureau (CFPB) is currently doing an investigation into these fees, which recent estimates have projected to reach closer to $38 billion annually. These numbers are significant when you realize how many transactions have to take place to generate these types of revenues. In fact, most customers who are assessed overdraft protection charges do not usually even overdraft more than the $30 or so that banks charge for the service. So, in effect, the banks have been profiting substantially. This has led to increases in promotion of the services as well as increases in costs of the services.

The Insufficient/Non-sufficient Funds (NSF) Fee Process: A transaction is sent to your bank requesting payment. These include requests by checks, debit cards, or Automated Clearing House (ACH) transfers. There is not enough money in your checking account to cover the total transaction request, and your account also does not have the bank's **overdraft protection** service.

The bank can, at its own discretion, decide whether to cover the transaction for you or simply reject the transaction. Whether the bank decides to reject or approve the transaction depends on the amount of the transaction, whether the transaction is a repeating ACH payment setup with online bill payments, the frequency of insufficient funds, and other company-specific criteria.

Option I: Rejection of Transaction:

If the bank decides to reject the transaction, then the check or transaction request is returned to the requestor stating that there was insufficient or "non-sufficient funds" in the account to cover the check. The transaction requestor's bank as well as your bank may assess a fee for the inconvenience.

If the funds requestor is your friend or is not a business, then he or she will almost always be upset that you wrote him or her a bad check that might have caused the check recipient to be assessed a fee that is sometimes $30 or more by the receiving bank. If you have written people bad checks, you can suggest that they try to cash the check at your bank in person rather than depositing the check into their account. That way, if there is not enough money in your account to cover the check, then they will simply refuse to cash it, and there will be no fee charged for a returned check. They might still be angry with you, but at least they will not be charged a fee.

If the requestor is a business, then that company will probably charge you a returned check fee of $30 or more per incident. If your checks or payments requests always "bounce," then that business might also report you to one of the national check monitoring systems, such as ChexSystems, Check Connection, TeleCheck, and the Shared Check Authorization Network (or SCAN). These systems will then add your account to their database so other businesses will know that you write bad checks or are not good for payments from your bank.

It may be considered a crime to repeatedly send bad checks to businesses depending on the frequency and amounts of the check. This can be serious if the business can prove that you intended to defraud them.

Option 2: Cover the Transaction:

If the bank decides to cover the transaction, then they will make the payment requested. Then they will put a hold on your account for the amount that your account did not have to cover the transaction. The bank will also charge you an insufficient fee or "non-sufficient" funds (NSF) fee.

Any amount that the bank lends your account to cover a transaction is similar to a loan, which means that it needs to be paid back. Therefore, you should be informed of your bank's terms for covering the funds. This includes interest charges as well as other fees.

A notice is sent to you detailing the insufficient funds incident. However, once you repay the fees and the temporary loan (the amount that your bank covered), your account will then return to good standing. If the bank offers a grace period and you deposit the needed funds into the delinquent account within that grace period, which is usually the same day, then the fees might be waived.

How the Overdraft Protection Service Works:

You must first enroll in the overdraft protection service provided by your bank and link to another credit or savings account to your checking account.

If a transaction is sent to your bank requesting payment, such as requests by checks, debit cards, or automated clearing house (ACH) transfers, and you do not have enough money in your checking account to cover the total transaction request, then the overdraft protection service goes to work.

Option 1: Your primary account is linked to another account

A transfer is made from the linked account to cover the transaction. If there is not enough in the linked account, then the bank will cover the account using the process outlined below in Option 2. A transfer fee may be charged for each incident or transfer. You should consult your bank's terms of service for this information.

Option 2: Your primary account is not linked to another account

Depending on the transaction amount, the bank will cover the transaction for you. They then put a hold on your account for the amount that your account did not have to cover the transaction. Just like the previous option, this is similar to a loan, and the amount must be paid back before your account returns to good standing. Your bank wants you to manage your account in a responsible manner. That means they can cancel your overdraft protection service if you use the service frequently.

Estimated Annual Revenue to Industry: Almost $38 billion was paid in overdrafts fees in 2011

New Fees/Annual Cost: The "courtesy" use of the overdraft protection service if you are not enrolled in the program can cost upwards of $35 per incident, plus other related fees. Some banks will charge you an NSF fee up to $35 per incident even if they return the transaction item unpaid. Most banks charge customers a fee for the overdraft protection service ranging from about $30 to $35 annually.

Transfer and other fees may be charged per incident depending on the terms of service. Some banks charge up to $10 or more per transfer for linked accounts. So you should compare rates across different institutions. If you are using the bank line of credit, then you should also review the terms of service for fee schedules.

Rumored Fee Increases: Increase to $40 to $45 if there is no customer push back or regulator intervention.

Bottom Line to Customer:

You have several options for overdraft protection:

- Find ways to monitor your balances
- Link checking or primary activity account to credit card or savings account
- Ask bank to waive the fees (usually as a one-time courtesy)

Customers must first be enrolled in the overdraft protection service, or their NSF transactions might be rejected. In order to avoid overdraft fees, it is prudent to manage your account balances. This means being aware of when deposits are going into your accounts and when money is being withdrawn from your accounts. Using your check register or a spreadsheet to track the deposits, withdrawals, and payments made against your accounts is a good first step. However, it is important to be aware of how long your bank takes to process different types of transactions on your account to manage your funds more efficiently.

A simple way to get an idea of your spending habits and your financial institution's timing of processing transactions is to look at previous monthly statements from your banks, credit card companies, as well as any monthly services that you pay for. Organize your income and expenses so you can see what time of the month that money is coming into or being withdrawn from your account and compare that to your initial entries made in your register or spreadsheet.

Once you have a schedule of the income and expense amounts and dates, ensure that you have are sufficient monies in your account when those expenses are being deducted. Setting up balance alerts and other reminders should let you know when your balance goes below a minimum.

Sometimes, overdraft protection service makes sense, but with smart options. You should still consider any annual fees charged for the service. Some financial institutions allow their customers to link their checking or primary activity account to a credit card or savings account. The cheapest option is usually your savings account, but check with your financial institution for its account requirements.

If you do get hit with an overdraft or a similar charge after you have taken these responsible steps, then give your bank a call or visit a branch to see if you can have the fee waived. Of course, you should have monies to deposit into the account to bring the balance into the positive again before going to the bank. However, even if you do not currently have the funds for whatever reason, it still makes sense to communicate with your bank and work out some plan to bring your account back into good standing. It is better to tackle the small problem now than to wait for it to grow into something unmanageable and probably more costly.

Account Maintenance Fee

What it is: Financial institutions charge monthly fees to customers who have an account with them. Many of these institutions suggest that the maintenance fee is to offset the cost associated with maintaining your account and providing you with the features and services requested for the selected account.

There are also a variety of ways that the monthly fee can be waived on a particular account depending on the promotions and practices of a particular financial institution. Here are some of the most common ways to lower or avoid monthly fees.

Direct Deposit: Some financial institutions will often waive account maintenance fees for customers who directly deposit a paycheck or make other types of frequent deposits.

Minimum Balances: Some accounts require that a minimum balance be maintained based on the institution's requirements. If those requirements are met, then the bank will not assess a maintenance charge on the account.

Minimum Transactions: If a certain level of activity can be maintained in your accounts or even through the use of debit cards attached to your accounts, then there is a chance that maintenance fees will be waived. Be aware that some banks charge you if you exceed the number of transactions for the particular account that you opened. Typically, these excess activities relate to withdrawal transactions from non-checking accounts.

Multiple Accounts and Services: If you open multiple accounts, such as checking, savings, and lines of credit, per the financial institutions' requirements, then monthly maintenance fees will be waived for some or all of the opened accounts. However, be aware that there might be other charges for creating and using other types of accounts.

Membership Waivers: Credit unions charge a membership fee, but they also tend to have lower maintenance charges for similar services at large commercial banks. Some financial institutions also have perks for shareholders. So you might want to see whether the long-term benefits of a small stock purchase might decrease the monthly or annual cost of maintaining your accounts.

Real Online Banking: There are traditional banks that offer reduced or waived maintenance for customers enrolled in their online banking programs, but be careful to read the fine print before signing up. Some traditional banks will still have a lot of fees associated with their online banking programs. They see it as an extension of the traditional accounts that they have in the branches and not a separate service. So ask a representative and read the account documentation for its fee schedule before opening up an online account with a traditional bank. Fees range from zero to about $10 if you have no other accounts with the bank.

There are also banks that are based in other countries with an online presence here in the United States. The Dutch bank ING is still popular for its competitive checking account rates and other perks. Of course, it is wise to do extensive research before sending your hard-earned money to an Internet-based bank. Make sure that it is not some guy operating a bank from his basement and funneling the funds straight into his overseas account. Most reputable banks have a physical building or office along with years of proven service and a history in the financial markets.

You have to be very cautious whenever you are enrolling in an online banking or bill-pay service, because this will more than likely end up being a long-term relationship. Therefore, it is imperative that you do your homework by looking at the bank's current and proposed fee schedules, reading about the company in the various media, and speaking frankly with a knowledgeable representative of that company. Remember, once the online or automatic deposit or payment systems are set up, detangling from that system can be very difficult and time consuming. It can take more than a month for certain vendors in a typical automatic payment setup to start and stop the automatic service. Therefore, be through and diligent.

New Fees/Annual Cost:

Some banks now charge fees as low as $4 to $20 a month. In extreme cases, accounts are being charged $100 or more for specialized features and services.

Rumored Fee Increases: Increase up to $170 if there is no customer push back or regulator intervention.

Bottom Line to Customer:

There are numerous ways to avoid paying monthly maintenance charges on your accounts. It will take some work to get the latest fee schedule and requirements from the various institutions, but it will be worth it over the long term. Fee waivers can save you hundreds of dollars or more a year, depending on the type of account or accounts you have opened. You should also check online for no-fee banks and financial service providers.

Excessive Withdrawal or Activity Fee

What it is: The Federal Reserve Board sets savings accounts' and money market accounts' preauthorized withdrawal and transfer limits under the Reserve Requirements for Depository Institutions (aka Regulation D). Regulation D limits special withdrawals from a savings account to six transfers within the statement-reporting period.

Eight Limited Withdrawals Allowed:

- ACH withdrawals
- Checks made to others
- Computer transfers
- Automatic transfers
- Overdraft protection
- Point of sale purchases
- Preauthorized electronic transfers
- Telephone transfers

Unlimited Withdrawals and Transfer Methods:

- At an ATM
- In-Person
- Through the mail

Some financial institutions might have other limitations for those types of accounts. Regulation D also requires that accounts that continuously violate the maximum-limit requirements be closed. Generally, a bank will aim to deter a customer from exceeding the preset limit by charging a fee when they exceed the allotted number of withdrawals. These limitations only apply to withdrawals. Regulation D places no limitations on the number of deposits you can make into these types of accounts. Financial institutions want you to keep those deposits in your savings account or similar interest-bearing accounts. This is necessary for the financial institutions to be able to make interest on those funds as well as to put it to work to create more money. If money is continuously removed from the account and you are receiving interest on the account, then the account becomes less profitable for the financial institution. Therefore, the bank may recommend closing the account, depending on the account balance.

New Fees: $9 per excessive withdrawal.

Some financial institutions have limits of less than the federally regulated six maximum before they start charging fees. So be careful and check with the fee schedule to avoid getting hit with such an avoidable fee.

Rumored Fee Increases: Increases if there is no customer push back or regulator intervention.

Bottom Line to Customer:

If you are making more than the required withdrawals or being charged fees for withdrawals, then it might make sense to talk to your financial institution to find a more suitable account or option for your needs. If no reasonable solution can be found, then look at your options online and in your community that may better suit your needs. These excess limitation guidelines are done through government regulations, not just bank policies.

Account Closing Fee

What it is: Banks tend to charge their customers a fee upon closing an account. The fees are supposed to cover the cost of closing the account, reporting necessary information to the correct financial regulators, and maintaining your records for the required period after your account is closed, which is usually three to five years.

Most financial institutions will waive this fee if your account is kept open and active for more than 90 days. However, some institutions have increased this probationary period to 180 days. So check these details before you close any accounts.

You should also check with your financial representative about the impact that closing a particular account will have on other accounts or services that you will still maintain. If certain accounts are linked through a promotion, then fees may increase on the accounts remaining open.

Be sure that all activity that was previously set up for automatic deposits (direct deposits) and deductions (online bill payments) from the account that you are closing has already been rerouted to its new account. Some banks will charge you fees if transactions continue to come in against the closed accounts.

New Fees/Annual Cost: If you close an account before it has been open for a required period of time, which is usually over 90 or 180 days, banks can assess a closing fee that ranges anywhere from $5 to $25 or more.

Rumored Fee Increases: Increases if there is no customer push back or regulator intervention.

Bottom Line to Customer:

If you must close your account before the probationary period is over, have a discussion with a representative from the institution to see if they can waive closing costs. Be mindful that there might be additional costs relating to closing your account if transactions and other services are still being used with that financial institution.

Other Bank Charges

Another Financial Institution's ATM (outside the United States) (Fee varies):

Fees can be up to $5, and other fees might be charged, depending on the transaction performed at the ATM.

Bank Check (between $4 and $10):

A bank check, also called a cashier's check, an official check, a demand draft, a teller's check, or a bank draft, is a check guaranteed to be paid by your bank. The guarantee usually occurs because either they withdraw the funds from your account or you present cash or other liquid payments to the bank before they will issue the check.

Some people prefer to use money orders instead of a bank check for amounts less than $1,000, because they are less costly. A postal money order costs less than $2, is good domestically and internationally, and never expires. It can also be replaced if it is lost or stolen and you have the receipt to make a claim. However, some institutions may require a bank check for certain transactions. It is probably wise to weigh your options before getting a bank check.

Check Image Service Fee (about $3 per month or $36 annually):

Provides an image of a canceled check with monthly statements

Replacement ATM or Debit Card Fee ($0 to $20)

Fees can be waived at certain institutions, but some charge up to $5 for replacements. Expedited delivery can increase costs up to $20.

Stop Payment Fees (up to $30 per incident)

A request made to your bank to stop payment on a particular check. Be aware that check might "bounce" depending on the circumstances previous to the stop payment request.

Domestic Wire Transfers (range $10 or more for regular delivery)

Making a transfer to another financial institution or vendor can be costly. Some considerations are transfer amount, urgency of transfer, exchange rates, and the transfer's final destination. Urgent delivery can add another $25 to the cost of the transfer. Make sure that you speak with a representative and get a detailed listing of all costs before you make the transfer. You do not want to be surprised by the final cost after the transaction is already completed. Also, wires can take minutes or days to reach the final destination if problems arise. Please bear in mind that some financial institutions charge around $10 or more to receive wires, as well.

International Wire Transfers (varies: up to $45 or more for regular delivery)

Making a transfer to another financial institution or vendor can be costly. Some considerations are transfer amount, urgency of transfer, exchange rates, commission fees, and the transfer final destination. Make sure that you speak with a representative and get a detailed listing of all costs before you make the transfer. In extreme and otherwise unfortunate circumstances, people have reported being charged more than $1,000 in fees relating to international transfers. This is why it is important to inquire and confirm in writing the fees relating to all your financial transactions. Please note that some financial institutions charge $15 or more to receive wires, as well.

CHAPTER 9

Leasing vs. Buying. . . The Discussion Continues

If you could name one financial discussion that has been held over and over again through the decades in homes, at car lots, and in appliance stores, it would have to be leasing versus buying. Is it more advantageous to lease a tangible asset or to buy it outright? The answer is never simple because so many factors come into play, such as purchase costs, taxes, depreciation, and even the intended use of the property.

A lease is defined as a contractual arrangement in which the rights to use assets are conveyed to another person for a designated period of time in exchange for periodic payments. At the end of the lease, the right of use ends and the property returns to the owner or options built into the lease are exercised. In a lease arrangement, property ownership does not change.

Leasing is different from buying in that a buyer purchases the asset in exchange for a certain amount of money. The buyer actually owns the property. The purchase amount can be financed, and the property can be used as collateral, but the buyer still owns the property. If a buyer defaults on a collateralized loan, the lender would have to go to court to take possession of the property in settlement of a debt.

As I mentioned, you can lease or buy tangible or intangible property. Intangible property includes things like copyrights, music rights, or other intellectual properties and competitive intangibles, like knowledge. Obviously, intangible property is mostly in the purview of commercial enterprises. This discussion addresses the tangible or physical assets that consumers most commonly lease or buy—personal vehicles, apartments, houses, home appliances, and furnishings.

Lease or Buy a Personal Vehicle?

Most days of the year, you could visit auto dealerships and find someone reading a window sticker in an effort to decipher the value of buying versus leasing the vehicle. This is not always an easy decision to make, because so many factors must be considered to determine the true cost of the lease.

Like most financial decisions, both leasing and purchasing vehicles have advantages and disadvantages. In the following sections, I will discuss the types of leases, the typical structures, and conditions of vehicle leases and purchase agreements. I will also compare the advantages and disadvantages of each and consider other factors influencing the decision.

A vehicle lease is an agreement in which you agree to pay a certain monthly lease amount for the right to use the vehicle during the leasing period. Since vehicles depreciate and lose value over time, the full lease amount is the equivalent of the amount the vehicle depreciates plus the finance fee and the sales tax.

Depreciation is the amount of value the vehicle loses over time due to wear and tear and mileage. The residual value equals the amount the vehicle is worth at the end of the lease period. The amount of depreciation used in the lease contract calculation is figured by subtracting the residual value from the price of the car. The Net Cap Cost (short for net capitalized cost) is the vehicle price less cash down payment less trade-in equity. The Net Cap Cost less the residual amount plus the finance fee and sales tax is divided by the number of months in the lease period to get the monthly payment.

Net Cap Cost = Vehicle Price – Down Payment - Trade-In Value

Monthly lease payment = (Net Cap Cost – Residual Value) + Sales Tax + Finance Fee/Term

<u>Types of Vehicle Leases:</u>

- Close-ended lease: In a close-ended lease, the lessee walks away at the end of the lease with no obligation to buy the vehicle. It does not matter how much a vehicle depreciates over the life of the loan or what the end-of-contract salvage value is compared to the salvage value used to calculate the lease payment.
- Open-ended lease: At the end of the open-ended lease period, you must purchase the car for an amount equal to the difference between the vehicle's fair market value and the salvage or residual value.

Since the lease value is determined by calculating the difference between the price of the vehicle and the residual or salvage value at end of the lease period, you should try to lease a vehicle with a high residual value so the lease payment is as small as possible. The finance fee is the equivalent of loan interest. On the lease agreement, it will appear as a grand total rather than as a monthly finance amount.

The costs associated with a vehicle lease can be paid up front, but many can also be capitalized or paid over the life of the lease. If you choose to capitalize these costs, then you are paying a finance fee for the privilege. Capitalized costs that could be paid up front will increase your lease payment. These costs include: (1)

- Taxes: state and local taxes.
- First monthly payment: lease payments are made at the beginning of the monthly lease period, so you usually have to make a monthly payment at the time you sign the lease.
- Security deposit: an amount set by the lessor that is meant to provide some financial guarantee in the event of a lease default or to cover amounts you may owe at the lease's end.
- Department of Motor Vehicle (DMV): Vehicle registration and title fees.
- Other costs: these can vary depending on the dealer, but usually include expenses like an administrative fee or prior balance amounts due on previous lease contracts.
- Capitalized cost reduction: an amount equal to the amount of cash down payment including trade-in allowance and rebates; this amount is deducted from the gross capitalized cost, which is the negotiated total of all the lease costs. The capitalized cost reduction is the equivalent of a down payment you would make if you were buying a vehicle instead of leasing.

The more you pay up front, the lower your lease payment will be. However, when comparing a lease to a purchase, a lease payment is normally less than a monthly financed payment on a vehicle loan because you are only paying the depreciation amount, plus some fees. With a financed loan, you are actually paying off the vehicle value, plus some fees. Since depreciation is only a portion of the vehicle's value each month, it would make sense that the lease payment is lower.

When you finance the outright purchase of a car, similar fees are included, but depreciation is not a factor. The calculation is simpler because you do not have to be concerned with residual value or depreciation.

The vehicle purchase price will include:

- Base selling price
- Title and registration fees
- State and local sales taxes
- Destination fee
- Other dealer fees for extra services or accessories

Rebates and your down payment or trade-in value are deducted from the total of the selling price and fees. Interest is charged on this net amount, and the loan is amortized for a set period of time. In an amortized loan, you make a fixed monthly payment, but with each payment you pay more toward the principal and less to interest. That is because the interest is calculated on the outstanding balance of the loan amount. That is why you pay more interest early in the loan period compared to later in the loan period.

Typical Lease Options and Conditions

The typical vehicle purchase agreement is simply a loan requiring you to make a designated monthly payment. Over the life of a loan, you are paying for the entire vehicle cost less any down payment you paid or rebates that were applied. There are few options found in the typical vehicle purchase arrangement. You have to make the payments or the vehicle will be repossessed. Some vehicle loans are written with prepayment penalty clauses. If you pay off the loan early, then you are charged a penalty amount.

Many vehicle leases do have early termination fees, but they have other conditions that do not apply to vehicle loans. In fact, one of the main features of a vehicle lease is that you must return the vehicle at the end of the lease period. Some leases are written with purchase options, meaning you can purchase the vehicle for the residual value amount or you can return it and walk away.

Most leases have a clause that limits the amount of annual mileage you may add to the vehicle. For example, a two-year lease agreement may state that you are allowed 12,000 miles per year to be put on the car. When the car is returned to the lessor after two years, the odometer should not read more than 36,000 miles.

Normally, the penalty attached to going over the allotted mileage is charged on a per mile basis, like 10 cents per mile. Using the previous example, if you have 40,000 miles on the leased car at the end of the lease period, you will be charged 10 cents x 4,000 miles or $400.

Another common lease clause addresses normal wear or tear. Leasing companies recognize that there will be normal wear and tear and will not penalize lessees for such. However, this also applies to things like tires. If the tires show more wear than should be expected under normal use, you may have to buy new tires. It is usually cheaper to replace tires or fix vehicle damage yourself rather than to allow the dealer to do so.

Comparing the Costs of Leasing vs. Buying

Clearly, the question of whether to lease or buy a vehicle involves more than just financial calculations. You can go through the calculations, of course, and compare things like how much up-front money must be paid or how much you are at risk of paying for excess mileage at the end of the lease. But the real comparisons involve looking at the depreciation rate and personal factors.

When you lease a vehicle and turn it in every few years, you are, in effect, continually paying the highest average annual depreciation expense in the vehicle's life. In addition, you will always have a lease payment unless you pay a balloon payment at the end of the lease and purchase the vehicle. You will never own the vehicle. A third disadvantage is that insurance rates on leased vehicles are often higher than on purchased vehicles.

Unfortunately, some vehicle lease agreements have restrictions on taking the vehicle out of state. Some lessors will not allow the lessee to take a leased vehicle to another state on a permanent basis, and cancelling a lease can lead to prepayment penalties.

The benefits that may offset these disadvantages when comparing leasing to buying include:

- You are able to get a new vehicle every few years
- No down payment is required (though you must pay the first month up front)
- Major repairs are the responsibility of the lease company
- They come with lower up-front expenses
- They have lower monthly payments
- The lessor assumes the risk of market decline in vehicle value

There are several disadvantages to buying a vehicle. For one thing, a vehicle may depreciate faster than the balance on your loan if you have a long-term agreement and make a small down payment. Annual depreciation is highest in the early years with 40 to 50 percent being incurred in the first few years. Early loan payments are applied mostly to interest. An upside-down loan is one in which the value of the depreciated vehicle is less than the loan amount. Equity loss is accelerated in the first few years because depreciation is high while principal payments are low.

Another disadvantage that greatly influences the decision is the fact payments on a vehicle loan are higher than lease payments. In other words, buying a vehicle reflects a higher commitment level than leasing does.

The advantages of buying a vehicle include the following:

- You can pay off loan and continue driving the vehicle
- You can do as you please with the vehicle at any time—keep it, trade it, sell it
- There are no mileage restrictions
- Paying down the loan builds equity in the vehicle
- Insurance rates are lower

It would be nice if there was a definitive formula for comparing leasing versus buying a vehicle. There is not, because you have to consider how much money you have for up-front expenses and monthly payments. Even when one clearly appears to be a good financial decision, considering your long-term goals is still necessary. If you intend to trade in a car every few years, then leasing may be the best choice. If you want to build equity in an asset and maintain complete control of your vehicle, then buying is the best option.

If you cannot afford to buy a new vehicle, but you do want to purchase your own car or truck, buying a used one is another option. There are certified used car programs, but you need to be aware they are not equal. There are dealer-certified and manufacturer-certified vehicles.

The manufacturer's certified used program is ideal, because it does not rely on the vehicle's location or dealer. In other words, the certification follows the vehicle no matter where you live and no matter which dealership is selling your type of vehicle. In addition, manufacturer-certified used vehicles are more rigorously tested. The original vehicle manufacturer backs up the warranty that comes with a quality certified used vehicle. Anything that was found wrong with the vehicle during the certification inspection was repaired by a factory-authorized service technician. (2)

The dealer-certified pre-owned vehicle programs that are not manufacturer backed are more like extended service contracts that the buyer must purchase. These "warranty" service contracts will have a number of terms you will need to study closely. For example, you may have to pay for all repairs up front and then claim reimbursement less a deductible.

Buying a new car with a manufacturer warranty included may often be cheaper in the long run. Before agreeing to buy a certified used car, make sure to research state laws because many have passed "Used Car Buyers Bill of Rights" laws. These laws invariably reference what qualifies a vehicle as certified. For example, California has specific conditions that must be met before a vehicle can be called certified. For example, the vehicle cannot have frame damage or have been repurchased by the manufacturer because of warranty problems. (3)

Unfortunately, what may seem to be a good deal may not be one at all once you know the whole story.

Renting vs. Buying

You are ready to move into a new apartment or house, but which should it be? Do you rent, or do you buy? In the United States, it is sometimes necessary for people to overcome the influence of culture when considering this question. A major goal of the American Dream has been to own a home, build some equity, and eventually use the house as a retirement asset whether by selling it for the money or accessing the equity.

The collapse of the housing market in 2007 and 2008 has forced people to rethink the American Dream. As millions of people lost their homes to foreclosure or discovered that their house was "underwater," renting took on new importance. An underwater home is one which the market value of the home is less than the mortgage balance. This is similar to the discussion on vehicle leasing versus buying concerning the rate of depreciation and the rate at which the loan principal is paid off.

In other words, some people are wishing they had rented an apartment or home instead of buying. Although you do not build equity in a rented property, you also do not have a long-term commitment with a value that is tied to market-asset values. Time plays an important role in the decision of whether to rent or buy.

The first step in evaluating whether you should rent or buy is to consider the advantages and disadvantages of each. Some people stop at this step and decide that the advantages of one or the other is enough to make the decision, but the second step even in these cases is evaluating financial options between like properties—apartment to apartment or house to house. If you decide that you could still consider renting or buying, then the second step is to learn how to financially compare the options of renting an apartment to buying a house.

Advantages and Disadvantages

Renting can be better than buying for many people without regard for the American Dream. A lot depends on a person's circumstances and goals, but as the recent recession confirmed, a lot also depends on what is going on in the marketplace. In a market where house prices are still falling, some properties present a major risk as a purchase while others may be great deals. However, when the housing market is declining, rent tends to rise. This is why "renters' markets" and "buyers' markets" exist. The relationship between the rental and housing markets is complex.

The first step is to consider the advantages and disadvantages of renting versus buying.

There are two main advantages of renting:

- No long-term financial commitment
- Able to move quickly if necessary without penalty

There are two main disadvantages to renting:

- No equity is accumulated
- Rent can increase over time

In between the advantages and disadvantages lay a host of other factors to consider. For example, renters do not have to pay for major repairs to apartments or rental homes. Those are the responsibility of the landlord. However, some of the advantages of renting concern convenience and practicality. Renting may:

- Place you closer to work, meaning less commute time and auto expense
- Provide more budgeting security since rent is often lower than a house payment. So people just starting their careers or those with variable incomes find renting more practical
- Enable you to save money that would go into house repairs if you purchased a home (opportunity costs)
- Make it much easier to relocate or change locations
- Be a more affordable option for those who cannot complete their own home repairs and maintenance

- Enable you to save more money for a larger down payment on a house

On the other hand, there are advantages and disadvantages to buying a house or condominium also. There are three main advantages of buying:

- Able to build equity in an asset if market conditions are right
- Freedom to manage property as desired
- Tax credits are currently allowed for home ownership

There are two main disadvantages of buying:

- Long-term financial commitment with opportunity costs
- Unable to move quickly

All Things Financial

The financial aspects of home ownership usually overshadow everything else. There are a number of them to consider also, ranging from the down payment to the tax benefits. Before you can compare renting to buying, you need to recognize the major costs:

- Down payment: percentage of the cost of the home paid up front, which typically ranges from 3 percent to 20 percent. In certain areas, the down payment required by some community boards can be even higher.

- Closing costs including down payment: partial monthly interest, home owner insurance for one year, real estate broker fees, loan fees including points and appraisal fees, escrow amounts for property taxes and utilities, title insurance, recording fees, attorney fees, and other costs. (4)

- Tax deductions and expenses: tax-deductible items include home mortgage interest, interest on home equity debt, real estate taxes, one-time tax deductions approved by law.

- Ongoing expenses: property taxes, home owner's insurance, home maintenance, and utilities.

Anyone renting an apartment needs up-front expenses that usually consist of a rental application fee or broker's fee, the first (and sometimes the last) month's rent, and a security deposit. The ongoing expenses include rent and possibly utilities. There are no tax deductions allowed for renting.

Condominiums have a couple of special features. A condominium is a residence that is like an apartment or townhouse, but you buy it like a house. Most of the closing costs and taxes are the same as those for home ownership, but you should be aware of additional financial facts.

- Costs include a monthly or annual condominium fee that covers building maintenance and maybe a special assessment fee for major building expenses
- Selling board or condominium association approval may be needed to buy or sell the property
- Some condominiums require payment of a flip tax or transfer fee if the property is sold

One other point is that buying and selling homes to make a profit will be viewed by the Internal Revenue Service as business activity. Buying and selling properties to make a profit is called "flipping." You will be subject to all of the taxes a typical business would pay, including state and federal income taxes on profits and employment taxes.

Following is a table summarizing the items to consider when deciding whether to rent or buy:

Rent vs. Buy Comparison

	Rent	Buy
Equity	No equity	Builds equity
Maintenance/repairs	No responsibility	Full responsibility
Mobility/Relocation	Flexibility	Must sell or rent home
Upgrades	None	Required, i.e. roof, siding etc.
Property taxes	Paid by landlord	Responsible for paying
Tax deduction	Not deductible	Interest is tax deductible
Payment	Rental rate can increase annually and faster than inflation	Fixed mortgage payment stable
Eviction	May be evicted	Must be foreclosed
Insurance	Not required	Required
Renovations	Not allowed	Allowed
Landlord rules	Must adhere to	None
Homebuyer tax credits	None	Available per current law
Flip taxes (for house flipping)	None	Subject to taxes if houses bought and sold as business
Flip Tax or Fee (New York coops and condos)	None	Transfer fee due upon sale
Upfront expenses	1st and last month's rent	Significant closing costs and down payment required
Selling board approval	Not applicable	May be required before selling co-op or condo
Financial commitment	Short term	Long term
Commuting to work	May rent closer to work	Requires longer commute
Opportunity costs	Only rent is committed	Money tied up in house cannot be spent elsewhere

Making a Comparison

How do you put all of this information together for decision making? Following is a basic comparison calculation:

Renting		**Monthly**	**Annual**
Monthly Rent		$950	$11,400
Renters Insurance			$300
Annual Rent Payments			**$11,700**

Buying			
Sale Price	$150,000		
Less: Down Payment @ 10%	($15,000)		
Amount Financed	$135,000		
Fixed-Rate Financing:			
Term of Loan	20 years		
Interest Rate	5%		
Monthly Payment		$565.33	
Annual Loan Costs			$6,784
1st year Interest on Mortgage	$5,766		
Homeowner Tax Rate	25%		
Less: Estimated 1st Year Tax Reduction			($1,442)
Adj Annual Loan Costs			**$5,342**
Other Annual Expenses:			
Property Taxes			$1,800
Homeowner's Insurance			$1,500
Estimated Maintenance			$700
Total Other Expenses			**$4,000**
Estimated Net 1st Year Cost			**$9,342**
(Note: all tax and interest rate calculations are estimates)			

Net Savings from Home Purchasing	**$2,358**

If the property appreciates in value, you will increase your net savings by the amount of appreciation. Appreciation is equity built up in the home due to marketplace forces. If housing market values should fall, which has been the case during the 2008 recession, the net savings will decrease, or there may even possibly be a net expense. (5) For example, if the house appreciated in value by 2 percent, you could add $3,000 ($150,000 x 2 percent) to the net savings or net expense, which would be a negative number in the example.

Where do the closing costs enter the calculation? The closing costs are lost opportunity costs. For example, if you spent $6,000 on closing costs, then that is $10,000 you did not earn interest on in an investment account or were not able to use to purchase a different asset. If you finance any of the closing costs, then they would be included in the total financed amount.

One final point to keep in mind is that the rate of appreciation of the property value will influence when it is better to buy or rent. In other words, the calculation year to year for annual expenses may be comparable for renting versus buying. But over a period of years, the cumulative picture changes as rent rises, tax rates change, and market values fluctuate. That is why many analysts recommend estimating the financial picture for the next five or even ten years based on current inflation rates. If rents rise quickly, then buying may become the right decision for long-term gain. The general rule of thumb is that you should plan on living in your home at least four years in a typical economy.

This discussion does not address every possible expense associated with an evaluation of renting versus buying. But it does give you a framework for assessing your options.

Home Appliances and Furnishings

You can rent appliances and furniture or to rent with the option to buy. Most of the financial principles that apply to renting versus buying vehicles or property also apply to appliances and furnishings. There are valid reasons for renting appliances:

- You gain access to items you could not buy otherwise but need
- You gain access to items that you need only for a short period of time
- You gain greater accessibility to brands you may not be able to afford otherwise
- Repairs are the responsibility of the retailer
- Most appliance and furniture rental vendors accept poor or bad credit
- You can choose the rent-to-own option in many cases
- You can return rented items

People often rent appliances and furnishings for four main reasons:

- Poor credit prevents financed purchase
- They do not have enough money to pay for the item in full
- They do not want to tie up money in the asset purchase
- They want to be able to return appliances or furnishings after a period of time rather than move them to a new location

When comparing the costs, you need to look at:

Renting

- Up-front expenses
- Monthly rental rate
- Actual price for the rental item
- Contract fees like late payment fees, damage fees, or repossession fees

If a refundable security deposit is required, there will also be an opportunity cost. Your money is not accessible for other purposes until it is refunded.

Buying

- Purchase price
- Interest rate, if you financed

Since retailers usually charge significantly more for rented items, buying is often cheaper than renting. However, using a high-interest rate charge account to pay for a purchase will also significantly drive up your costs. The important point is to include all costs, including opportunity costs, in your calculation.

Typical Agreement: Rent a Washer and Dryer

Weekly Rental Price		$30
Own it Term Length	130 weeks	
Total Weekly Amounts by Contract's End		$3,900
90-Day Same as Cash		$2,100
Retail Purchase Price		$1,400

Rental agreements will almost always be more expensive than a purchase. However, using the previous example, if you charged the appliances on a charge card with a 10 percent interest rate and paid $30 per month, paying off the balance would take fifty-nine months. That is about 256 weeks and almost double the contract period.

59 months x $30 per month = $1,770

$1,770 paid - $1,400 Retail Price = $370 interest charges

$370 interest charges/$1,400 Retail Price = 26.4 percent effective interest rate

Taking the Time

One point you must remember after reviewing lease or rent versus buying options is that you must take the time to identify all of the expenses associated with any transaction. It is also important to consider opportunity costs, because money spent is money you cannot use elsewhere.

Many times, though, the decision to lease or rent instead of buy will be a matter of convenience or personal preference. You may want to be able to drive a new car every few years, move out of an apartment within six months, or return appliances you will not need after a few months. In these situations, renting or leasing just may be the right option. Yet even in these situations, you should always make a decision only after studying the entire financial picture.

SECTION 3

Real Estate

CHAPTER 10

Real Estate Investing: Buying a Home

If there has been one common dream for American families, it surely has been to own a home. The housing industry has its ups and downs, but the advantages to owning a home have always kept it at the top of the list of preferred living arrangements.

The process of buying a home is fairly complex because so many factors come into play. For this reason, a number of professionals are usually involved, including the real estate agent, attorneys, lenders, and many others who work as a team of sorts. The first-time home-buying process involves a lot of negotiating, calculations, and documentation. In the following sections, I will review this process under normal conditions and then briefly discuss the second home purchase and the short selling and foreclosure process.

Overview of the Process of Buying a Home

Home prices are not immune to economic fluctuations. The best way to approach the process of buying a home is to assume that normal economic conditions will persist. Under normal conditions, there is an adequate level of housing inventory in the marketplace as well as a variety of financial institutions to provide the necessary financing. The home market prices are equal to or higher than existing mortgages, so you are not trying to buy an "underwater" house. Buying an underwater home can greatly complicate the buying process. Fortunately, most people do not buy property that is underwater when they buy it, but financing choices and declining market prices create the environment for mortgages to become underwater.

Finding an Agent

The process of buying the first home begins, of course, with finding the house. Normally, people use a real estate agent who has access to local property listings. The agent should be a licensed professional who can narrow the search to those properties that would seem to best fit your criteria. Typical criteria include:

- Location
- Price
- Square footage
- Number of bedrooms
- Number of bathrooms
- Floor plan
- School District

As the buyer, if you hire a real estate agent, the agent must represent your interests and not just the seller's. If you decide to search for a home without using an agent, remember that the seller's real estate agent represents the seller. In other words, the real estate agent will work to obtain the best deal for the people who retained him or her. In fact, a real estate agent legally must disclose whether the buyer's or seller's interests are being represented during the negotiating process.

Making an Offer

Once you find a house that fits your criteria, the next step is to make an offer. You and the real estate agent will discuss what to offer the seller, which is seldom the seller's asking price. If you hired an experienced real estate agent, the professional will know how to determine fair market value. This is where it is important to know whom the agent is representing. Obviously, the seller's real estate agent will want to sell the house for as much as possible, while the real estate agent you hire will want to negotiate a price that is as low as possible while still remaining within the range of fair market value.

When the offer is made, it will consider other factors that affect price, such as:

- General condition of the house
- Cost of necessary repairs
- Price of home in relation to nearby properties
- How long the house has been on the market
- Items to be left in the house like appliances and curtains

In addition, the offer should make the price conditional on the house passing a professional home inspection and a termite inspection to make sure the house has no hidden problems or flaws. The law requires disclosure of problems, but even the home owner may not be aware of certain problems, like a termite infestation. The offer you make the seller can include a requirement that the seller make necessary repairs or fix serious problems. You may decide to cancel your offer, too, if the home inspection uncovers an expensive problem or potentially recurring problem that can prove costly over the long term.

The offer may also be structured to indicate whether you are pre-approved for a loan or whether you will need time to find financing. If you have not been prequalified for a mortgage amount, then your offer will be made contingent on a loan approval. In addition, a good-faith deposit will often be included with the offer as well as a statement of how much down payment will be made. This is referred to as an earnest money deposit and it should only be made to the real estate firm and never directly to the seller for your own protection against loss of funds. The real estate brokerage firm will hold the money in a trust or escrow account until the purchase is completed, at which time the money will be given to the seller.

Finally, your offer will include a time period for the sale closing. The wait for the closing date is usually at least thirty days and is often longer. However, buyers might ask for a faster closing because they need a place to live immediately. Usually, though, a mortgage takes at least thirty days to be approved and finalized.

The Counteroffer

Once the real estate agent presents the offer to the seller, the home owner will either accept it or make a counteroffer. In fact, the offer-counteroffer process can last as long as the buyer and seller are willing to negotiate. For example, you may offer $150,000 for a house, while the seller was asking $175,000. If the market is hot for selling homes, meaning that home prices are steadily climbing, then the seller might reject your bid since it is lower than the asking price. However, under normal market conditions, the seller will not reject a low offer as long as the offer is reasonable and the seller does not have another buyer offering a higher price. So rather than reject your offer outright, the seller might counteroffer with $170,000. The counteroffer is made in writing, but usually states that the original terms stand and that only the price is changing. The seller may want to negotiate other items you have included in the lower offering price at that time also. For example, the seller may not want to include the refrigerator, chandelier, or water softener in the lower selling price, but may include those items at the higher asking price.

Closing the Deal

After an offer is accepted by the seller, the closing process begins. The closing is triggered by the signing of a binding agreement called a Residential Purchase Agreement or a Contract to Purchase Real Estate. The down payment is also submitted with the purchase agreement to an escrow holder. Usually, preparations for a closing will take thirty to forty-five days but can require more time if any issues arise. For example, the title company may discover liens on the property that must be cleared before the sale can be completed.

The escrow holder is a third party who is neutral to the real estate transaction. Escrow is made up of the money deposited, the purchase agreement, and other instructions relevant to the sale. Normally, an escrow holder is a title company or a business that specializes in escrow accounts. Real estate attorneys also manage escrow accounts.

The escrow officer is the person who ensures that:

- All required paperwork is assembled
- Down payment money is deposited in escrow
- Appropriate signatures on documents are obtained
- Title search is completed
- Seller meets requirements of the purchase agreement
- Property has been appraised
- Lender requirements are met
- Appropriate home owner insurance is in place
- Deed transfer is prepared and filed

The escrow company will also prepare a final statement of the closing costs you will need when you sign the title transfer paperwork. If you are considering financing certain closing costs, then the escrow agent can give you an estimate of those costs ahead of time. Once all of the documentation is completed, you will be contacted by the escrow agent, who will schedule the closing meeting and let you know if you need to bring additional funds to the closing.

The closing cannot occur until financing is settled, of course. Many people decide to speed up the process by getting prequalified by a financial institution for a particular amount before even seeing a property. During the prequalification process, the lender will verify the buyer's credit, income, and bank accounts. Once a house offer is made, the lender finalizes loan amounts as well as other changes in the loan documents. However, not everyone gets prequalified for a loan for a variety of reasons. If not prequalified, you will need to secure financing and be able to produce signed loan papers and lender funds before the closing can be completed.

If the financing has been secured, the contingencies have been taken care of, and other requirements have been met by the buyer and seller, then it is on to signing day. On signing day, you and the seller will meet at the escrow company and sign all the forms. Most states require a three-day waiting period before the process is considered complete. At that point, you will get the keys to your new home if you have not already received them.

This is a bird's-eye view of the home-buying process. Naturally, there are a lot of complex details, and since it is a legal process, there are also a lot of people involved whom you may or may not actually meet. In the following section, I will expound on the purchasing process.

More Details on the Home Buying Process

Participants

Most of the people involved in the home buying process are experts who play a specific role. Since each person is responsible for making sure the process is thorough, accurate, and legal, choosing experienced people and companies with excellent reputations is critical. The closing documentation should be as close to perfect as humanly possible. There are many horror stories about house titles not properly cleared or repair issues that were hidden from the buyer or not fixed properly. Buying a real property is a long-term investment, so take your time and invest in finding the right property, working with the best professionals, and negotiating an agreement that will serve you well, even after the buying process is over.

The main professional participants include the following:

- Real estate agent: You should only use a state-licensed agent whose license can be verified with an agency in your home state. The agent should be familiar with the workings of the real estate market in general and the local market in detail and know property values. The agent should also have property listings and access to the Multiple Listing Services (MLS), which lists properties for sale by thousands of real estate agents. In addition, the agent should have a network of contacts who can help find the house that meets your requirements.

- Real estate broker: Like the real estate agent, a real estate broker must be state-licensed. In fact, a brokerage firm cannot call itself a broker unless it is licensed as such. The broker oversees the activities of the real estate agents who join the brokerage firm. Real estate agents are independent contractors working on commission, and the broker is an important fail-safe agent who is responsible for the agent's activities. Real estate agents work under the supervision of the real estate broker. Should the agent not perform as expected or required, you can discuss the issues with the broker.
- Real estate inspectors: The house offer should be contingent upon the completion of an independent inspection by a licensed property inspector. The licensing requirements vary from state to state, but the real estate agent should have the information you need, which can be verified at the state agency level. The property inspector will assess the condition of all the house components. The inspector's report should be carefully reviewed to ensure that the house has no expensive or dangerous issues. Any major repairs should then be included in the sales contract, regardless of whether they will be repaired prior to closing. It is better to have stipulations and conditions written into the sales contract than to depend on personal assurances. If the seller promises to make repairs, then the contract should ensure that dates are included to stay on schedule. Some closings drag on longer than necessary because the buyer and seller did not agree on firm dates for issues to be resolved.
- Lender: Unless the buyer is able to pay cash for the house, a loan is necessary. Loan can be structured in a variety of ways in terms of the percent of the total selling price that is mortgaged (for example, 70 percent, 80 percent, or 100 percent), the amount of down payment required, the type of interest rate (fixed or variable), and payoff term, to name just a few. The standard mortgage is called a conventional mortgage, which is what this discussion is based on. The lender is called the mortgagee. Some communities and developments (such as co-ops and condos) might require that specific down payment amounts, closing costs, and other financing amounts be paid directly by the buyer rather than financed

through the bank. In some major cities such as New York, some co-operative developments require prospective buyers to have up to two years of maintenance fees in an escrow account in addition to a 25 percent or more down payment as well as closing costs. So confirm these types of details while reviewing various properties.

- Underwriter: The lender sends loan documents to an underwriter who does the actual detailed analysis of the loan. The underwriter analyses documentation, verifies information, and actually approves the loan. Once the package is analyzed, it is returned to the loan officer or loan processor with approval, denial, or conditions for approval.
- Appraiser: The lender will order an appraisal of the property to ensure that the house is worth at least as much as the sale price. The appraiser is also state licensed and will gauge the value of the home based on several factors that include square footage, house features, size of the lot, and the value of similar properties in the area.
- Escrow agent: The escrow officer handles the money and documentation related to the transaction. The escrow agent should be a disinterested third party who does not represent the interests of the buyer or seller. There are independent professional and legal firms that offer escrow services.
- Insurance agent: It is necessary to have homeowner's insurance that becomes effective the minute you actually own the home. Home insurance coverage is provided by a licensed and regulated insurance company. You can choose the deductible and add special coverage, but the insurance amount on the house must cover its full actual cash value. You can also buy replacement coverage that insures the house for full market value replacement cost as opposed to only covering the house's value less depreciation at the time loss occurs. Sometimes, financing terms will require certain types of insurance, depending on how much equity will be in the property after the closing.

The person who is borrowing the money for the house purchase is called the mortgagor. Sometimes, an attorney is needed if the sale is complex, but escrow officers work for companies that have attorneys on staff or contract for specified services. Other people may provide services like termite inspections or specialized inspections for more detailed evaluation of certain house components such as the foundation or electrical. The lender may also require that the property be surveyed or that the septic system be inspected in certain regions of the country.

It is so important to give yourself a way out of a real estate transaction before closing by including contingencies in the earnest money agreement. Adding one or more contingencies to the Earnest Money Agreement will ensure you can get your escrowed deposit money back if things do not go according to plan. Contingencies can vary and may include conditions such as:

- You must be able to close the sale of your existing home
- You must be able to secure suitable financing for the purchase
- The buyer must ensure that the property appraises for at least the selling price
- The house must pass all required inspections

Possible Closing Delays

Buying a first home is exciting, and it is natural to want everything to go smoothly. However, several things can prevent a home sale from closing quickly. These include:

- The property appraisal amount is less than the selling price
- The title search discovered encumbrances or unreleased liens on the property
- New encumbrances are assigned to property before closing
- A problem, like new debt, arises concerning the buyer's credit report that now disqualifies the buyer
- Missing documentation such as an insurance policy
- A problem that should have by law been disclosed to the buyer is discovered in the home
- Mistakes in the documentation are found and must be corrected
- The underwriter requires additional information before approving the loan

Remember, prequalified buyers will usually be able to close faster than buyers who must still find financing after the process has begun. However, do not underestimate how long the closing process can take. Closings can take over six months if the buyer and seller have conflicts. In those cases, if the delays are caused by the buyer's or seller's contingent charges that were written into the contract, then the delays are at least more acceptable. Imagine if you had a stipulation that if the seller misses the closing date deadline, then he or she will have to pay $200 per day until deal is closed. After two weeks, you will have $2,800 in delay costs payable to your escrow account. The seller and buyer generally want to avoid additional costs and such contingencies in order to at least guarantee that an earnest effort will be made to close on time.

Financial Issues

There are many financial issues to consider. The buyer cost-estimate sheet details possible expenses that need to be taken into account before closing. The estimate sheet will give the buyer a best estimate of the closing costs, insurance and tax reserves, real estate broker commissions, and all the other fees and charges involved in a real estate sale. At the actual closing, you will be presented with a HUD Settlement Statement, which is required by federal law. (1) This statement provides the final details of the sale transaction and shows a debit and credit ledger for the amounts to be paid by borrower and to the seller. The escrow agent will notify the buyer of the amount to bring to the closing in the form of a cashier's check.

There are two categories of closing costs:

- Nonrecurring: Fees charged once at the closing
- Recurring: Prepaid or ongoing fees deposited in an escrow account that is maintained as long as the buyer owns the home

Nonrecurring fees include the fees already discussed and many more:

- Lender origination fee: paid to the lender for preparing a loan. It is expressed as a percentage. Each percent represents 1 percent of the buyer's mortgage amount
- Discount points: additional funds paid to the lender to buy down the interest rate. It is expressed as a percentage, and each point paid on a thirty-year mortgage equates to approximately a .125 percent reduction in the interest rate, which may be beneficial if the buyer expects to be in the home a long time. Average points range anywhere from 0 percent to 3 percent
- Appraisal fee: ranges from $263 to $444, depending on the selling price of the home (2)
- Inspection fee: ranges from $300 to $500, depending on the inspection services needed (e.g., house, water quality, septic tank) (2)
- Underwriting fee: a loan documentation processing fee covering the cost of the loan approval process

- Escrow fee: usually based on charging so many dollars per $1,000 of the selling price
- Title insurance fee: there are two types of title insurance: one to insure the lender against title flaws after the purchase, and one to protect the buyer. It is usually calculated based on a cost per $1,000 of the house value with a standard policy costing approximately 1 percent of the purchase price (3)
- Recording fees: usually inexpensive, these are the fees to record the deed and mortgage at the courthouse
- Broker commission: an average of 5 percent to 6 percent of the selling price that is paid to the real estate broker (4)
- Other fees include: credit report fee (approximately $55), application fees (average cost is $365), wire transfer fees, and others (2)

The recurring fees are also paid at the time of closing and are usually deposited in an escrow account. These fees are calculated in two steps: 1) from the date of closing to the first of the month, and 2) the monthly amount to be paid into escrow. Often, the monthly fees are paid with the mortgage payment, and the lender divvies up the payment between escrow and the lender. The escrow agent then ensures that the buyer's taxes and insurance are paid as required. In some cases, the buyer has the option of paying a full year of taxes and insurance up front to keep the mortgage payment as low as possible. Most people choose the monthly payment option.

- Private Mortgage Insurance (PMI) or Mortgage Insurance Premium: insurance that covers the lender in the event that the borrower misses payments. PMI is only valid when 22 percent of the home's equity has been accumulated. It is paid with the mortgage payment.
- Prepaid Interest: since interest begins accruing at the time of settlement, the lender will calculate the interest owed for the partial month of settlement; after that, the monthly interest is paid through the mortgage payment.
- Home owner's Insurance: the cost of insurance protecting the owner in the event that the house incurs physical damage. The cost depends on the value of home, type of coverage, location, and other factors. Average cost is approximately $744 per year. (2) The buyer may prepay the insurance company for a required number

of months and include a monthly amount in the mortgage payment that is deposited into escrow for payment to insurer.

- Taxes: like interest, city and county property taxes are usually paid on a monthly basis into an escrow account through the mortgage payment process. When the taxes are due, the escrow account disburses the payment.

Many other fees are possible in a first-time home purchase, depending on the home being purchased or the type of loan that has been obtained. For example, if you are assuming an existing mortgage, there will be an assumption fee. If you are buying a home with a Veterans Administration (VA) loan, there is a VA funding fee.

The seller also gets a cost estimate leading to another point. Traditionally, in most states, some costs of buying a home are prorated between the buyer and the seller. A few states have addressed closing costs legislatively. For example, Kentucky law requires the seller to pay the closing costs. Elsewhere, many of the fees are split between the buyer and the seller based on local customs, meaning the split is negotiable. For example, title insurance may be paid by the buyer or the seller or split 50/50.

Typically, the escrow fees are split between the buyer and seller, with the seller paying the prorated amount of property taxes and insurance up to the closing. The buyer then pays an amount to cover the time period from closing to the first of the month. The seller will also cover the expense items that are associated with proving the property is as described. In one example, the seller will pay the appraisal fee, termite inspection fees, and for required repairs. However, the buyer usually pays for home inspections.

In almost every case, the seller will pay the real estate commission to the real estate broker. The seller has hired a real estate agency to find a buyer for the house, so they have a contractual arrangement between them. The buyer and seller brokers must come to agreement on how the commission will be split between the agents and the amount paid to the brokerage firm.

Typically, closing costs will cost about 3 percent to 5 percent of the selling price plus the down payment. The total amount of cash outlay can easily add up to 15 percent to 25 percent of the selling price. For certain selective or affluent developments, the cash outlay can be as much as 50 percent of the sales price due to a larger percentage down payment and other up-front escrow requirements.

The First Year of Ownership

The first year of home ownership can be a bit disconcerting, because a house can seem quite expensive to maintain compared to renting. It is important to understand qualifying for a mortgage does not mean you will be able to afford the higher expenses associated with home ownership. In fact, the mortgage payment may be less than what you were paying for rent but now there are other costs that need to be paid on a monthly, quarterly, or annual basis that need to be prorated in your monthly budget.

Compared to renting, you will now have to pay:

- Higher utility expenses due to more square footage
- Water, sewer, and garbage expenses that were included in your rent but are not included in the mortgage
- Property taxes
- Home Owner's insurance

After the closing, the home owner is also usually responsible for all maintenance expenses. If the purchase is within a development, then a fee may be charged for certain communal services. However, in general, there is no landlord to call to fix the leaky plumbing or to replace the shingles or seal the driveway concrete that began cracking. Many times, people deplete their emergency fund or savings account to cover closing costs or to pay for the cost of moving and making necessary changes to the house, like adding locks or lighting. In addition, many new home owners need to buy a washer, dryer, furniture, and window coverings and make general repairs, like painting.

For this reason, qualifying for a loan may require that you show that you have enough cash on hand to pay for closing costs, the down payment, and several months of mortgage, insurance, and tax payments. You should also have enough money saved to pay for the maintenance and repair expenses which will average 1 to 3 percent of the house value annually. (5)

There is simply no way to anticipate all of the unforeseen expenses associated with house repairs and maintenance. For this reason, you should develop a household budget that includes a house emergency fund and set aside an amount each payday. The budgeted amount for the home mortgage and home repairs and maintenance should represent no more than 30 percent of your gross income. If these costs represent more, then you should begin looking for ways to trim your other expenses to ensure you can afford your home after you have purchased it.

Government and Other Credits

The housing industry constitutes a large portion of the country's economic activity. For this reason, the government periodically offers programs to help people interested in buying a home, especially for the first time. For example, there was a first time home owner tax credit offered to those who purchased their first home in 2008, 2009, or 2010. These types of programs have expiration dates, so you should always research current programs when you are interested in buying a house.

If you itemize on your income tax return, you can take long-standing tax deductions such as:

- Mortgage interest
- Points associated with a mortgage
- Interest on a loan used for home capital improvements
- Interest on a home equity loan up to a stated limit
- Property taxes
- Mortgage Credit Certificate (MCC) home buying program tax credit
- Residential Energy Efficient Property Credit (through 2016)
- State tax credits for homebuyers

The Mortgage Credit Certificate allows first-time homebuyers who are also low income to take an additional tax credit equal to 20 percent of the mortgage interest payments. The credit is deducted dollar for dollar from the income tax owed and has a maximum of $2,000.

The Residential Energy Efficient Property Credit allows a tax credit of 30 percent of the cost of property that is qualified as alternative energy equipment. Alternative energy equipment includes solar water heaters, geothermal heat pumps, and wind turbines. The certificates are issued by state.

State tax credits for homebuyers vary and are usually income restricted. In other words, most of them are geared toward helping low- and middle-income families buy their first home. The states that allow tax credits usually allow a percentage of annual interest.

Other programs include assistance with the down payment, savings programs for a down payment that have tax advantages, and assistance with obtaining a low-interest fixed rate loan. For example, the state of Minnesota offers the Community Activity Set Aside Program that requires a homebuyer to attend an education program to quality for $4,500 in assistance for closing costs or the down payment. The $4,500 is interest free and payment free and becomes a lien on the property that is paid back when the house is sold. The state also offers the Home ownership Assistance Fund and the Home owner Entry Loan Program. (6) Your state housing agency can tell you about any current programs available.

The discussion on mortgages also assumed a conventional mortgage is the source of funding for the first-time homebuyer. There are other funding sources such as the federal government Federal Housing Administration (FHA) loan. First-time homebuyers may find an FHA loan is better structured to meet the needs of families who do not have a lot of available cash. Though you must meet income and credit score requirements, the FHA loan advantages include:

- Easier qualifications
- Government guarantees
- Smaller down payment (3.5 percent)
- Possibility of including closing costs in mortgage

In addition to the government financial credits, many developers and homebuilders offer incentives and credits to convince people to buy their homes. These incentives are available on a builder-by-builder basis, so never hesitate to ask about them. The incentives can take many different forms.

- Allowance amount for finish materials like paint
- Percent taken off base price
- Cash incentives
- Allowable upgrades

Second Homes

Sometimes, people decide to purchase a second home and keep the first home, as well. For example, a buyer may have a main residence and a vacation home. As long as the second property is used as a second home, the mortgage interest is deductible in the same manner as the interest on the first home. You can also deduct the property taxes on your second home. You do not have to actually use the home, but you cannot rent it out due to the requirements for certain government incentives and deductions.

The rules change once you rent out the first or second home for more than fourteen days a year. It then becomes income or investment property, and rental income is reported. You also have to calculate the percentage of days it is rented to the days the house is used. That percent is then applied to the mortgage interest, taxes, interest, and other expenses, and the prorated amounts are deductible as rental expenses.

Per the IRS, to qualify for the residence interest deduction when you rent, the house must be used for personal use for more than the "greater of fourteen days or 10 percent of the number of days you rent it." (7) If you do not meet these conditions, you cannot deduct the full amount of the mortgage and taxes as personal residence expenses. If you rent the property, you may still be able to take a tax deduction for the prorated mortgage interest and taxes.

A word of caution: tax laws are regularly amended, so you need to verify current laws and regulations with a competent attorney or knowledgeable professional before purchasing a second home.

Foreclosure Process and Short Selling

There are two types of properties buyers sometimes consider in the hopes of getting a good price: a foreclosure and a short sale. In both cases, the current mortgagor is in financial distress and has fallen behind on making the mortgage payments. The foreclosure and short sales processes both represent methods for ending the mortgage contract.

The foreclosure process is a legal proceeding in which the lender attempts to recover the money owed on the mortgage by forcing the house to be sold. The property served as the collateral for the loan. When the borrower defaults, the lender can then try to obtain full ownership so that the house can be sold and the mortgage can be paid. The laws on how this process must proceed vary by state. In general, the process works in the following way:

- Mortgagor misses a payment and loan goes into default
- Late fees are charged
- Mortgage company begins foreclosure process if payment is not made
- Public notice of default is issued

- Mortgagor is notified
- Property is sold at auction

Three Types of Foreclosure

Judicial Foreclosure: In a judicial foreclosure, the lender must file suit in court. If the borrower does not make the demanded payment, the court orders the sale of the property at auction. The auction is conducted by the sheriff or the court. The lender can buy back the house, or someone else can buy the house and pay off the mortgage.

Strict Foreclosure: The strict foreclosure is not as common. It also begins with a lawsuit filed in court. If the mortgagor cannot pay the mortgage, the property is directly returned to the lender and no auction is held. The lender then resells the property in the hopes of recovering as much of the mortgage balance as possible.

Statutory Foreclosure: If the mortgage has a power of sale clause, a statutory foreclosure process is followed. When the home owner defaults on payments, the lender notifies the mortgagor that payment is due. After the allowed waiting period, the mortgage company can hold a public auction without using the court or local sheriff.

Liens on the Property

Generally, foreclosure proceeds are distributed based on encumbrance date. There are junior and senior liens, and the senior liens are paid first. Senior liens are those recorded against the property before the foreclosure process began. Property liens are paid off according to their date of filing for the most part. However, in practice, property sale proceeds will be used to pay property taxes first (to the local government) and then the first mortgage holder (usually a bank), followed by the second and third mortgage holders. These proceeds also pay the foreclosure expenses, which can be significant.

In most cases, the IRS has the right to seize or put a special lien on all of a debtor's personal property in order to collect on monies owed. An IRS lien, however, is treated like other liens, and its payment from proceeds of the sale of the property thus depends on the date the lien was filed. In fact, even if the IRS were to seize property for payment before a foreclosure proceeding commences, it must pay the lender what the property owner owes them on the home mortgage and other senior liens on the property before recouping its monies from the property owner.

Unpaid liens will remain with the property, making it more difficult to sell. The lender will usually buy the house at auction if the auction bidders do not offer enough to pay the mortgage. A homebuyer can bid on homes at foreclosure auctions. It is possible to buy properties for less than market value since it may not be necessary to pay the equity value. In the unlikely event that there are undistributed proceeds after all the liens are paid, the property owner is paid. This is only a quick summary of the foreclosure process. Many foreclosures can be quite lengthy and complex.

Short Sale

An alternative to foreclosure is the short sale. The short sale is a process in which the lender agrees to accept less than the mortgage balance in order to sell the property quickly. It is a process often used when the mortgage payments are delinquent and the owner wants to prevent foreclosure or bankruptcy.

When you buy a house as a short sale, the home is purchased directly from the mortgage at a discount. For example, a home owner has a first mortgage for $200,000 and is about to go into foreclosure. You offer the lender $160,000, and the lender accepts in order to limit the loss or to avoid auction fees. Short sales are best when they are completed before a foreclosure, because there will be fewer fees. Owners who have been notified that they are in default are highly motivated sellers.

The lender will often be willing to waive many of the fees normally associated with closing costs in order to recover the mortgage balance. A short sale requires negotiating with the lender to get the best possible buy. The lender will only agree to a short sale if the senior and junior lien holders agree.

One of the main disadvantages of buying foreclosed properties or properties on short sale is that the process can take months longer than a normal sale. Mortgages and liens can be extremely complex and the lender will have to work through the details one by one. Another major disadvantage is that a short sale can abruptly end if a lien holder refuses to cooperate or the lender decides not to follow through. It is therefore important to do more thorough research and to work with professionals who will have the time to focus on you in these types of transactions. Distressed sales can be wrought with headaches, disappointments, and unforeseen complications. It is, therefore, crucial to have an expert in that area to guide you through the process.

Buying, Owning, and Enjoying a Home

This discussion lays the foundation for the home-buying process. The home-buying process can be complex, but a successful end result makes it all seem worthwhile. It is not a decision to be taken lightly, though, because owning a home is a long-term financial commitment. Once you decide to purchase a house, the first step is to do some research on the real estate market so you know what to expect while undertaking the search for the ideal property. And remember that the location, education system, and taxation are all integrated and important.

CHAPTER 11

International Real Estate Investing

We tend to think of international real estate investors as big corporations investing in commercial property, but many people in the United States purchase residential real estate overseas. Generally, there are four main reasons for these purchases:

- Vacation home
- Home for retirement
- Generate rental income
- Job relocation

Like most investment markets, real estate markets vary from country to country. One country's property may be experiencing price increases while a country on the other side of the world may be in a period of declining prices. However, the current and expected real estate prices are just two factors that go into a decision to invest in international real estate. Deciding to buy property outside of the United States is a serious decision that requires a lot of thoughtful research and preparation to ensure that you invest in property that meets all your needs and that you are shielded from potential loss as much as possible.

When buying property that will be part rental and part residence, you should consider how it will produce income. Property can generate profit in two ways: rental income and capital appreciation through market value increases such as renovations.

Collecting data on how many Americans own residential real estate in other countries is difficult because the IRS does not require this information to be filed with their agency upon purchase. It is safe to say, though, that international travel was a much bigger event than it is now. For the most part, pre-baby boomer generation real estate purchases were made by the wealthy who wanted vacation homes or homes where they could live while conducting business overseas.

In the 1980s, the number of international home buyers grew when they were able to take out second mortgages on domestic property that had significantly appreciated.

Unfortunately, in the 1990s, a recession led to many of these same people losing their homes because they were unable to make the payments.

Between the late 1990s and 2008, Americans purchased unprecedented amounts of international real estate. Most buyers purchased properties in warm-climate locations in the Caribbean and Latin America, such as Panama and Brazil, with the intention of using the property for retirement or vacation. (1) International real estate purchases accelerated because of declining air fares, rising property values, and declining interest rates.

The global recession that began in 2008 had a significant negative impact on the global real estate markets. Real estate markets collapsed, and home values trended downward in most locations. However, the economic disaster also created a real estate market loaded with unsold residential properties and foreclosed homes, townhomes, and condominiums. It is still a buyer's market in many locales, meaning you have a choice between buying a new property or a resale and can negotiate a good price.

Anyone considering international real estate should be familiar with the term "off plan." Buying off plan means buying the property based on the design plan of a house that is not yet built. Off-plan buying also indicates that the financing is arranged before building begins. Some countries require off-plan purchases by foreign real estate buyers.

Advantages and Disadvantages

Buying real estate in another country has its advantages and disadvantages. With an international purchase, you cannot just drop by to see how the area operates at particular times of the day, month, or year. For example, it may be difficult to figure out what traffic congestion is like close to the property or to determine the noise level in the morning, afternoon, night, or on the weekend. However, there are still good reasons for international real estate investing. Let us take a look at some of the good and the bad.

Advantages

- Property prices can be quite reasonable in many locations
- Property can have great potential appreciation value
- Favorable currency exchange rates offer advantages
- You may be able to get more value for your money
- Properties with amenities and special incentives that would be unaffordable in your home country are affordable internationally

Disadvantages

- Not all countries carefully preserve property rights like the United States does
- Economic and political conditions abroad can be very different from the domestic economy
- The property may be subjected to new, unfavorable international laws and taxes
- You would be unable to get to the property quickly in general or in cases of emergency

There are also other considerations that you should bear in mind when considering international real estate. One of the first decisions is deciding where you want to own property, as a lot depends on the how the property will be used. For example, if you are buying a home where you hope to one day retire, then the year-round climate will be a critical factor. If, on the other hand, you only intend to spend the winter months in the home, then you should choose property in a location where winter weather is mild. If you want to spend skiing vacations in your own home, then the location needs to offer plenty of winter snow and access to ski slopes.

Most people would love to buy property with a view, but a view will almost always increase the price of property. A beach property, a view of a beautiful valley, or breathtaking mountain scenery may sound great, but the higher price of the property will reflect the value of the view.

Special Considerations

A number of special considerations come along with the purchase of international residential property.

Legal Requirements

Every country has unique laws concerning foreign investments, purchase of real estate, taxes, documentation, fees, licenses, and so on. If you choose to use an international real estate agent or attorney, you should make sure their credentials and reputation are valid. It is easy to get into trouble in some countries when legal requirements are not carefully adhered to. This is especially true in under-developed or emerging economies where economic and political stability is questionable. Americans and many Europeans are used to living in stable countries where properties cannot be seized by the government. However, in times of social, economic, or political instability, such expectations might be illusory in some countries.

Exchange Rates

The exchange rates can greatly impact the cost of a mortgage or your payments if the loan is funded in another country but you are paying with money in the currency of your homeland. The mortgage or financing can be taken out in the currency of your homeland or in the country where the property is located. One of the advantages of securing a mortgage in the currency of your homeland is that you get some protection against devaluation. If the currency of the country in which the property is located declines in value, then the value of your international property should increase by the same percentage when converted into your homeland currency value. Let us take a closer look at exchange rates to see why this happens.

Exchange Rate's (F/X) Impact on Mortgage Payments

When exchange rates or foreign exchange (F/X) fluctuate, they will affect the value between two currencies. As an investor, you can be negatively or positively impacted by these fluctuations depending on which currency you hold.

For example, let us assume you have US dollars and want to find out how many Great Britain pounds (GBP) you can get for your dollar. You will look at the exchange rate for your homeland's currency, and you might see something like this:

1 US dollar (USD) = 0.6353 GBP

Or 0.6353 GBP/1 USD = 0.6353 GBP to 1 USD

This is considered your homeland's foreign exchange rate if your country's currency is the US dollar. If you have Great Britain pounds and want to find out how many US dollars you might get, then you would look up the rate for GBP/USD and get something like this:

1 GBP = 1.5741 USD

Or 1.5741 USD/1 GBP = 1.5741 USD to 1 GBP

If you were from Great Britain, then this is what the foreign exchange rate would look like if you were converting to US dollars. Although they are written differently, the underlying currency rate is the same—the difference is in what currency you have and what you want to exchange it for. From the above example, it should be clear that the GBP has more value. If you have one US dollar, then you will not get one whole GBP, because the GBP is more valuable. The US dollar is worth a fraction of a whole GBP, so you will only get about 0.64 GBP. Now if you held one GBP and wanted to convert it into dollars, then you would get $1.57, because a dollar is only a fraction of the GBP value and you need to add up the dollar equivalents until it equals a whole GBP. Here is a breakdown:

1 whole GBP = 1 whole dollar + 0.5741 dollar fraction = 1.5741 US dollars

Let us take a look at a real estate example. Say that you live in the United States and want to buy a property that costs 100,000 GBP in the countryside of Britain. In order to compare this investment to other comparable properties in the United States, you will want to have everything in US currency. This means you will want to convert the British property purchase amount from British pounds to US dollars.

Converted value = amount foreign currency x appropriate F/X rate

Converted value in USD = 100,000 GBP x 1.5741 USD/1 GBP

Converted value USD = $157,410

If you are given the USD equivalent and the GBP purchase price, but not the currency exchange rate, it is simple to figure out what the underlying F/X rate is. If you divide the two values together, you get the appropriate F/X rate. So if you were told by a real estate broker that the US purchase price is $157,410 and the British equivalent is 100,000 pounds, then you can find the F/X rate as follows:

USD Value/GBP Value = F/X rate

USD Value/GBP Value = 157,410/100,000 = 1.5741

Now let us assume that you finance the whole purchase amount through a private bank in Great Britain because they are offering lower interest rates and overall better loan terms than US banks. Due to the property being held in Great Britain, your loan is a lower risk to the British bank in case of default on the mortgage if it becomes necessary to seize the property.

Also bear in mind that in reality, most real estate transactions will require a percentage down payment and might have restrictions on financing 100 percent of the purchase price. But to make this example a little simpler to follow, we will assume you have financed the whole purchase amount. Now that you have financed and purchase the property, let us take a closer look at what happens to the financed or mortgaged amount in a variety of scenarios as the F/X rate changes.

Decrease in Home Country Currency Value

What happens to a mortgage's estimated value if the GBP value gets stronger against the dollar?

Assume: 1 GBP = 2 USD or 2 USD/1 GBP

Converted value = amount foreign currency x appropriate F/X rate

Converted value USD = 100,000 GBP x 2 USD/1 GBP

Converted value USD = $200,000

As you can see, if the foreign property's currency value increases or your home currency value decreases, then your mortgage amount owed will increase when converted to your home currency. In this case, you will be paying more in your USD currency over the life of the mortgage if nothing else changes. This might amount to an additional $42,590 or about 27 percent more if there are no further changes.

Mortgage difference = current value - original value

Mortgage difference = $200,000 – $157,410

Mortgage difference = $42,590

Increase in Home Country Currency Value

What happens to a mortgage's estimated value if the GBP value gets weaker against the dollar?

Assume: 1 GBP = 1.3 USD or 1.3 USD/1 GBP

Converted value = amount foreign currency x appropriate F/X rate

Converted value USD = 100,000 GBP x 1.3 USD/1 GBP

Converted value USD = $130,000

As you can see, if the foreign property's currency value decreases or your home currency value increases, then the foreign mortgage amount owed will also decrease when converted to your home currency. In this case, you will be paying less in your USD currency over the life of the mortgage if nothing else changes. This might amount to a reduction of $27,410 or about 17.4 percent.

Mortgage difference = current value - original value

Mortgage difference = $130,000 – $157,410

Mortgage difference = ($27,410)

If you have taken out a loan from a US dollar-based financial institution, then you will not have to worry about the F/X changes impacting your mortgage payments. However, your bank might charge other fees in regards to them taking on the currency, legal, political, and other foreign risks that the foreign bank would otherwise be assuming. Therefore, the savvy investor will compare various scenarios that might include taking out a loan in the home country or the foreign country in order to determine which would prove more financially profitable over the period that the investment will be held.

As you can see from the previous example, you can take out a foreign currency loan, but it does have risks associated with most foreign investments. Changes in currency exchange rates can occur rapidly and without warning. Currency rates are impacted by interest rates, fees, and economic and political actions. A foreign currency loan payment usually costs the borrower fees or commissions to convert domestic currency into foreign currency needed to make the mortgage payment. (2) Getting into financial difficulties due to currency rate movements is easy to do, so keep a watchful eye on currency rates as well as other factors that might affect your investment.

Scams

Any sound advice that international real estate buyers listen to will always include this: beware of scams. Each country has laws concerning property, but they vary widely. Unfamiliarity with laws makes buyers susceptible to scams. In addition, some countries with a lax judicial system or cultures riddled with corruption make foreign real estate frauds and scams much more commonplace. You should never pay money to anyone without doing thorough research, viewing the property, and consulting with a trusted and knowledgeable attorney.

Scams can vary. They include:

- Selling a property that is worthless
- Selling an "off plan" and then failing to build to specifications
- Collecting a down payment and then disappearing
- Selling property which is not legally owned by the seller
- Failing to properly register a real estate sale
- Selling the same property more than once
- Selling property that has undisclosed governmental restrictions

Economic Environment

The economic stability of a country should be considered when deciding on international property for purchase. Economic stability includes a stable currency, a reliable and regulated financial system, and clearly established laws and regulations concerning land purchases and related transactions.

Political Environment

Properties in some countries may be truly desirable bargains, but if the political environment is unstable, then the purchase is risky. The government should have a history of stability and should not condone fraud. Buying property in a country where payoffs to government officials are an accepted practice is an unnecessary risk that international property investors should avoid. That is why it is important to do your own in-depth research and to consult with professionals and organizations that are knowledgeable about the country where you are planning to buy. And again, government policies on foreign ownership of real estate need to be evaluated by a qualified attorney.

Language

In the age of technology, handheld language translators make managing different languages less of a barrier. However, you should use an attorney and trustworthy translator to interpret all real estate documents. Legal jargon is complicated even when it is in your native tongue.

In addition, if you plan to live in a foreign country, you will probably want to learn the language. Some languages are easier to learn than others are. For example, it is generally agreed that learning Spanish is easier than learning Chinese. If you have difficulty learning languages, you may want to consider property in countries that speak a language similar to your home country's language.

Infrastructure and Access

The condition of the infrastructure and access are closely tied together. Infrastructure plays a big role in the decision concerning where to buy international real estate. There are a lot of questions to ask before making a decision. For example, if you will be traveling to the property often, then easy access is needed. Does the country have an airport that makes travel back and forth possible all year? How long does it take to get to the property? If you want to be able to access it for short periods of time like a few days or a week, you do not want to buy property that will take you two days to reach one way. How much will it cost you to reach the property? If you plan to visit regularly, travel costs can accumulate rapidly.

Another access issue is the condition of the roads or highway system. You may be willing to buy property in the backcountry or mountains, but if the roads are closed all winter, then you will not be able to access your property during those times. Many countries also offer properties for sale in areas where the infrastructure is still being installed. The government may have plans to pave unpaved roads, but future plans should be verified with reliable sources.

In addition, while living in the international locale you will want to be able to access local attractions, restaurants, grocery stores, and so on. In some countries, the roads may be unpaved from the main highway to beach property, for example, but the climate is such that accessibility is not an issue. If you are considering buying a home near a big city like London, Paris, or Frankfurt, then you are going to be more concerned with traffic congestion than the condition of the roads.

Other infrastructure items to consider include:

- Communication system: telephone, cell phone, and Internet
- Sewer or septic systems
- Utilities: electrical, gas, water, and waste disposal

Paying for the Property

Generally, the best approach is to obtain pre-approved financing before looking for property. That way, you will know how much you can afford and have a negotiating tool. People use several methods to pay for international real estate purchases:

- Cash
- Loan at home
- Loan in property's country
- Offshore banking centers
- Local financing from property developer

The requirements for obtaining loans differ from country to country, but a domestic loan is often the ideal choice simply because its terms will be easiest to understand. If you choose to pursue a loan in the international country or offshore banking center, it is critical to use an attorney familiar with the real estate laws who is accessible even after the initial transaction is complete. Most countries will not loan more than 70 to 80 percent of the property value, but in some cases, there are lower percentages designated by law for foreign buyers. Borrowing domestically also means that you can be certain that your payments will not be negatively affected by fluctuations in exchange rates.

Rentals

Verify that the country does not restrict rentals. For example, some countries might not allow short-term rentals before holidays. Some places have favorable rental terms for investors, especially the traditional vacation locations, which legally are not allowed to protect local hotel and motel revenues. From another perspective, if you do not want to take a chance on living near property where renters come and go, then you want to avoid buying in a location that allows short-term rentals.

Property in cities usually makes better rental property than rural real estate does. Rents are also higher for properties near sought-after attractions such as golf resorts, ski slopes, major attractions, mountains, and beach areas.

If you are planning to rent out the property, be sure to verify that the rental income estimates are accurate. This estimate often influences the property's sale price. Good practices include researching the real estate market where you want to buy property. Some useful information to have on hand includes rental trends, planned growth in the area, historical property sales in the area, and projected short-term and long-term resale values.

Taxes

The United States permits the purchase of residential property in foreign countries, and the purchase does not have to be specially recorded. If the first home in the United States is ever sold, though, the gain on the property will have to be reported.

In the foreign country, there may very well be taxes due at time of purchase and property taxes due annually. An attorney may recommend opening a foreign bank account to make tax payments simpler, but that may trigger new United States reporting requirements.

Buying a new home in some countries may cost you a value added tax (VAT) or consumption (sales) tax. China and India as well as many Asian, African, South American, and European countries have some form of the VAT tax. The good news is that countries charging the VAT tax usually do not add many other, if any, fees in addition to the purchase price.

Traditional or Hot Spots

Finding an "overseas paradise" or "dream retirement home" is often the kind of description you hear from people interested in buying international residential property. There are hot spots where sales are robust, and the reasons for their popularity vary. Often it is a combination of warm climate and reasonable prices. However, there are plenty of hot spots in cool or cold climates, as well.

A hot spot is also defined as a location where property values are expected to rise. For example, maturing properties or rising economies often create hot spots. Following are some of the recently popular areas where housing markets are hottest and the primary reason:

- Brazil: real estate prices are expected to rise over next five years
- Costa Rico: inexpensive property and warm climate
- Dominican Republic: inexpensive property and warm climate
- Guatemala: inexpensive property and warm climate
- France: low interest rates with expected real estate price increases
- Morocco: emerging market
- Panama: inexpensive property and warm climate
- Thailand: zero- to low-interest government-backed loans

Because of the drop in real estate prices at the start of the recession, real estate bargains are available in plenty of other countries. Investment opportunities include places like Croatia and Bulgaria. However, what one person considers a hot market actually depends on the reason for buying the property, and that may not appeal to others. If you are looking for a hot housing market for rental income or because you enjoy big-city activity, then Hong Kong is hot. If you are looking for a quiet retirement home, then Brazil or Costa Rico are desirable locations. That is precisely why the first thing to do when considering buying international real estate is to decide your ultimate goal.

Since the recession, real estate prices have dropped precipitously. However, high unemployment has risen, and consumer confidence in the global economy is low, which has led to a reduction in international real estate buying. The depressed global real estate market is showing some signs of recovery, but prices are expected to remain low for a much longer period of time. Therefore, bargains exist for those in a position to purchase real estate.

Getting Assistance

A fairly recent development emerging during the 2008 to 2010 recession is the formation of travel groups specifically organized to showcase real estate for sale in specific countries. Some of these travel organizations also organize the trips on the behalf of a real estate company or developer. The trips are designed to help buyers find good deals on properties while also providing a wealth of information about issues pertaining to real estate ownership in particular locations. These issues include getting title insurance, meeting insurance requirements, maintaining the house from a distance, and legal and tax issues concerning foreign real estate purchases. (3)

There are also domestic and international real estate companies that assist real estate buyers. However, it is critical that you use only verifiably reliable companies. Most areas have realtor associations that use licensed real estate agents. In some countries, the real estate agent is allowed to represent both the buyer and the seller. Other intermediaries include attorneys and property managers, but the same rule applies as far as checking credentials. Property developers also arrange tours of various developments with the hopes of selling you real estate. Once again, always check with an attorney before buying property, and always retain an attorney to handle the actual purchase.

Some possible information sources on buying property overseas include:

- Association of International Property Professionals (industry group)
- International Pathfinder
- International Living
- National Association of Realtors

Alternatives to Buying

If you want to be able to access property in a foreign country without purchasing real estate, you have basically two options. First, you can rent property. A second option is to buy into a timeshare-type of arrangement in which you use the property for a designated period of time.

Buying international real estate is complex because so much depends on your needs and the country where the real estate is located. As you begin your search, it is important to take your time and do plenty of research on locations of interest. Making any real estate commitment requires careful planning, but it becomes a necessity when the property is located in another country.

CHAPTER 12

Refinancing

Like most things in the financial world, refinancing a loan has two sides. Generally speaking, it makes good sense to refinance if the interest rate and monthly payments decrease and lead to significant savings over the life of the loan. That is a generalization, though. There are many factors to consider when refinancing, including your reasons for refinancing. Refinancing can be used improperly and cause more financial problems than it solves over the long run.

The first step in the refinancing process, therefore, is to define and understand the purpose of what refinancing means. For our purposes the term refinancing is when a person or a business revises a loan payment schedule or replaces one loan with a completely different loan that has more beneficial terms. Refinancing is sought for many reasons. For example, people refinance their car loans or mortgages to obtain additional loan funds or to consolidate debt.

Deciding when it makes sense to refinance is not always obvious. A lower interest rate on a new loan does not automatically make refinancing a good decision. The reason is that you have to consider the type of interest, the loan fees, taxes, and a host of other factors. Before deciding to seek refinancing, you need to ask yourself what you want to achieve. If you want to lower your interest rate or shorten a loan term so you can pay off the loan more quickly, then considering refinancing makes sense. If you want to refinance your mortgage so you can go on an elaborate vacation, the refinancing probably does not make sense. This is not a moral judgment. It seldom makes sense to borrow long-term funds for short-term, one-time needs. In other words, you do not want to pay for your one week vacation for fifteen or thirty years.

In the following sections, I will guide you through the advantages and disadvantages of refinancing, the true cost associated with refinancing, and the various factors to take into consideration.

Advantages and Disadvantages of Refinancing

There are generic advantages and disadvantages of refinancing and specific ones associated with the type of loan involved. For example, refinancing a mortgage is different than refinancing a car loan. A mortgage has a longer term and can have significant refinancing fees, and so your plans for staying in a house or selling it must be taken into consideration.

The advantages of refinancing a loan may include the following:

- Lower interest rate
- Possible change in type of interest (i.e., from variable to fixed)
- Lower monthly payment
- Can pull cash out of loan based on property equity
- Possible reduction in loan amortization period
- Possible acceleration of equity building in property if the new loan is paid off sooner than the old loan would have been
- May consolidate debt into a single loan payment

The disadvantages of refinancing a loan may include:

- New loan fees are charged, increasing out-of-pocket costs
- Possible extension of loan amortization period
- Longer loan payoff period can make it difficult to get a new loan at a later date
- If loan amortization period is extended, lower interest rate may still result in higher total interest payments over life of the loan
- Early repayment penalty fees may have to be paid on original loan
- Equity on property is used now to cover refinancing and sales costs, making it unavailable at the time property is sold

Clearly, the advantages and disadvantages that apply to your situation depend on the type of loan, your reason for refinancing, and the terms of the refinancing. That is the reason why refinancing may result in either a shorter or longer loan amortization period.

True Cost of Refinancing

Since most loan refinancing is associated with mortgages, the following discussion on the cost factors uses a mortgage loan as an example. However, many of the same cost principles apply to all loans.

Refinancing may cost as much as 6 percent of the loan principal. If that is the case, you have to figure how much savings you will generate with a lower interest rate and compare those savings to the additional loan expenses incurred. In other words, how long will it take you to recoup the loan fees? If it takes many years and you intend to sell the home, there is no need to refinance. You will be spending money on loan fees you will never recover. In other words, the break-even point—how soon the lower monthly payments will recapture the loan costs of refinancing—should be calculated.

The true cost of refinancing must take into account a number of factors:

Payback Period: The payback period is the amount of time that it takes to recover an investment. The payback period adds up the monthly payment savings on the new loan earned because of a lower interest rate and then compares that number to the total cost of refinancing to determine when the costs are paid back. If the month of payback is month thirty-six of the loan period and you plan on selling your home within twenty-four months, then refinancing is not economically feasible.

Principal: The principal is the amount of the money borrowed. Notice the payback period does not consider the principal of the loan. The amount borrowed on the new loan is compared to the amount remaining on the existing loan to determine the change in the home owner's net worth.

Interest: The cost of borrowing money. There are a number of different types of interest methodologies used today, and the cost of refinancing must take into account whether the calculation of interest changes from old loan to new loan and the amount of interest paid over the life of the new loan versus the old loan.

The two primary types of interest rate calculations are called fixed interest or variable interest. On a fixed interest loan, the interest rate that is charged over the life of the loan does not change. The result is a fixed payment each month. A variable interest rate loan has a changing interest rate over the life of the loan and the rate is tied to the underlying interest rate which is usually the prime rate. There are many different variations of interest rate calculations but they are variations of the fixed and variable interest rates.

Up-front Costs: The up-front costs of loan may be, but are not necessarily, out-of-pocket costs, meaning you pay for these expenses and do not include them in the total loan amount. These are real expenses that must be prepaid before you can obtain the loan and thus are part of the true cost of refinancing. Typical up-front costs include expenses like home inspection fees, appraisal fees and application fees. Up-front costs are sometimes rolled into the loan amount, but they are still up-front costs.

The Federal Truth in Lending Law requires that an annual percentage rate (APR) be disclosed on a loan. The APR is different from the loan interest rate because it takes into account the prepaid finance charges like the origination fee, loan points, loan broker processing fee, insurance premiums, and closing fees. The APR is not used in calculating the monthly payment, but it is used to equalize loan calculations so you can more easily compare loans issued by different lenders. The APR helps you identify the true cost of refinancing.

Net Worth: The net worth was mentioned in the discussion on principal. One of the considerations in determining whether refinancing makes sense is the change in the borrower's net worth due to refinancing. When a mortgage balance increases, it is usually due to the fees added to a loan and household liability balance increases, which also tends to lower net worth. Net worth can also be decreased if you will pay more in total interest over the life of the loan than you would have paid on the original loan. This can happen when you refinance at a lower interest rate but for a longer loan period.

Out-of-Pocket Expenses: These are expenses you pay that are not included in the loan balance. They may or may not be up-front costs. For example, you usually must pay a credit report fee or you may have to pay an attorney fee to resolve a loan-related matter.

Loan Fees: Many different types of loan fees may be charged. Loan fees include a loan-origination fee, loan points, discount fee, processing fee, underwriting fee, escrow fee, wire fees, prepayment penalty (if applicable), and others. Most of these fees are included in the loan balance unless you pay them as up-front out-of-pocket expenses.

Other Expenses: Other expenses on the loan include the title insurance, property insurance, hazard insurance, flood insurance, property taxes, and recording fees. These are usually included in the total loan amount.

Points: There are two different types of points: discount points and origination points. The points equal 1 percent of the loan amount. The origination points are the amount paid to the loan processor. Discount points are the same as prepaid interest. Each point purchased will then lower the interest rate on the life of the loan by .25 percent. So if you pay two discount points, your loan interest rate would be decreased by half a percentage point.

Taxes: Some loan fees are deductible on your tax return, which means you may recover some of the loan costs through a lower tax liability. For example, most points are deductible, but it is always important to consult with your certified accountant or attorney regarding what is currently deductible based on your financial circumstances.

Deciding to refinance is a complex decision based on finding the break-even period at which you will recover the cost of refinancing and then comparing that period to your plans for the loan collateral. The fees may be different for different types of loans but the principals are the same. In the case of a house, you would consider how long you plan to stay in the house. If you are refinancing a vehicle, you would have to consider how long you plan to keep the vehicle. In addition, you will want to compare the full cost of the new loan to the cost of the old loan.

Following is a simplified example of a break-even period calculation: (1)

Break-Even Period Calculation

1 Current mortgage payment paid monthly		$1,199
2 Minus: new monthly mortgage payment		($1,073)
3 Savings each month		126
4 Calculate 1 - tax rate (assume 28%)	0.72	
5 Multiply savings each month times after tax rate	$126 x 0.72	$91
6 Figure total of loan fees and closing costs		$2,500
7 Divide total fees and costs by after tax savings	$2,500/$91	27.5
8 Months to recover refinancing costs		27.5 Months

In this example, it will take you about twenty-seven months to recover the refinancing costs. The first question to ask yourself is if you plan to stay in the house for more than twenty-seven months. If you plan to sell the house within twenty-four months, you should not refinance. A second calculation involves figuring the total costs of a new loan for a specified period and comparing those costs to the total costs of the existing loan for the same period. This will ensure that you have included all the loan costs in the calculation.

Comparing the Old Loan to New Loan Worksheet[2]

Current monthly payments	$__________	(1)
Number of months borrower expects to own property	__________	(2)
Total payments (1 x 2)	$__________	(3)
Payments at the lower interest rate	$__________	(4)
Number of months borrower expects to own property	__________	(5)
Total mortgage payments (4 x 5)	$__________	(6)
Difference between old and new payments (3 minus 6)	$__________	(7)

Net savings using refinancing costs

Prepayment penalty	$__________	(8)
All costs + points on new loan	$__________	(9)
Increase in taxes due to lower tax deduction		
For interest	$__________	(10)
Total costs (8 + 9 + 10)	$__________	(11)
Net savings over life of mortgage (7 minus 11)	$__________	(Net)

There are two important points to make about this worksheet. First, you will only use the number of months you expect to keep the loan and not the number of months remaining on the loan. If you do not plan on keeping the loan until it is paid off, you would not calculate savings for the entire loan period.

The second is that the net savings are calculated for the life of the mortgage, and once again, the life is the amount of time you expect to keep the mortgage. For example, if you expect to keep a loan with a remaining twenty-year balance for another five years, you would use the five years of sixty months to calculate the net savings or net loss of refinancing.

Interest, Principal, and Extra Payments

The mortgage amortization schedule shows how much of the mortgage goes to principal and how much goes to interest. Though you will pay something on principal with each payment (unless you have an interest-only loan for a period of time), most of the payment goes to interest for at least the first five years and much longer on a longer term loan. It can easily take more than half of the life of the loan before you are making payments where the principal and interest are paid equally.

There is often a question about whether it pays to make extra payments on a loan in order to pay it off faster. If you make additional payments, it should be specifically used to pay down principal only because interest is figured on the principal. Not only will you pay off the principal faster with your extra payment, but more of your required monthly payment will be distributed to principal, too. Since the first half of the loan has slow equity gain, paying additional principal will increase the rate of gain earlier in the loan.

However, there is one disadvantage. The tax deduction for interest will be lower because you will be paying less interest each month and more on principal, which is not deductible.

When is the Best Time to Refinance?

This question almost always comes up at some point when discussing this topic. There is no specific answer to the question of when it is best to refinance. However, it may be time to consider refinancing if one or more of the following scenarios is possible:

- You can lower your interest rate by approximately 2 percent
- You can reduce the monthly loan payments without extending the term
- You can reduce the term of the loan
- You can pull out equity that can be used to pay off higher interest debt
- The cost payback period is less than the time you intend to keep the loan

Each one of these factors must be evaluated in terms of all loan costs and loan features. As David Laibson, Harvard University professor, discussed, the ideal refinance rate must consider all of the factors, including closing costs, tax impact, the remaining number of years on the mortgage, and so on. (3) You cannot look at just one factor.

If you are considering refinancing, the best thing to do is to consult with a financial advisor or mortgage expert. So many factors go into calculating a refinanced loan, and each person's circumstances are different. Refinancing can be a smart or not-so-smart decision.

SECTION 4

Education and Jobs

CHAPTER 13

Financial Education for Kids

Setting goals gives you and your child an opportunity to measure real progress. Goals should be selected based on your child's learning ability and your aspirations for your child. It is important to not do a one-size-fits-all lesson plan, because kids learn in a variety of ways. For example, some children might prefer to look at pictures of bills and coins to learn the differences between currencies. Other children might not fully grasp the concept that way and might need additional reinforcement for this lesson. These children might benefit from a hands-on approach that allows them to identify money by depositing correctly identified coins and bills into a piggy bank.

A recent national personal finance survey found that teens starting out at college will be offered an average of eight credit cards within their first week of education. It also put the average level of debt that a student would hold upon graduation at over $28,000.

Research results gathered by www.credit.com show that 91 percent of undergraduates own at least one credit card and that 50 percent own more than four cards. Additionally, the average credit card debt held upon graduation is now over $4,000, and 7 percent of college dropouts are directly related to debt or financial pressure. At a time when they should be laying a sound financial foundation for the rest of their lives, young people between eighteen and twenty-four are increasingly paying over 30 percent of their monthly income in debt repayments. Nearly nine out of ten undergraduates who were asked said that they needed more financial management education. Sadly, many high school and college students are clueless about the long-term effects of their financial decisions. The lack of good financial programs in our schools can be attributed to the financial apathy in society and the belief that it is up to parents and guardians to teach their kids about money.

Does that make sense? We expect our educational system to teach our kids other practical lessons they will need as they grow older and become adults. Schools teach sex education and driver's education, but very few schools take the time to develop a financial education program. This is a poor reflection of our societal goals and should be changed to empower our kids to become financially educated adults. We need a financial education program.

The use of credit cards is also increasing, particularly as spending at online marketplaces becomes more accessible to the average consumer. From the research results published by credit.com, 45 percent of teens use credit cards, though only 26 percent of these young consumers understand how credit card fees and interest work. This is a very dangerous practice with long-term ramifications if it is not managed correctly. And what happens if these teens cannot pay for their purchases?

As they fight huge fiscal debts and decreasing revenue streams, the government and businesses are also moving the responsibility of retirement saving and investing onto workers. Our young people either currently make or will soon have to make decisions about college funds, retirement planning, savings, and investments. Without a foundation in place, many of these individuals will not make decisions that are in their best long-term interests. The fortunate ones of the group who have either the financial resources or access to guidance might get the help they need, but what about the rest?

Why Financial Education for Kids?

The proliferation of credit cards, store cards, and debit cards, coupled with the low level of understanding of fees and other charges has, undoubtedly, fuelled the increase in personal debt levels. Learning the right way and wrong way to use these tools of the modern financial world will empower today's youngsters to be tomorrow's responsible and more financially mature consumers.

Easy credit, the buildup of debt, and the changing financial environment are impacting personal finances more so now than they ever have before. Our youth has greater access to financial instruments than ever before. However, most of these instruments are geared toward spending rather than planning for the future. The "buy now, pay later" mentality can leave you owing more money than you had originally spent. That is because most teenagers have no concept of interest rates or how they affect current and long-term debt balances. Some Internet companies base their business strategy on the "buy now" or "one-click" shopping experience because they know that customers spend more on impulse buys. This all goes to the company's bottom line and is conversely removed from the consumer's bottom line.

Similarly, research shows that today's young people do not realize that the value of the dollar in their pocket today will decrease over time. They understand that prices rise and goods and services get more expensive, but they lack appreciation that inflation negatively impacts money value. Such understanding would increase the worth of saving and investing wisely, either for a rainy day or for future financial needs. These are basic financial concepts that society should have in order to become better consumers and more responsible citizens.

Ignorance is bliss only when it does not affect you. If you think that most decisions being made by businesses and governments directly benefit you, then you will be surprised to learn that this is not always the reality. Ignorance, my friend, is no longer bliss. Ignorance, nowadays, is costly for everyone.

Young people who are starting to make their own way in the world, will need to consider the financial impact of rent or mortgage, insurance, and long-term financial requirements such as pensions, overdrafts, and borrowing. They will also need a basic knowledge of how financial instruments, investments, savings accounts, and financial transactions work. A good appreciation of the importance of budgeting will also aid sound financial judgment from the outset of a life independent of parents. A parent's ultimate goal should be to have self-sufficient children who can not only survive in the world, but hopefully add something to it, as well.

Finally, when the parents of today retire, the kids of today will be relied upon to make the big financial decisions that impact society. Tomorrow's pensioners and the wider community will need today's kids to be more financially productive than they were as a greater dependence on Social Security benefits and the needs of an aging population kick in. If we are just thinking of ourselves and not of the legacy we are leaving our younger generations, then we as a society are in trouble. Today's unresolved problems will inevitably become a burden for our children and grandchildren. I think we owe it to them to at least do the best we can to ensure that the burden we leave them was not something we could have resolved in our time.

There used to be a time when a civilized society took only the resources that were necessary to sustain its population and ensure that resources were still available for future generations. Those who wasted our scarce and declining resources were penalized and even exiled from civil society, but times have changed. Today, many businesses and people in society are encouraged to live in the moment. Accountability and responsibility is often disregarded in the pursuit of selfish goals and profits. Greed is hailed as good. But the worst aspect of our current state is that penalties for offenses have become so trivial that they have become merely another cost in achieving our goals. Our system is, for lack of a better word, broken. And we can start to fix it by teaching ourselves and our children forgotten lessons that will make us better humans so that the next generation does not repeat our mistakes. If we learn our history, then it becomes less likely we will be blindsided by mistakes that were made by previous generations.

Key Stages in Financial Education

In a financial literacy study conducted by the Allstate Foundation in 2011, 92 percent of teens said that they learned about money management (or mismanagement) from their parents, though only 43 percent said that they have discussed it as a family. In the survey, 81 percent said that financial education should start as early as kindergarten and be on the education curriculum until twelfth grade.

There is clearly an identified need for financial education, but also an unsatisfied dependence upon parents to provide it. In reality, parents and the education system can work together, both formally and informally, to cater to the growing needs of society's youth to become financially literate. By setting realistic goals, parents and teachers can progress the financial knowledge of their children and students at an achievable pace appropriate to age and learning ability. The following is a rough guide with some suggestions from financial consultants, nonprofits, and organizations such as the Family Education Network. It is up to the parents and teachers to create customized and achievable plans based on the needs of their kids and students. We all learn differently, so sometimes, different strategies might be appropriate to reinforcement the core lessons.

Elementary School Age (Five to Ten)

Key Goals: Identifying money and learning how money is used.

Reinforcing Activities:

- Piggy bank management
- Explaining lessons when shopping or banking
- Giving a gift of colorful framed stock certificates or currencies

These are the years when the foundation for later learning is put into place. Just as children will learn to count and then add, subtract, multiply, and divide numbers, they should also learn about money value and the value of money.

Through the use of shopping trips, where parents can let children hand over money and accept change and identify notes and coins, the relative value of money will be taught. The value of goods and services will start to formulate in a child's mind, and the need to have money to pay for those items will be solidified. Explaining not being able to afford things or prioritizing expenditures will help children learn the necessity of money in today's world. Simply saving for a desired toy in a piggy bank will teach children financial responsibility, and the need to pay for goods will be cemented in their thoughts. The impact of not having enough money will be plainly exposed: no money, no toy.

A trip to the bank will help a child know how money is kept safe and how money earned is paid. The concept of "no free money" and the need to work and earn can be discussed and explained. Sources of money can start to be identified as the children get older: gifts, allowances, and work.

At school, educators can employ various techniques to reinforce lessons learned from parents. The telling of stories, picture coloring exercises, and talks by visitors are all enjoyable activities through elementary school years. A supervised "school bank," with pupils acting as tellers, can be used to help teach money identification and management.

Middle School and Junior High School Age (Eleven to Fourteen)

Key Goals: Understanding costs, managing allowance, and saving concepts.

Reinforcing Activities:

- Allowances tied to chores
- Opening a savings account
- Discussing college savings activities
- Buying a stock or bond and explaining the purchase
- Taking on supervised neighborhood jobs

The foundations of earlier learning should be built upon through the pre-high school years. Encouraging saving for desired items will lead to a "save to spend" mentality. The idea of regular allowance income and irregular income can be introduced by parents using a scale of payments for jobs. For example, a child's allowance could be tied to chores: $5 to tidy the yard, $6 to clean the car, and $2 to wash the dishes. Children could also participate in supervised neighborhood jobs such as operating a lemonade stand or having a paper route.

This can also lead to increasing savings, and spending on presents for others for Christmas or birthdays as well as saving for things that kids want themselves can be budgeted into those savings. It is important to not just give gifts to kids, but to teach them that they should also give gifts, as well. Saving to buy a birthday present for a sibling or other relative can teach a valuable lesson. The realization of needing money for different things will have started to take shape. Decisions on how and when to spend their money and on what will form the foundations of self-budgeting and planning future spending.

At this age, children will have the maturity to begin to understand family budgets. The payment of rent or a mortgage as well as utility bills and other household expenditures could be discussed and evaluated. Some parents are embarrassed to discuss certain financial matters with their children. Remember, it is better to explain certain things when appropriate than for them to incorrectly assume the reasons for certain financial decisions.

Junior high or middle school children, in particular, will start to grasp the cost of necessary items. They will also become aware that money can be saved by frugal use of goods and services and that such savings will affect disposable income for spending on luxury items. Turning on this light may make kids turn off the electric light in their bedroom when it is not in use. My mother always used to say," "Save a watt—turn off that light!"

At school, teachers can deepen understanding of the banking system by increased participation in a school bank programs. In some schools, a local bank helps this process and can also give employees time to supervise or talk to students about the role of a bank in the money system. Math teachers could introduce the concept of interest in language that a child can understand. The effect of interest rates on debt and savings could be introduced in theory, and discussion with parents should be encouraged.

A sense of wider community and the need for money to filter through to more needful causes could be promoted by charity-raising activities. This could also be used to introduce the Social Security system and the concept of how the government spends our taxes. The lessons are only limited by the teacher's creativity and the student's ability to grasp the concepts.

High School Age (Fifteen to Eighteen)

Key Goals: Understanding income, savings, basic budgeting, investment concepts, and financial security.

Reinforcing Activities:

- Reduction of allowances
- Landing a summer or part-time job
- Creating a simple budget
- Opening checking account
- Balancing a checkbook/Reviewing checking account transactions
- Discussion of college savings activities
- Discussion of financial situations: such as credit cards, paying taxes, bills, credit scores, etc.
- Researching, buying, and explaining stocks and bonds
- investment diversification concepts after they grasp basic concepts

By this age, kids should have a keen level of understanding of rudimentary financial items and will be ready to be introduced to the financial tools they will need in their adult lives. Some kids will have a high level of savings or regular income from a part-time job. Many parents will, at this time, choose to reduce or even cut allowances. This is usually accepted as a part of life without much argument. After all, the child now knows that money has to be earned and does not grow on trees. Once the child has a basic grounding of the workings of banks and bank accounts, it will be time to open an account in the child's own name. Parents can discuss the difference between checking accounts and savings accounts as well as introduce the concept of Internet banking.

A meeting with the bank, parents, and the new account holder can be used to set guidelines and explore the differences between credit and debit cards. The parent should not allow the child to underestimate the importance of pin numbers and chip and pin technology as an aid to account security. The concept and danger of financial fraud can be discussed.

When the child opens an account and receives his or her first banking card, parents should discuss responsible card use and the concept of credit ratings and credit scores. Most children will have ambitions of owning a home, owning a brand-new car, or taking exciting holidays. Borrowing money to do such things is commonplace, and this would be the time to talk about responsible borrowing, the ability to pay debts, and how poor credit scores negatively impact the ability to borrow and achieve life's dreams.

As the child starts to see the wages from work go into the bank, encouraging him or her to keep a written record and a budget is a good idea. This will help the child to be financially disciplined as an adult and hopefully avoid the debts that many college graduates accumulate.

Future requirements, such as college fees or mortgage payments, can be discussed in detail, and children can be encouraged to take some financial responsibility themselves. Some families will find it easy to discuss their joint income and the impact of regular payments on disposable income. Such discussion can be used to generate debate and learning of state and federal taxes and how they are deducted from paychecks.

Children at this age crave independence and will see financial responsibility bestowed upon them as co-operative rather than destructive. They will also now understand the importance of saving on a regular basis toward things that they want to buy or do.

With the end of high school in sight and a college education a possibility for many sons and daughters, this is a good time to begin to expand financial discussions with children to saving for their further education. This could include looking at relevant 529 or other college savings plans that are tax advantaged for savers. High schools are likely to lead here and could also have a large part to play in encouraging saving and investing for future needs.

Many schools run investment clubs or have investment competitions. These give their students the opportunity to learn about the stock market, how companies use it to raise money, and how individuals invest in those companies. A good scheme will encourage participants to conduct research on traded companies and then "buy and sell" shares accordingly. Parents do not need to worry, of course, because all buying and selling is conducted with fantasy funds. Such programs not only teach children the importance of knowing their investments, but also that they may incur losses as well as making gains.

From this starting point, parents might wish to allow children to make limited investments using real money. Investments made with their own cash will teach about risk, profit, and loss and will make better investors for the future. Some investment firms have low minimum balance requirements for parents who want their children to learn about and invest in the financial markets.

From such an investment starting point, the learning curve can be extended to cover other financial instruments. The investment potential and risk of government bonds, their place in the economy, how they add funds to government income, and the long-term costs of issuing those bonds can be a lesson attached to the story surrounding taxes.

Advantages of mutual funds for investment purposes, the disadvantages and costs of using them as investment vehicles, and other investments such as currencies, commodities, gold, and silver can be introduced over time. Hopefully, the money we are paying into the educational system will assume some of the burden of teaching our kids these advanced lessons.

Conclusion

The aims of giving kids a well-rounded and solid education in financial matters can be summed up as:

- Giving individuals a personal advantage at the start of a life filled with financial decisions and considerations
- Creating a more financially literate educated society that will be better placed to make the big financial decisions that affect everyone.

A well-designed financial educational system will form children's financial foundation and prepare them for the real world, where they will have to make financial choices daily. They will also be less susceptible to the temptation of relying on easy credit or succumbing to regrettable spending opportunities.

CHAPTER 14

Higher Education: Will Your College Degree Pay Off?

How Higher Education Impacts Your Income

In today's dismal economic environment filled with layoffs, downsizing, and long-term unemployment, more and more people are debating whether a college or post-graduate degree will pay off in terms of finding—or keeping—a job or changing careers. The current conventional wisdom says that the degree pays off. But for a better understanding, I will take a closer look at some of the key numbers and facts in this debate.

Why a college degree is important

Today's educators and employers seem to agree that higher education is a must. Writing in Harvard University's publication *Pathways to Prosperity*, Sarita Brown, president of Excelencia in Education, says the following:

> This report "opens the door to new strategies that can help a broader range of Americans, including the rapidly growing Latino population, gain the meaningful work and educational experiences they need to earn degrees and higher salaries, helping to create better jobs and a stronger workforce. The report reminds us that in order to close achievement gaps, we must develop a more effective and holistic strategy to develop human capital." (1)

This study indicates that over the past thirty years, all of the net job growth in America has been generated by careers that demand at least some post-high school education. So what does this tell us? In the job market of the twenty-first century, education beyond high school is quite probably the pathway to realizing the American dream. And while such education seems almost mandatory for all segments of the population, it is doubly important for racial minorities and women. For example, the report remarks that teenage high school graduates across the board are facing unemployment at Depression-era levels. But unemployment among black teenagers is four times greater than it is among white teens from affluent families, and it is two times greater among Hispanic teens.

According to the US Labor Department, higher education affects the labor market most significantly by increasing worker productivity and thus increasing earnings for the business. As workers acquire more education, they are better able to absorb new information, acquire new skills, and utilize new technologies. Many of today's employers stress the need for their workers to acquire "soft" as well as "hard" skills; critical thinking, collaboration, and conflict resolution are in increasingly higher demand.

If higher education benefits individuals and families through higher lifetime earnings, it can also benefit society at large in somewhat less tangible or obvious ways. For example, people with higher levels of education tend to be healthier than those with a lower education level are. Better educated people are more likely to make an investment in themselves by taking preventive measures to maintain better health. Annual physical checkups, mammograms, and regular exercise are all seen as investments in the maintenance of human capital and personal wellbeing.

Higher education further contributes to economic growth through the creation of new knowledge, thus increasing the value of human capital. Having more highly educated individuals means that society has more scientists, analysts, and inventors, who, in turn, increase human knowledge by developing new processes, reshaping old ideas, and innovating new technologies.

Additionally, education affects economic growth through the dissemination of knowledge. For example, increases in education levels have helped both invention and innovation in the computer industry over the past thirty years. Yet without schools to teach people how to use computers and other new technologies, the effect of such innovation would be reduced.

Over the course of the twentieth century, formal education has become more integral to the labor market, and there is no reason to believe that this trend will not continue in the twenty-first-century economy. In fact, the need for more education, whether in a formal classroom setting or in a workplace setting, will become increasingly important as technology and the global economy change. Besides contributing to enhanced economic productivity, investing in higher education enables people to become more knowledgeable citizens and parents. On average, higher educated people tend to command higher salaries than their less educated counterparts do. However, bear in mind that there are salary exceptions in both groups.

What the degree will cost

As with any kind of investments, the venture of earning a degree involves cost. In the case of education, depending on the individual's financial resources, the cost can be paid up front, paid periodically, financed, granted, or any combination of these options. According to recent reports by the College Board, Georgetown University in Washington D.C. was the most expensive college choice in 2010, with an annual tuition of $40,437. The least expensive choice was the University of Nevada, with an annual tuition of $2,682. Nationwide, the average annual cost of a bachelor's degree at a private college is around $25,143. At a public university, the average is $6,585. These costs are for tuition only and do not include room and board.

Tuition increases in recent years have outpaced inflation, and that trend is expected to continue. The rise in costs of a college education has been nothing short of explosive since the 1950s. Harvard, arguably one of the best universities in the world, was a little more than $500 in 1950 or about $4,700 in 2011 dollars when adjusted for inflation. The cost of Harvard's tuition was forecasted to grow to about $52,650 for the 2011-2012 academic years. That is an astonishing increase from the 1950s considering non-inflationary and inflationary values from the 1950s for comparison.

1950s vs. 2011 Tuition at Harvard University

52,650/500 = 105.3 x100 percent = 10,530 percent

Adjusted for Inflation: 1950s vs. 2011 Tuition at Harvard University

52,650/4,700 = 11.2 x100 percent = 1,120 percent

In 2007, David W. Kirkpatrick restated a comment from Karen Heller's "Smart Money" article that I am sure others can agree with. In his piece, appropriately entitled "Student Aid and College Tuition: The Upward Spiral," David states:

> Six years ago, I co-authored a series on why tuition costs had almost tripled over fifteen years, increasing at a rate higher than cars, housing, or even health care . . . The real reason schools charge what they do, we discovered, is deceptively simple: Because they can. (2)

Harvard and other Ivy Leagues are not alone in the mind boggling increases in education tuitions. Over the past decade, tuition costs have averaged increases of 6 to 9 percent per year. To put this into personal perspective, it means that if you have a child today, you will pay tuition of more than $25,000 per year at a public university when he or she is ready for college.

Of course, there are some viable alternatives to the four-year college degree. Whether they are comparable to the four year colleges value might still be debatable, especially when looking at individual cases and including overall cost, incurred debt, salary returns, and overall career performance after completion of degree programs. Depending on your career choice, you can get the post-secondary education you need by attending cheaper technical schools or two-year associate's degree programs at a community college. These programs focus on real-world knowledge and skills that can be applied directly on the job. This saves you the time and expense of having to take a year or two of liberal arts classes that provide the "core" of a typical four-year degree program.

While tuition costs have outpaced inflation, the payoff for higher education has increased, as well, but clearly not at the same pace as tuition costs. Information published by the National Bureau of Economic Research would indicate that a tremendous increase in the value of schooling has occurred since 1979. They found that the return for one additional year of education rose from 6.2 percent in 1979 to nearly 10 percent in 1993. Although the future is unknown, the demand by firms for high levels of human capital seems to be increasing, tending to increase the prospects for future financial returns to education.

The investment vs. the payoff

A Census Bureau study estimated that the average lifetime earnings of a bachelor's degree holder was $2.7 million (in 2009 dollars), 75 percent more than the amount earned by those with just an average high school education. It should be clear, then, that having a college degree is important to having more economic opportunity. However, even with a degree, the level of economic success varies widely by race and gender. Consider the following:

- On average, women earn 25 percent less than men with similar degrees do at all levels.
- At all degree levels, African Americans and Latinos earn less than whites do.

- African Americans and Latinos with master's degrees earn less than whites with bachelor's degrees do.

Current enrollment in degree programs may signal a change in this trend, at least where women are concerned. Women now account for 57 percent of the college degrees awarded and 57 percent of college enrollment. Women also currently make up 60 percent of the enrollment in graduate degree programs.

The education gap in median income is varied, as well, regardless of race or gender. For someone who has not finished high school, the median lifetime income averages $973,000. On the high end, someone with an advanced professional degree such as an attorney or physician can anticipate a median lifetime income of $3.7 million. Individuals with a master's degree can expect to earn about 25 percent less than the physician or attorney, while those with a doctorate in a different field will earn about 16 percent less.

Not only is the income gap significant, the career-opportunity gap is substantial, as well. Those with less than a high school diploma will be likely to work as truck drivers, janitors, retail salespersons, and health aides. With some college education, people may find jobs as administrative assistants, supervisors, and even sales managers. Once the college degree is obtained, career choices can include teachers, nurses, accountants, and a variety of managerial roles. A master's degree may lead to careers as education administrators, software engineers, or certified public accountants (CPAs). Doctoral or advanced professional degrees will produce lawyers, doctors, scientists, and top-tier business executives.

These figures show that when it comes to education, more is generally better, especially when it is in a focused or specialized field known for its lucrative earning potential. Earning at least a two- or four-year degree provides a sizeable economic return. The 33 percent of bachelor's degree holders who continue on to obtain graduate and professional degrees have even more prosperous futures ahead.

Education not only pays off for the individual, it pays off for society, as well. So a nation that wants to compete effectively in a global economy must have a knowledgeable and flexible workforce who can adapt as the world changes. Discrimination or restrictions on segments of a society may serve short-term goals of a selected few. However, long-term growth and competiveness will depend on the overall productivity of society, which increasingly relies on rigorous educational requirements for the jobs of the future. If a society does not work as one, then it is doomed to eventually fail. Racism and other discrimination have no place in a forward-looking nation.

Is one degree better than another?

Of course, no one should make a career decision or degree choice based on monetary prospects alone. Working at a job you hate simply because it pays well can be psychologically and emotionally damaging, and that situation benefits neither the employee nor the employer. Before his death in 399 BC, Socrates realized that the unexamined life is not worth living and that one should shape his or her life accordingly. I say do what you love, have a natural talent for, or have a natural passion for, and the money will eventually come. And even if you are not as wealthy as you hope, you might at least be a little happier with your choice. Just be wise and do not be afraid to seek help or guidance in the areas where you might not be strong. Having said that, it is certainly useful to note that there are differences in income potential among various degree choices.

In general, the technical or practical fields tend to have long-term earning power. The engineering field usually comes out on top, with petroleum engineering leading that group. Petroleum engineers can expect a median starting salary of $97,900 per year and a median mid-career salary of $155,000. Other engineering specialties round out the top five professions and are prominent throughout the top tier. In the bottom 10 percent are professions in areas such as elementary education, child and family studies, culinary arts, theology, and athletics. These professions offer a median starting salary in the $30,000 range with a mid-career salary in the mid-to-high $40,000. Professions such as medicine, law, and accounting generally fall in the middle of the pack.

Using the degree to change careers

A college or advanced degree can be key to a successful redirection or a coveted promotion, especially for people in the later years of a career. Online education blogger Cathy Goodwin is correct when she suggests that an MBA degree can provide three important assets to mid-career growth and change. It can:

- Supplement skills in a field where you are already experienced
- Help you find a career in a totally new, but related field
- Help you get promoted or reassigned within your own company

If you are considering going back to college for an MBA or any other college degree, it is important to be thoughtful about the process. If your intentions are career retraining, do your research and make sure you pick a new career path that will have the potential to lead to a sustainable job and a satisfying new career. Investigate the current and long-term prospects of the job's market and its industry segment. If the goal of the degree is financially motivated, then your strategy will be important. Ideally, you want to make a change to a career that is in high demand. Then when your education is complete, ideally, you will be able to find a job with relative ease.

When you are looking for that new job, be aware that—especially for salaried positions—a degree plus experience ranks highly among the traits, skills, and characteristics identified as needed and desired from people selected to fill most of the leadership positions in organizations. This is often the case because a college degree and the coursework associated with earning it show a prospective employer that you are a well-rounded, knowledgeable individual who can analyze and solve problems. By obtaining the required degree, you have proved that you can stick with a goal and complete it.

How to find the money

Whether you are a mid-life career changer or a first-time prospective college student, you will need to spend money to get where you want to go. Before you get down to the nitty-gritty of getting the needed funds, you can take a few steps to improve your chances.

- **Start early.** Most scholarship programs are "first come, first served." Many states run out of grant money long before the school year starts in the fall. Last year, the state of Illinois ran out of its grant money on April 18 and turned away more than 138,000 qualified students who had waited too long to apply.
- **Move away.** Many well-respected private colleges in the Midwest and Northeast are suffering from a decline in the numbers of eighteen-to twenty-year-olds in their immediate geographical area. Schools in those states are therefore offering comparatively large scholarships to recruit students from other regions.
- **If it sounds too good to be true . . .** Cash-strapped students are staying away from expensive schools, so a number of lower quality colleges are starting to attract students by offering bigger scholarships. But wasting four years at a school that does not challenge you or has a poor reputation with prospective employers is a

waste, no matter how little it costs. I cannot stress enough to prospective students that they should carefully evaluate all costs, future job prospects for their chosen degree, school's partnership with the business community, and the quality of the education being offered before making a final decision. Be smart. Prospective students should do their homework before making make any decisions that will more than likely have a major impact on their lives.

- **Raise your GPA.** To cope with the exploding demand for scholarships, many financial aid programs are setting competitive targets that require higher grades and better test scores. Programs that used to require a *B* average may now require an *A*.
- **Watch your bottom line.** Every dollar you save by choosing a less expensive university or finding cheaper housing is a dollar you do not have to borrow or raise in scholarships. Look for local city or state schools that might offer a competitive quality education at a lower price. Why go into unnecessary debt if your local state school is churning out successful grads?

In addition to scholarships, there are a number of other ways to pay for a college degree. Many members of the military are eligible for tuition reimbursement programs. If you are already employed, your employer may fund all or part of your education if you can show that it improves your value to the company. However, this may require you to sign an agreement that you will either remain with the company for a certain period of time or repay the money if you choose to leave. Some companies that downsize will also include education or retraining as part of a severance package.

There is an important tool you should know about when researching the cost of your prospective degree. By a federal mandate, every college and university now has an online net price calculator, which you can use to estimate how much you will need to pay for college. You can generally find these calculators on the university web site, usually under the financial aid section. They might be called something like "personal cost estimator" or "financial aid calculator."

Once you use that calculator to figure out the total cost, if you are like most students, you will probably end up considering the student loan. Recent studies show that the debt levels of students who graduate with loans continue to rise. Unfortunately, cost varies considerably by state as well as by college. The sky is the limit when it comes to tuition increases as it continues to outpace many of the cost of living indices, including wages. This point was clear to two-thirds of college seniors who graduated in 2010 with student loan debts averaging $25,250, which was up five percent from the previous year. Given the rise in unemployment, declining income, and the need for retraining in today's economy, this figure is not surprising. In fact, if the economic climate continues to be bleak, the level of student loan debt default could become a major problem for society.

Substantial information is available about student loan programs, either online or through the financial aid office of most colleges and universities. Before going into debt, however, it is a good idea to figure out the total cost of your intended education. How much will you need to borrow? At what interest rate? And what is the time period for repayment? And most important, could this debt become a burden that will diminish the positive impact of your degree? Nobody wants to spend the next twenty to thirty years paying off a loan that will not be beneficial.

There are several interesting behavioral connections between students' academic environment, their debt load, and their perceptions of its impact on their financial future. Prospective students should have a strong understanding of their financial situation in order to avoid potential financial distress and to maintain their psychological well-being.

One recent study found that students' main sources of financing their education came from family assistance, personal savings, and student loans. However, the students' lack of financial awareness in acquiring debt was somewhat alarming. A sample question regarding a hypothetical student loan obligation of $10,000 indicated that only 65 percent of the students came up with a reasonable estimate of what the monthly payments would be. This indicates that many students may lack a proper understanding of personal finance and are likely to overextend their financial obligations. Parents or guardians should guide those under their care so that prospective students realize the ramifications of these financial decisions. You would not give a teenager the keys to your car without first ensuring he or she has adequate training behind the wheel, is licensed, and can drive responsibly. Even then, you might hesitate. Why would you let your children take on debt before they are aware of how it will impact their lives? If we do not adequately prepare the next generation, they might end up relying on you as they get older and are burdened by debt versus you relying on them as responsible taxpayers.

Conclusion

In today's tight job market, higher education is and will continue to be an important component of career success. Before making the decision to seek a college or advanced degree, it is important to understand both the personal and financial cost as well as the potential payoff in both lifetime income and personal satisfaction. A higher education begins before you get to college. Learn how the higher educational system works, so you do not fall prey to its various pitfalls.

CHAPTER 15

Student Loans and Bankruptcy

More and more Americans are finding themselves dealing with an expanding and unmanageable debt burden. This may be because of unemployment, medical expenses, educational expenses, and irresponsible spending. Current rising prices, along with an enduring recession and a slower-than-expected economic recovery, have also aggravated these debt problems. Long-term unemployment, unmet household expenses, and repayment of debt incurred prior to the recession have significantly compounded these individuals' situation.

Many of these individuals experiencing unprecedented debt burdens are surprised to find themselves in such a financial predicament. In some cases, they were just following a predetermined course that their family members, teachers, government, and career counselors had so thoughtfully laid out for them. Like most Americans, this group bought into the notion that college was a necessary burden on the way to a successful life.

However, many of these advocates of educational debt did not realize and failed to appreciate that the global and domestic economies were going through an unprecedented shift that was transforming the world, creating jobs, destroying some jobs, and redistributing other jobs from one country to another. When the global crisis began in late 2007, it further destabilized the global economy and reduced many of the jobs that were held primarily by Americans.

Most consumers, households, and businesses went into defensive mode at the outset and have reduced spending and unnecessary costs wherever they can. However, one group in particular was on a predetermined path, and in most cases, its members had no choice but to continue to rack up more debt on the way to completing what they had already started.

Millions of students were attending colleges and universities when the economic crisis gripped the nation. Some of these students had taken out student loans, expecting to be able to find decent-paying jobs that would enable them to repay the debt. Instead, most of these individuals now belong to the group of Americans with some of the highest unemployment rates according to the US Bureau of Labor. As of January, 2012, the age group consisting of people aged twenty-five to twenty-nine is experiencing 10.2 percent unemployment. Another four million never entered the labor force or dropped out of the job search. (1) So the real unemployment rate is significantly higher than 10 percent for this group. Many of these millions of young adults are recent college graduates who have incurred tens of thousands of dollars in student loans.

However, student loan repayment issues are not just a concern for people under age thirty. According to government and private organization research, many people borrowed $50,000 or more to attend undergraduate and graduate programs and are still paying off those loans fifteen and twenty years after graduation. The difference, however, is that the newer grads often do not have the necessary employment and hence income to begin paying down these loans. And bankruptcy is becoming an increasingly popular option. However, this choice has been met with extraordinary opposition from the student loan industry, education institutions, and other critics.

These critics spent considerable time and money lobbying legislators to establish student loans as different from other debts. Consumer bankruptcies may be one alternative to relieve financial distress, but unfortunately, student loans are rarely allowed to be discharged during bankruptcy proceedings.

In this discussion, I will review the bankruptcy process, the laws governing student loans, and the reasons students are incurring ever-increasing amounts of debt to pay for their education.

Consumer Bankruptcy Process

A consumer bankruptcy is a legal process that enables a borrower to eliminate some or all of his or her current debts or establishes a reasonable debt repayment schedule. Filed in a bankruptcy court, the process enables consumers to get a fresh financial start while also protecting creditors in terms of fair distribution of debtor assets or payments.

Many people believe the bankruptcy process is a cure-all for debts and that everything is eligible to be discharged or written-off. However, many debts are not dischargeable for a variety of reasons. Ineligible debts include criminal or civil obligations, certain taxes, and domestic support payments like alimony and child support, fraudulent debts, divorce settlement obligations, and student loans.

Debts that can be discharged include unsecured debts like department store accounts, medical bills, gas accounts, signature loans, certain lawsuits, credit card debts, and certain taxes. They also include secured debts like home mortgages, property loans, and auto loans. However, secured loans have underlying assets, and the court will determine the appropriate method for asset disposal or return of the asset to the creditor for debt settlement. There are two types of consumer bankruptcy filings: Chapter 7 and Chapter 13.

Chapter 7 Bankruptcy

A Chapter 7 bankruptcy is usually the best choice for an individual who has an average to low income, few assets, and a high level of debt. Also called a "straight bankruptcy" or "liquidation," Chapter 7 allows the individual to discharge debt with the exceptions that I have already noted. Debts excluded from the bankruptcy will remain the responsibility of the consumer. Some debts, especially secured debts, can often be renegotiated with the creditor so that reasonable payments are established.

In the Chapter 7 filing, you will list all of your liabilities (debts or possible debts due to current actions like lawsuits) and all of your assets. Assets include your home, bank accounts, retirement accounts, income, and any other personal property of value. Some assets can be exempted or shielded from creditors. Both federal and state bankruptcy laws impact which assets can be treated as exempt, but they generally include home equity, one vehicle, a certain amount of personal property, benefits like Social Security or disability payments, and a burial plot.

Exemptions vary considerably between states, and the federal bankruptcy court will determine which assets and liabilities are exempted. If the asset value is sufficient, the bankruptcy court trustee will liquidate all or some of the assets to pay back the creditors.

Chapter 13 Bankruptcy

The Chapter 13 bankruptcy is called a "reorganization" or "wage-earner bankruptcy." This type of bankruptcy allows an individual to repay a portion of debts according to a repayment plan approved by the bankruptcy court. These individuals can keep their assets. A Chapter 13 filing is designed to provide debt relief for people who have regular income and unsecured and secured debts below a designated amount.

Under a Chapter 13 filing, you are paying debts out of expected future income. The court will normally extend repayment plans up to five years. At the end of the period, you will either have satisfied the debts or have paid an amount equal to your disposable income for that period. Disposable income is the amount of income remaining after paying living expenses and priority claims like income taxes and child support. At the end of the bankruptcy period, your debts are discharged.

Like the Chapter 7, a Chapter 13 does not accommodate the discharge of all debts; some debts cannot be discharged. This includes taxes, domestic support obligations, criminal and civil fines and restitution, and student loans.

Bankruptcy and Secured Loans

Secured loans are treated differently than unsecured debts for a couple of reasons. First, there are assets serving as collateral for secured debts, which means the consumer owns only part of, not the entirety of the asset in reality. Second, special legal methods deal with secured assets like homes and autos that can be incorporated into the bankruptcy process or managed as a completely separate process.

Generally, homes and vehicles are exempt assets, but that does not mean you have less obligation to the lenders. It only means that they are special cases that involve more complex treatment than a simple discharge judgment.

Homestead Exemption and Foreclosure

In a bankruptcy filing, you can exempt a certain amount of equity in your home. This is called a homestead exemption. It will be credited to the home owners in most legal cases when calculating debt that needs to be paid to creditors from the legal proceedings. This exemption essentially allows you to deduct this exempt amount from the amount you owe. The actual exemption amount is calculated and determined according to state laws.

In some states, the exempt amount is a percentage of the equity in the property. For example, if the home is worth $100,000 and you owe $55,000 on a mortgage, then you have $45,000 of equity in your home (($100,000 to $55,000). This equity represents the value of your ownership interest or stake in the property. This amount will also be used to determine how much you have to pay to creditors in the legal proceedings.

Assuming that the exempted equity amount in a bankruptcy for a married couple is $36,000, the exempt amount is then deducted from the equity ($45,000 to $36,000), leaving $9,000 as non-exempt equity. This is the amount that must be paid in the bankruptcy proceedings. The couple must pay the $9,000 to the bank, or the house will be sold to pay the non-exempt amount. If the house is sold, then the couple will keep the $36,000, and the rest of the sale proceeds will go to pay off the creditors.

In general, the home owner's exemption will permit the home owner to remain in his or her home by reducing the amount that creditors can legally go after in the bankruptcy proceedings. However, they must still make regular mortgage payments, or they will risk foreclosure.

Home exemptions also vary quite a bit from state. Some states have an exemption cap, while others have low limits. In a few states, such as Florida and Texas, your home is completely exempt from consumer creditors. However, federal law limits the homestead exemption to no more than $125,000 of equity if the house was purchased within forty months of filing bankruptcy. In addition, the home owner must have lived in the state for at least two years to claim a homestead exemption.

In a Chapter 7, you must make payment arrangements to catch up past due payments, and the mortgage company must agree to the plan. In a Chapter 13, it is possible to negotiate an agreement with a creditor to pay delinquent mortgage payments while also paying current monthly amounts. However, at the end of the bankruptcy period, you will still owe the mortgage balance. Mortgages are not discharged.

The thought of losing a home is stressful, and there are ways to keep your home if you continue making mortgage payments under either Chapter 7 or Chapter 13 bankruptcies. However, you can lose your home under a Chapter 7 bankruptcy if your payments are already delinquent. The mortgage company can foreclose during bankruptcy or at a later date. If there is a significant amount of equity in the home, the trustee may take possession and sell the house to raise money to pay unsecured creditors.

Vehicle Loans and Repossession

In a Chapter 13, you will continue making car payments on an auto or truck loan. The dealer may also lower the interest rate and restructure the loan as part of the negotiation process. In special cases such as a "cram down," the loan company agrees to lower car payments by only asking that you pay for the car's current worth instead of what you owe on it. This can be coupled with a lower interest rate.

There are several options for filing a Chapter 7:

- Re-commit to the current loan: confirm with the lender that you will continue making payments for the loan's duration and that you need the vehicle for work
- Redeem the vehicle: pay the creditor an amount equal to the value of the vehicle, which may be less than the loan amount
- Surrender the vehicle and the loan: return the vehicle to the lender and end the loan

When vehicle loan payments are delinquent, the lender has the right to repossess the vehicle without warning. There are laws, however, that limit how the lender can resell a repossessed vehicle and how the money must be used for full or partial debt settlement. A vehicle repossessed before bankruptcy is filed and then sold may result in a "deficiency judgment," which is the difference between what is owed on the loan and the net proceeds from reselling the vehicle. It is important to include this deficiency amount on your bankruptcy list of liabilities. Once bankruptcy is filed, an automatic stay is put into effect that stops collection efforts, which would also include vehicle repossession efforts at that time. Vehicle repossession laws, whether or not a bankruptcy is involved, also vary from state to state.

Debt Reaffirmation

Re-committing to pay a debt during a Chapter 7 or Chapter 13 bankruptcy is called reaffirmation. Reaffirming a debt must be completed before the bankruptcy is discharged. The debt will also be included in the final bankruptcy agreement. Reaffirming a debt means agreeing to continue paying the debt and that the creditor has a right to collect on the debt even after the bankruptcy discharge. If you fall behind on your payments, the creditor has the right to foreclose on the house or repossess the vehicle. If reselling the collateral does not settle the debt, you can be sued for outstanding balances on reaffirmed debt.

Most of the time, the only reason a consumer would want to reaffirm a debt is to retain possession of collateral like a house or vehicle. The creditor must agree to the reaffirmation, and a legal document will be filed with the bankruptcy court. Either the agreement is automatically accepted, or the bankruptcy trustee may ask the judge to approve the agreement. Once the reaffirmation is accepted, the loan arrangement continues as originally agreed, as if it were left out of the bankruptcy. Lenders may even continue reporting timely payments to the credit-reporting agencies, which can help your credit score.

If you do not reaffirm debt, the creditor can enforce the lien held on the house or vehicle. Due to these lien rights, the creditor retains the right to recover its collateral even if you do not reaffirm the debt. This means a creditor can foreclose on the house or repossess your vehicle should your payments become delinquent. However, since you did not reaffirm the debt, the lender will not sue you for money. In other words, you can live in your home or drive your car, but if you cannot make payments at any point, then you can "walk away" and lose the asset without being faced with a collection lawsuit. So it might be wise to consult with both your attorney and accountant to carefully consider the ramifications of a decision to reaffirm debt.

The Special Case of Student Loans

Student loans play an important role in making higher education accessible. However, increases in tuition rates and fees coupled with decreasing amounts of grant funding have led to an increase in student borrowing.

The first direct, unsubsidized federal student loans using US Treasury funds were authorized by the National Defense Education Act of 1958. The first federally guaranteed (subsidized) student loans given by banks and other non-government lenders were created in 1965 by the Federal Family Education Loan (FFEL) program.

Pre-1976: Bankruptcy Act of 1898 in Effect

Before 1976, educational debt could be discharged under the laws established by the Bankruptcy Act of 1898. The 1973 Commission on the Bankruptcy Laws of the United States recommended that government loans to students be prohibited from discharge unless five years had passed since the first payment was due or where undue hardship could be proven. These recommendations were included in 1976 in the amended Higher Education Act of 1965 by adding Section 439A. This law amended the bankruptcy laws and made government student loans non-dischargeable.

1978 Education Amendment to Bankruptcy Reform Act of 1978

In 1978, the Bankruptcy Act of 1898 was repealed, and a new law called the Bankruptcy Reform Act of 1978 was passed. Referred to as the Bankruptcy Code, the Education Amendment from 1976 was also adopted in section 523(a)(8).

1990 Education Amendment to Bankruptcy Reform Act of 1978

In 1990, the five year rule was extended to seven years. Until October 1998, student loans could still be discharged through a Chapter 7 bankruptcy if the first loan payment had been due at least seven years before the bankruptcy filing or if undue hardship could be proven.

1998 Education Amendment to Bankruptcy Reform Act of 1978

The law was drastically changed in October 1998 when President Clinton signed the 1998 Education Amendment to Bankruptcy Reform Act of 1979 into law. This disqualified all government student loans from discharge except in cases of undue hardship. However, private loans were still easily dischargeable with some limitations.

The Bankruptcy Abuse Prevention and Consumer Protection Act of 2005 (BAPCPA)

In 2005, Congress passed the Bankruptcy Abuse Prevention and Consumer Protection Act (BAPCPA), which made government-backed private student loans ineligible for bankruptcy discharge except when undue hardship could be shown.

In summary, under the current BAPCPA legislation, the following rules apply:

- Broadened scope of student loan exception to discharge to include all student loan programs, including government-guaranteed and private loans
- Undue hardship is the only standard for student loan discharge
- There is no longer a time limit

Undue hardship has been defined only by the courts and not by statute. In general, most courts use the Brunner Test, named after the 1987 *Brunner v. New York State Higher Education Services Corp.* court case. It is a three-pronged test: (2)

1. Debtor is unable to maintain a minimal standard of living if required to repay loans
2. Circumstances indicate that this state of affairs will continue for a significant time period during which loan repayment would be required
3. Debtor has made a good faith effort to repay the loan

Why Are Student Loans Not Dischargeable?

The current laws on discharging student loans have evolved over time, and there are several theories as to why student loans are not eligible for discharge at this point. The discussion originally started, like many laws, when some system abuses were discovered. Reports showed that a number of students who had gone on to become doctors, lawyers, and other professionals with large incomes were not paying back their students loans. This was not the only reason for changing the law, though.

One of the primary rationales for making student loans dischargeable is that these loans cannot be collateralized. And often, these unsecured loans amount to as much as mortgages and other large traditional collateral or secured loans. Repayment is based on the assumption that the borrower will be able to utilize the human capital accumulated and financed while in school. However, that assumption may prove to be false. Some argue that students cannot be forced to work after graduation and creditors might be left on the hook for huge sums of money. Behavioral theorists also suggest that making it too easy to discharge student loans will lead to high student default rates and high interest rates.

However, these critics do realize that the system is filled with problems and needs to be reformed. The problem is the rapidly rising tuition and fees that are outpacing inflation and are exacerbated by students being forced to accept loans they cannot afford to repay in order to stay in school. In addition, making the student loans non-dischargeable promotes private lending. Lenders might be reluctant to lend to students if those amounts can be easily discharged in bankruptcy proceedings. Eliminating the ability to discharge student loans may also reduce government costs. Since the borrower is always held responsible, the guarantor (the government) is not. Therefore, neither the government nor the taxpayer has to absorb the cost of student loan discharges.

Options Prior to Defaulting

Student loans must be repaid whether or not the student graduates or is employed after graduation. In general, a loan will come due once the funds are disbursed, unless there is a grace period. A loan default can begin about nine months or 270 to 360 days after failing to make payments on time. In that period, a borrower can look at their options to prevent an imminent default. Once in default, the whole amount is then due. It is extremely difficult to prove an undue hardship, even if you are disabled. For one thing, you have to show that you have already made a good faith effort to repay the loan. However, many students have some options besides defaulting available to them.

- ***Deferment:*** A deferment postpones the start of principal payments until you resolve temporary financial difficulties. Interest either does not accrue or can be capitalized. Deferments are usually granted for cases of unemployment, economic hardship, disabled students in rehabilitation programs, and students still enrolled in school.

- ***Forbearance:*** Forbearance refers to a postponement or reduction of payments while interest continues to accrue. Forbearances are also granted for cases of temporary hardship.

- ***Federal Loan Forgiveness Programs:*** Government-funded loans like the Stafford and Perkins loans are eligible for loan forgiveness if certain conditions are met. Some or all of a loan is eliminated. There are also programs that erase all or part of a loan based on specific service like military service (National Defense Student Loan), teaching service (Teacher Loan Forgiveness Program), or health care service in designated locations.

- ***State Loan Forgiveness Programs:*** Many state programs will help you repay part of your student loans in exchange for doing a certain type of work. For example, many states have loan forgiveness programs for doing medical research, setting up practice in a rural area, or working on an American Indian reservation or in inner-cities.

- ***Consolidation Loan:*** You can apply for a consolidation loan that combines all of your education loans into a single loan. This might allow for better debt management and increased leverage in terms of interest and other term modifications.

While student loans are not easily dischargeable, it is still possible to obtain some relief from student loans under a Chapter 13 bankruptcy with the help of an attorney. For example, debts including student loans can be consolidated, or an interest free repayment arrangement can be negotiated as part of the bankruptcy.

This discussion is not just an academic exercise. Students leaving school or graduating with staggering student loan debt is a growing problem. According to *Project on Student Debt,* "two-thirds of college seniors graduated with loans in 2010, and they carried an average of $22,250 in debt. They also faced the highest unemployment rate for young college graduates in recent history at 9.1 percent." (3)

The US Department of Education reported in 2011 that the student loan default rate rose to 8.8 percent based on loan payments that first came due between October 1, 2008, and September 30, 2009, and are in default as of September 30, 2010. Out of 3.6 million borrowers in repayment status, there were 320,000 defaults. (4) As of 2011, there was more student debt than credit card debt as student loans exceeded $1 trillion.

Addressing Student Loan Default Issues

Many societal and personal consequences are associated with young adults incurring unmanageable student loan debts. Two laws are currently being considered by Congress that could restore the ability to discharge private student loans in bankruptcy.

The first piece of legislation is the Fairness for Struggling Students Act of 2011. This bill revises the federal bankruptcy process by repealing the exemption for student loans funded by the government or nonprofit institutions and other education loans incurred by other debtors for the taxpayer, taxpayer's spouse, or dependents. Protections for private lenders are removed, and private student loans could be discharged through bankruptcy if the bill passes. The bill has been considered since 2010 and has yet to pass. The argument for maintaining non-dischargeability of government-backed student loans is that publicly funded loans are actually taxpayer-funded debt. Therefore, debtors should not be able to discharge the debt out of consideration to taxpayers.

A second legislative bill, the Private Student Loan Bankruptcy Fairness Act of 2011, makes private student loans dischargeable through bankruptcy. It repeals the section of the bankruptcy code that makes education loans non-dischargeable. Government-guaranteed loans are left non-dischargeable, but the bill ensures that nonprofit-backed loans remain dischargeable only if the entire fund is provided by the nonprofit. This clause was added because current law states that any student loan is non-dischargeable if any part of the funding comes from a nonprofit. It appears the bill will not be discussed again until the 2013 Congress meets.

Proponents of the bill had hoped that the Bankruptcy Abuse and Consumer Protection Act (BAPCPA) would bring reform to an ailing student loan industry. When the law was passed, "promises" were made concerning benefits that would accrue as a result of the bill's passage. For example, the bill was expected to slow student default rates, and that has clearly not happened.

In addition, supporters of the student loan inclusion in the legislation claimed that fewer student loan bankruptcies and lower losses would lead to lower interest rates on student loans as a result of the savings. In reality, interest rates increased after the legislation passed. The same promise was made concerning credit card debt. The expectation was that BAPCPA would reduce the losses to creditors and the creditors would then pass on the savings to borrowers as lower interest rates. In reality, credit card rates also increased significantly. It seems to these supporters that the credit industry cannot be held accountable to promises they make to borrowers unless it is tied to laws or there are legal agreements and enforcements in place.

Reasons for Providing Student Loan Relief Options

There are opposing opinions as to the best way to deal with rising student loan defaults. The opinions depend a lot on whether you accept the psychologically debilitating impact of student debt. Students graduating with as much as $100,000 of debt are not just debtors faced with long-term loan payments. The money invested in loans represents lost opportunities. This money could have been spent on housing or developing businesses, for example. Allowing the bankruptcy process to work could free up potential economic resources that could benefit the economy.

In an economy like the post 2008-2010 economy, where mostly low-skilled jobs are available, the situation is looking grim for our younger generations. In fact, young adults are now facing low earning power or unemployment. Student loans have always been presented as an investment in the future. However, high unemployment rates for new graduates and students reduce or eliminate the return on some higher education investments. Pre-recession students are experiencing 4.5 percent unemployment while new graduates are at 9.1 percent unemployment. Saddled with debt and having no way to repay it, the country's most educated youths have no recourse when they are unable to repay student loans. The 8 percent default rate on student loans represents a psychologically debilitating situation where the only choice is to turn an investment in the future into a bad debt and stop making payments since the debt is not dischargeable.

The long-term consequences of defaulting on a student loan are severe. Consequences include: (5)

- Possibly being sued for the loan amount
- Negative credit reporting on default for up to seven years
- Inability to get additional financial aid
- Loan may be turned over to a collection agency leading to additional collection charges
- Inability to qualify for deferment
- May be unable to obtain a professional license
- May be prevented from enlisting in the military
- Difficulty qualifying for other loans like a house or vehicle loan

Even if students are able to make payments on the student loans, they are burdened with debt for decades. Some students have been known to repay these student loan debts for more than twenty years.

The arguments for giving students relief from student loan debt also address the fact that some of the borrowing is out of their control if they want to complete their education. Uncontrollable tuition increases make it necessary to borrow increasing amounts of money. The cost of going to college is rising faster than wage increases and inflation, and expenses are taking a larger share of household income.

In 2011, tuition and fees increased an average of 8.3 percent at public schools. Less than half of all public university students are able to pay the full price of college without financial assistance. (6)

Even if a student tries to avoid default by applying for a deferment, the deferment fees are high. In addition, deferment does not lock in an interest rate. When the borrower begins making payments again, the interest rate may very well have gone up, which will increase the payment amount. Deferment also extends the amount of time it takes to finally pay off the loan.

Unfortunately, there is no adequate loan modification program in place for student loans like the one the government has instituted for mortgages. Yet some student loan balances are as high as some mortgages and have mortgage-sized loan payments. A home purchase used to be the largest financial investments for adults, but it appears that student loans are competing to be that large investment, and if students default on that loan, it might be the only large investment that these individuals ever see.

Some of the arguments for allowing student loans to be dischargeable are also based on experiences from the recent 2008-2010 recession. It is widely known that the government spent over $2.5 trillion helping the auto manufacturers, financial institutions, home owners, and even the states when they needed help. However, student loan holders with defaults of approximately $880 billion were given no relief. There is a sense of injustice among proponents for student loan relief programs.

The passages of the Fairness for Struggling Students Act of 2011 and the Private Student Loan Bankruptcy Fairness Act of 2011 have been delayed partly due to the lobbying efforts of the influential financial institutions giving student loans. In the past, these lobbyists have managed to get priority over the IRS in terms of debt collection or discharge potential. So it will be a very difficult to get discharge and other modifications programs in place. It will take a lot of political pressure and money to create real change for those who need relief.

Reasons for Not Providing Student Loan Relief Options

Just as there are those who support relief programs for student loans and inclusion of student loans as dischargeable bankruptcy debt, there are those who oppose any such actions. Most of the opposing arguments have one of two themes: economics and responsibility.

Economically, allowing students to discharge student loans could cost taxpayers. Since most student loans are guaranteed by the federal government, discharges would equate to taxpayers footing the bill. Since taxpayer dollars would not be collectible, the cost of student loans would rise based on market pressures from the supply side as well as the demand side.

In addition, discharge would cost private lenders of student loans since debts would not be collected. The student loans would have to be written off as bad debts. The financial institutions will have to absorb higher costs that will be passed on to future borrowers.

The suggestion that student loan forgiveness will free up spending by borrowers and thus serve as economic stimulus is rejected by opponents. They argue that the people who cannot afford to pay their student loans are having financial problems and do not have money to spend on other goods and services. They are not making student loan payments, so there is no money to be redirected in the economy.

As I have discussed, there are bankruptcy discharge options for those who can meet undue hardship requirements. These critics of change suggest these are the most logical and viable options for responsible borrowers. In terms of personal responsibility, opponents of bankruptcy discharges for student loans believe that people accepting student loans have a responsibility to meet their debt obligations. The opponents are of the opinion that making it easy to discharge student debt will encourage excessive borrowing while students are in school. This sets a bad precedent for incurring financial obligations and sends the wrong message about accountability for personal and taxpayer debt.

They further argue that though the economy is sluggish and unemployment is high at this point, the economy will eventually recover. Making a long-term public policy concerning student loan forgiveness based on a temporary business or economic cycle can have unintended consequences.

Skyrocketing Tuition and Fees

The cost of attending college is rapidly rising, and this is contributing to the increase in the number and amounts of student loans and thus student loan defaults. In 2011 and 2012, the average increase in tuition and fees at four-year schools of higher education rose 8.3 percent for in-state students. From 2001-2002 to 2011-2012, tuition and fees rose an average of 5.6 percent annually beyond the inflation rate. Two-thirds of college students also get some kind of financial aid.

Much research has been done to identify the reasons for skyrocketing tuition and fee increases over the decades. One of the factors influencing the rise in tuition and fees is the fact that state and federal contributions to public schools have not been adequate to keep up with rising operational costs and enrollment growths. As a result, the universities must raise tuition to cover costs.

In addition, state funding for higher education has been declining over the last ten years. From 2011 to 2012, state funding fell by 7.6 percent across the nation. (7) The recession has taken a toll on state budgets, and there is less revenue available for higher education. This creates a domino effect. The school raises tuition and fees, which forces students to borrow more money to cover expenses.

Other reasons for rising tuition and fees include:

- Increasing administrative and labor costs, including health insurance and retirement expenses
- Cost of technology upgrades to remain competitive
- Increasing cost of infrastructure upgrades needed to support campuses
- Increasing costs of financial aid as more students need assistance
- Higher costs of specialized programs that include remedial programs, career counseling, and others
- Additional expense of adding services like student security
- Rising labor costs to pay for top faculty
- Rising labor costs in general for a labor-intensive operation
- Increasing costs of doing research

Reasons Given for Increases by Students

Naturally, students have a different opinion as to why colleges and universities keep raising tuition. For example, many students believe that higher education is too autonomous and that there are no regulations requiring capping increases. This group has often said that the schools raise tuition and raise it as much as possible for one simple reason: because they can.

In addition, many people believe higher education institutions are wasteful and that they have no incentive to become more efficient. (8) The schools compete for high-priced faculty, spend money on events and activities that are not essential to education, award scholarships that are not based on need, and build or upgrade facilities in a way that suggests "empire building."

This empire building also attracts profit-driven individuals into these institutions' management ensembles. This group sees opportunities to make profits from multiple sources of funding that include federal and state grants, donations, tuition, and fees. They are driven to increase wealth for the institutions and themselves at the cost of others.

Reform-minded groups also argue that lobbying is another contributing factor to accelerating tuition and fees. The idea of lobbying lawmakers for legislation that is friendly to the education industry has been a central part of the industry strategy for decades. In 2008, colleges and universities spent over $102 million on lobbying Congress and other federal agencies. This makes it the seventh-most powerful lobbying industry in terms of spending.

The truth is that the reasons given by the educational institutions and the students for tuition and fee increases are all contributing factors. The question now is how can tuition and fees be controlled, student debt lowered, and student loan defaults managed so that there is not a whole generation of young adults burdened with unmanageable debt half their lives?

These are complex problems that will need innovative solutions and effort by all involved—the higher education institutions, state and federal governments, and the students themselves.

CHAPTER 16

Salary Trends: Compensation in America

Salary Trends in a Changing Economy

According to recent compensation studies, some CEOs of large US companies make as much money in one day as the average worker makes in a year. Other CEOs can make more in one day than an average family makes in a year. An ABC report in 2010 showed that the CEO of Wal-Mart, Michael Duke, makes about $16,826.92 every hour when his salary is converted to an hourly figure. This is in sharp contrast to some of his employees who make about $13,650 in a year (about $8.75 an hour). (1)

CEO pay scales have been on the rise for decades, jumping more than 45 percent in the past ten years alone. In contrast, the federal minimum wage gives entry-level workers roughly 7 percent less money, in real terms, than they were making ten years ago. Many critics question whether this pay distribution is justified. Others wonder when exactly the wage gap between the top of the business chain and the bottom rung became so divergent.

One can argue that we live in a capitalist society. So, technically, there is no limit to how much money a person can earn. In fact, our free market system is set up to reward the biggest risk takers. If the CEO of a company actually dreamed up a business concept and put in long hours and hard-earned capital to create and grow the company, shouldn't he or she be rewarded accordingly? Many free market advocates will agree that, given these circumstances, CEOs should receive higher compensation.

However, nowadays, some CEOs are not founders of the companies in which they are supposed to serve. In fact, some of these CEOs and executive team members are hired and subsequently fired when the companies they manage do not meet market expectations. And it is widely noted that some top executives have and continue to get increasing compensation in the face of declining shareholder value.

Meanwhile, what of the little guy and the slowly disintegrating middle class? Famed billionaire investor Warren Buffet has spoken recently about the unfairness between executives and staff. In one of his famous quips, he suggests that in addition to commanding astonishing larger annual earnings, he and other executives are paying taxes at a lower tax rate. In his case, he pays about an adjusted 17.4 percent, while his secretary who makes substantially less than he does pay taxes at more than double his tax rate or 35.8 percent. (2) In line with being fair, Warren Buffet has only taken a salary of about $100,000 over the last thirty years. However, Buffet is the exception rather than the rule. The fact is that the pay system is not working well for society as a whole. In this discussion, I will take a closer look at some of the details of compensation in America and why the pay gap is increasing.

Notable CEOs

Did the national attention and discourse on the issue of rich vs. poor all start with the CEO of Wal-Mart or with Warren Buffet and his secretary? Probably not. This discussion—and often passionate debate—has been going on for almost a century or more—was it not worker dissatisfaction with management that started the whole labor movement in the early 1900s? The difference today is that the gap has grown beyond any justifiable comprehension, and the system at the beginning of the century looks fairer than the one we see today.

Let us take a look at some top executives and see if we can understand the compensation divergence a little better. Let us start with the top earners in the country today and the industries they represent.

Forbes Highest Paid Ceos 2011					
Ceo	Company	Industry	Compensation	Co Earnings (TTM)	CO Returns (1Yr)
John Hammergren	McKesson	Pharmaceuticals	$131.2 million	$1.2 billion	20%
Ralph Lauren	Polo Ralph Lauren	Apparel	$66.7 million	$630 million	50%
Michael Fascitelli	Vornado Realty	Real Estate	$64.4 million	$830 million	-16%
Robert Iger	Walt Disney	Entertainment	$53.3 million	$4.55 billion	-6%
George Paz	Express Scripts	Healthcare	$51.5 million	$1.29 billion	-15%
Jeffrey Boyd	Priceline.com	Internet	$50.2 million	$720 million	48%
Lew Frankfort	Coach	Apparel	$49.5 million	$880 million	35%
Stephen Hemsley	UnitedHealth Group	Healthcare	$48.8 million	$4.93 billion	35%
John D. Wren	Omnicom Group	Advertising	$45.6 million	$900 million	-1%
Michael Watford	Ultra Petroleum	Oil and Gas	$43.7 million	$373 million	-33%
John C. Martin	Gilead Sciences	Biotech	$42.7 million	$2.73 billion	10%
James Dimon	JPMorgan Chase	Financial Services	$42 million	$18.6 billion	-19%
Leslie Moonves	CBS	Broadcasting	$41.5 million	$1.2 billion	32%
John C. Plant	TRW Automotive Holdings	Auto parts	$41.1 million	$977 million	-7%
David Zaslav	Discovery Communications	Broadcasting	$40.7 million	$936 million	-7%
Laurence Fink	BlackRock	Investment Management	$39.9 million	$2.4 billion	-13%
Richard Adkerson	Freeport-McMoRan Copper & Gold	Materials	$39.5 million	$5.59 billion	-26%
James Hackett	Anadarko Petroleum	Oil & Gas	$38.9 million	$845 million	14%
John Chambers	Cisco Systems	Technology	$37.9 million	$6.49 billion	-24%
David Pyott	Allergan	Pharmaceuticals	$33.8 million	-$2.5 million	23%
Gregory Lucier	Life Technologies	Biotech	$33.8 million	$365 million	-22%
Charles Davidson	Noble Energy	Oil & Gas	$33.4 million	$592 million	4%
Louis Camilleri	Philip Morris	Tobacco	$32.7 million	$7.9 billion	16%
Joseph Tucci	EMC	Computer Services	$31.6 million	$2.12 billion	15%
Gregory Boyce	Peabody Energy	Coal	$30.7 million	$895 million	-27%

The annual compensation among this group ranges from a high of $131 million to a low of $30 million. Although there are some similar fields represented, in general, these executives represent the varied compensation packages across American businesses.

Let us contrast these financial behemoths' outsized compensation packages with what smaller enterprises pay. It has been difficult to accurately give an average number that best describes the annual income for small and midsize business owners. This is because there is a wide spectrum of business formation types, revenue bases, and therefore annual income expectations for this group. In Salary.com's 2006 Small Business Compensation Survey, it was suggested that the average small business owner in America has an annual salary of $233,600. However, Smallbiztrends.com writer Scott Shane put forth the suggestion that there is not just one number that should be reflective of the small business group. Shane's article "How Much Money do Small Business Owners Make?" puts forth the idea that the 2008 IRS figures show that the average revenue of a sole proprietorship ranged from $11,862 for unclassified establishments to $1,073,406 for coal mines and that the average net income ranged from $47,455 for coal mines to $117,685 for dentists' offices. (3)

This is evident also in employee salaries across a variety of businesses. In fact, considering pay scales by industry, the highest paying jobs tend to be found in engineering, with medicine a close second. Petroleum engineers lead the field with annual salaries in the mid $200,000 range. In the medical field, surgeons and anesthesiologists bring home $220,000 to $250,000. Many reasons are given for earnings at this level. Simply put, it is a most likely a combination of education and demand. Physicians spend four years in medical school, plus a year of internship, and anywhere from two to five additional years before they become board-certified in their specialty. This substantial investment of both time and money commands a reasonable return.

Government Pay: Washington and Beyond

Government leaders, especially in Washington, do fairly well themselves, although they cannot hold a candle to our top ten list above. These salaries explain why many politicians are very reluctant to leave once they are in office. Contrast that to the earlier days of the nation when politicians had jobs other than their government posts to support their lifestyles. Here is the current average run-down of some well-known government positions:

- President of the United States: $400,000 per year, plus $150,000 expense account, $200,000 non-taxable travel allowance, and $19,000 for entertainment
- Members of Congress: $174,000
- Supreme Court: Chief Justice, $223,500; Associate Justices, $213,900 thousand
- The average Washington lobbyist makes between $79,000 and $136,000
- State governor salaries vary widely. New York's and California's governors are the highest paid at $179,000 and $206,000 respectively. Maine's governor makes the least at $70,000, and Maine's governor has not had a raise in twenty years. Some governors choose not to accept a salary, and most governors' salaries have declined in the past four years while Washington salaries have risen

Compared to those government workers who labor in relative anonymity, the average wage for federal civilian employees grew from $51,000 in 2000 to more than $80,000 today. Most of these increases at the top levels were meant to attract talented employees considering higher paying private sector positions, which can sometimes come with double the salary of a government job. During that same period, the average private industry worker's salary grew from $38,000 to $52,000. Total compensation today (including wages and benefits) is more than $120,000 for government workers and only $60,000 for private sector employees.

The once-high total compensation packages are decreasing across some private industries, because employers are finding ways to creatively reduce benefits and perks to employees. A pension guarantee is rare in the private sector nowadays as employers shift the burden of these retirement plans to their employees. Some private firms have shifted from providing health and other benefits at a discount to getting rid of them altogether. These burdens, which can be thousands of dollars a year, are now shouldered by the employees. In addition to a much higher compensation level, government workers also enjoy far greater job security than those in private industry, especially in today's uncertain economy.

What is a living wage?

Obviously, the individuals and groups discussed above are making a living wage, perhaps even a "living very well" wage. Living wage is a term that is tossed about with great frequency in the media. But what, exactly, does it mean?

Across the country, individuals working in low-wage jobs often make insufficient income to provide for their families, given the local cost of living. Some community organizers and activist groups have argued that the prevailing wage offered by the government and businesses doing business with the government should reflect a wage rate required to meet minimum standards of living. This required wage varies widely by geographic area. For example, the living wage for a single individual in Los Angeles should be $11.99 per hour. For supporting a family of four, it should be $34.07. In Maine, the living wage for an individual should be $7.84, and for a family of four, it should be $26.45. By comparison, the average minimum wage in California is $8.50. In Maine, it is $7.25, which is also the federal minimum wage amount that was enacted in 2007. This was the first increase in the federal minimum wage in almost a decade.

Many argue for raising the federal minimum wage as well as for paying the living wage. Eighteen states, led by the state of Washington at $9.04 an hour, have already enacted higher minimum wages. The minimum wage, unlike Social Security, is not required by federal law to enact an annual inflation adjustment. Thus inflation eats away at the buying power of low-income Americans every year that Congress does not raise it. In the more than three years since Congress passed the last increase, the buying power of the minimum wage has eroded by 11 percent. To contrast, congressional (house and senate) salaries have increased by about 5 percent during our most recent economic downturn alone. In fact, congressional members' salaries automatically add annual cost of living adjustments (COLA) unless they vote against the increase that year. Many wonder if there is not an inherent conflict of interest in allowing this group and others to essentially set their own salaries. Maybe a fairer system would be for the voting public (comparable to shareholders in a company) to be the ones setting their elected officials' salaries. However, this is an unlikely possibility, and legislators will most likely push back against the voters' right to dictate their salaries—much like executives in a private company fighting similar-minded shareholders. No wonder society questions whose interests are being served by government officials.

So how does the federal minimum wage compare with the federal poverty level? Currently, a single individual earning minimum wage would gross $15,080 per year. The federal poverty level is $11,170. So a single individual earning minimum wage would be just above the poverty level. If that individual were supporting a family of two, he or she would be right at the poverty level of $15,130 for a family of two. However, a family of four trying to live on one wage earner's minimum wage would be well below the poverty level of $23,050 for a family of that size.

The ethics of compensation

The recent corporate accountability scandals have drawn substantial attention to what some see as excessive compensation of a select group of high profile CEOs. This leads to the generalization that these individuals represent a major trend. But is this argument correct?

In an effort to put CEO pay in perspective, Lee Hecht Harrison, a global human resources consulting firm, conducted a study of over one hundred publicly available employment agreements and proxy statements (75 percent of which belonged to Fortune

500 companies) filed with the Securities and Exchange Commission. These CEOs had a median annual salary of $950,000 and received bonuses up to $16.5 million. Their direct reports had a median annual salary of $500,000 and bonuses of up to $6 million. Interestingly, there does not seem to be much controversy about the second level group. Although the sums are not a pittance, they are hardly the "obscene" salaries reported by the media. Perhaps the real obscenity occurs when highly paid chief executives preside over the demise rather than the growth of the corporation or lower rank-and-file employees.

Some argue that if these huge payoffs are the result of excessively large returns to the shareholders, then those who created and managed those returns should be compensated. In fact, they argue that most shareholders are likely quite content with their personal gains in these situations. This is true to a point, because when everyone is getting a piece of the pie, there are fewer complaints. However, as the people's piece of the pie is reduced and their expected portions are redistributed up the food chain in the organization, resentment—and sometimes riotous behavior—might ensue over time. And that kind of outcome is unlikely to be pleasant.

Other observers argue that CEOs *themselves* have a duty deriving from their moral fiduciary duty *to decline* excessive pay from their firms—as is Warren Buffet's approach. Furthermore, these corporate managers are responsible for seeing that workers at all levels of the corporation are fairly compensated and given an opportunity to benefit from the firm's success.

Clearly, the business culture needs reform in America—and globally, as some will also suggest. The arguments regarding wage disparity have existed for decades and likely will continue to exist for decades to come. While wage earners at all levels should be compensated fairly for their contributions to corporate success, fairness cannot be legislated by the government or created by taking from one group or class and giving to another. It would seem, therefore, that it is the responsibility of each business, both management and rank-and-file workers, to work toward a system of fair compensation within its own unique environment. This should be bolstered by adequate legislation from within the government that creates a more equitable compensation system based on business profits, employee contributions, and economic value. The goal should be to build a wealthy nation where the prosperity is created not just for a few, but also across the board.

SECTION 5

Financial Products

CHAPTER 17

Insurance Overview

Insurance in one form or another is a factor in the lives of most Americans. Some forms of insurance, like car insurance, are required by law. Others are optional, depending on your individual needs. If you live in California, for example, you probably need earthquake insurance. You might not need that if you live in South Dakota, where the risk of earthquakes is much lower.

The dictionary definition of insurance is "a promise of compensation for specific potential future losses in exchange for a periodic payment." In other words, you pay someone to protect your financial well-being in the case of an unexpected loss.

Insurance is built upon the principle that it spreads the risk around among a large group of people so that a single person does not assume all of the risk. For instance, if there is one house fire in your town each year, you could just sit tight and hope your house does not burn down. Or everyone in town could get together and pay a fire insurance premium each month that could be used to rebuild whichever house burns down.

In order to understand how insurance works in terms of your own financial situation, it is useful to understand a couple of terms unique to the insurance industry. The first term I will look at is *indemnity.* To be indemnified means to be made whole again or returned to a former state. In the case of an automobile accident, for example, your insurance policy would repair or replace your car so that it was as good as it had been before the accident.

Then there is *insurability.* In order for you to be considered insurable, the insurance company must charge you a premium that is high enough to cover both the potential loss and the company's own expenses. In other words, the company's risk could be neither catastrophic nor so great that the cost could not possibly be paid.

How Insurance Companies Work

Like all business entities, insurance companies are in business to make a profit. They do this through a combination of underwriting and investing. First, they must determine the amount of premium to charge for insuring against loss. This amount is determined by both the risk involved and what the consumer is willing to pay. The company then *underwrites* your policy.

The insurance company collects policy premiums from the individuals or companies it insures. While the company is required to hold money in reserve against future losses, it invests the money in the meantime. This is known as using the "float." Insurance companies make more profits on their investments than they make on the premiums alone.

Types of Insurance

A policy exists somewhere that will insure almost anything. Lloyd's of London, a British company founded in 1774, is well known for insuring rather strange, often high risk items such as a violinist's hands or a movie star's legs. Most insurance covers far more commonplace things, however.

The everyday kinds of insurance that most individual consumers are familiar with include automobile, home owner's, health, disability, and life. Businesses utilize some of these, but businesses may also be concerned about business interruption, worker's compensation, key personnel, and general or product liability, to name a few. You can buy health insurance for your pet, drought insurance for your crops, and even alien abduction insurance (although substantiating that particular type of claims may be a bit difficult)!

Consumer Insurance Basics

Here is a list of brief explanations of each type of insurance that an individual consumer might use:

- **Automobile Insurance.** Automobile insurance has three components: liability, collision, and comprehensive. Liability insurance is required when you license your car in any state. This may be fault or no-fault insurance. Fault insurance pays based on who was at fault in an accident, while no-fault pays regardless of who was at fault. This is important in case you are involved in an accident with an uninsured motorist. If your car is financed or leased, you will probably be required to carry some level of collision and comprehensive insurance. Full comprehensive coverage usually covers most common damages whether they are caused by collision, weather, acts of nature, man-made accidents as well as theft of the insured vehicle, damages done to the property of others involved accident, and medical expenses for anyone involved in the accident.

- **Home owner's Insurance**. This covers both the structure of your home and your personal possessions stored there. You may also obtain liability insurance that will cover medical bills for accidents that occur on your property. Renter's insurance is similar, but it would only cover your personal property since your building should be insured by the owner. You would add riders (additional specific coverage) to your original policy if you have high value items to insure, such as jewelry or antiques.

  Important note: You can often save money by "bundling" two or more types of insurance with the same company. The most common practice is to bundle your automobile and home owner's policies.

- **Health Insurance.** Health insurance provides coverage in the event of illness or accident. Some companies provide this as a benefit for employees and their families, often on a shared-cost basis. Private health insurance is available for seniors who may wish to cover costs that are not paid by Medicare. Many states provide insurance coverage for uninsured children through statewide programs. This coverage is for families with modest incomes who make too much money to qualify for Medicaid.

- **Disability.** Disability insurance insures your income in case a disability makes working uncomfortable, painful, or impossible. Coverage usually includes paid sick leave as well as short-term and long-term disability benefits. While businesses often provide this type of coverage to employees, it is even more important to self-employed individuals whose entire way of life may be in jeopardy if they are unable to work.

- **Life Insurance.** These policies come in two types: term life and whole life. *Term life insurance* is the least expensive alternative and is designed to provide a benefit that will compensate the family of someone who dies for financial obligations such as consumer debt, funeral expenses, college education for children, and mortgages. As the name implies, the cost of this insurance is based on the time period (term) covered by the policy.

  Whole life insurance is a policy that lasts for the whole life of the person who is insured. It is actually promoted as a type of investment, because it builds cash value and pays a guaranteed interest rate. It pays your heirs in the event of your death. However, if you elect to cash out the policy before you die, you would forfeit the death benefit.

Business Insurance Basics

While the kinds of insurance necessary to a business would depend somewhat on the type of business involved, this is a brief discussion of some types of insurance that many businesses might use:

- **Liability.** Liability insurance protects a company's assets if it is sued for causing property damage or personal injury. Lawsuits are so commonplace in today's business environment that even small mistakes can result in big legal bills. So general liability insurance is critical for most companies. Some companies may purchase an umbrella policy, which picks up where general liability coverage ends. It provides additional coverage for any liabilities that standard liability policies do not cover.
- **Worker's Compensation.** Worker's compensation insurance provides wage replacement and medical benefits if you are injured on the job. However, in order to receive worker's compensation from your employer, you usually would have to agree not to sue your employer for whatever caused your accident.
- **Business Interruption.** Business interruption insurance protects against the cost of repairs after a disaster strikes. If your place of business becomes unusable due to fire, earthquake, or other disaster, this insurance covers the income your business would have made while the property is unusable. It also covers the fixed costs and expenses you may continue to incur as well as the costs of moving to a temporary location if that becomes necessary.
- **Key Employee.** Key person insurance or key employee insurance protects a company if a top salesperson, executive, or owner dies or becomes unable to work. This type of policy enables the business to continue operation without a major disruption, and so it provides peace of mind to owners, shareholders, and employees.

Insurance Cost Factors

How much you pay for insurance varies widely and depends, first of all, on the kind of insurance you are buying. Here are a few of the cost factors associated with each type of insurance I have discussed.

- **Automobile.** What your policy costs will be based on your age, where you live, your driving record, and the kind of car you are insuring. Other factors the insurer may consider include your occupation, how far you drive to work, your credit rating, and your education level. You can often get lower rates if you are a non-smoker or have safety or theft-protection devices on your car.
- **Home owner's.** Home owner's insurance is based on where you live and the value of your home. It is usually wise to insure to replace your home at the current value, rather than at original market value, which could be too low. Your cost will depend on the amount of your deductible and on what types of perils you are insuring against. Whether you insure against fire, flood, earthquakes, or other disasters can vary widely, depending on your home's location. Newer homes generally cost less to insure than older homes do.
- **Health.** Assuming that you are buying your own health insurance, rather than using a plan provided by your employer, you must consider several factors when analyzing health insurance costs. The health care law that was passed in 2010, and which may or may not go into effect in 2014, will change the health insurance picture substantially. However, at the present time, there are several things to consider. If you choose a policy with a high deductible and co-pays, your premiums will be lower. Conversely, low deductibles and low or non-existent co-pays will lead to higher premiums. Other determining factors would be your age, your profession (whether you are in a high-risk job, for example), and whether you have any chronic health conditions.
- **Disability.** Self-employed individuals or others not covered by a company disability policy may want to purchase disability insurance as a protection against loss of income due to illness or injury. Again, the first determining factor is your age. The younger you are, the lower the premium. Women will pay more than men will, and non-smokers will pay less than smokers do. Those in white-collar jobs, such as attorneys or CPAs, will pay less than blue-collar workers do. You may also adjust your premium by determining a waiting period before you receive benefits. The waiting period can range anywhere from thirty days to one year.

- **Term life.** Like many other types of insurance, the main factor in determining life insurance costs is your age. For example, a healthy forty-year-old man who buys a twenty-year term policy with a fixed annual premium might pay $350 a year for a $500,000 death benefit. A healthy fifty-year-old man who buys the same policy might pay $1,000 a year. If he waits until he is sixty, the policy will cost about $3,000 a year. (1)

- **Whole life.** Insurance agents may say that buying a whole life policy is a great way to force you to save money. While it does involve saving, it can be a very costly way to do it. First of all, whole life costs more than term life for the same level of coverage. The money you put in does grow tax-deferred, but so does an IRA or 401(k). Different kinds of fees apply to whole life policies; these include commissions, annual fees, investment management fees, and surrender fees if you decide to cash out your policy. So even though you are saving, you may be able to realize a higher return by using a different savings vehicle.
- **Liability.** The cost of liability insurance for your business depends on the type of business you operate, how long you have been in business, how much coverage you want, and what kind of deductible you choose. Relatively inexpensive policies are available, of course, but you often get what you pay for, and cheap liability insurance may leave you in a dangerous position if the worst should happen. You may even find yourself with a policy that really does very little for you.
- **Worker's compensation.** Rates for worker's compensation insurance are set by each state. Risk is determined by two factors: the frequency of on-the-job injury and the severity of injury. Severity is measured by both medical payments and payments made directly to the injured employee for losses suffered as a result of an accident. Insurance companies can adjust the rates based on a number of factors, including the employer's safety history and whether or not the employer offers health insurance to its employees.
- **Business interruption.** This particular type of policy is generally based on the gross earnings of the business in question. Because there are many different definitions of "gross earnings," it is best to work with a competent accountant and a trustworthy insurance agent to get the level of coverage you need.
- **Key person.** This is essentially a life insurance policy for anywhere between $500,000 and $5 million. Usually, these are ten- or twenty-year term policies. Costs may range from hundreds to thousands of dollars per year. The costs vary, in large

part, according to the covered individual's age. If the executive in question is fairly young and in good shape, costs can be quite reasonable.

What is Wrong with Insurance?

While insurance is important to most individuals and companies, the industry does have its critics. As an informed consumer, you should be aware of both the pros and cons. What do the critics say?

One of the most common complaints is that because insurance policies and related documents are written by lawyers, only other lawyers can understand them. The paperwork is simply too complicated for ordinary consumers who risk being misled about coverage or buying something they do not need. The best way to deal with this problem is to use an insurance broker or agency that you know and trust. Ask questions if you do not understand something, and have the agent explain your policy in ordinary English or layman's terms as clearly as possible.

Some people think that having an insurance policy makes people take more risks than they would otherwise. For example, if you have home owner's insurance that covers theft, you may not be always being careful about locking your doors and windows every time you leave the house. You may keep your jewelry in plain sight instead of locked in a jewelry box or safe. Insurance companies have their own safeguards for occurrences of this type. If you fail to take reasonable precautions to protect your insured property, then they have the right to deny your claim. For example, if your house burns down and the insurance investigator finds that you did not have working smoke alarms, you may be the loser.

Criticism regarding denial of claims on the part of insurance companies is widespread. Insurers are given bad grades for processing claims too slowly as well as for seeming to find ways to deny legitimate claims. For example, some companies have what is called a "concurrent cause" provision. This means that if there are two causes for a claim, but only one cause is covered by the policy, the claim can be denied. Let us say your home is in the path of a hurricane. Your policy might cover wind damage, but does not cover the damage from the flooding that comes after. So even though some of the damage was caused by wind, your entire claim could be denied because you did not have flood coverage. As I have mentioned before, awareness is the key to avoiding this type of problem.

Working with insurance companies and agencies

Insurance companies are generally divided into two basic types:

- Life insurance companies, which sell life insurance, annuities, and pension products
- General lines companies, which sell all other kinds of insurance, such as automobile, home owner's, health, disability, liability—and many subcategories of each of these.

Informed consumers understand the importance of knowing the basics about the types of insurance. You should learn enough to know the right questions to ask and how to compare quotes and coverage from different companies. Then find an insurance agent you can get to know and trust. There are two types of agents. A captive agent represents a single insurance company, while an independent agent may represent many different companies and lines. Once you find a good agent, you can then work with him or her to obtain the best possible coverage at the most reasonable cost.

CHAPTER 18

Understanding Life Insurance

When you purchase a life insurance policy, you are essentially buying peace of mind for your heirs. Your policy is a contract between you and an insurance company where the company promises to pay a specific amount of money upon your death to your designated beneficiary. In return, you pay premiums to the insurance company, either in a lump sum or on a regular payment schedule. Within the general definition of life insurance are several different types of policies, each serving a different need or purpose. The two major types I will consider are term life and cash value life.

Term Insurance

As the name implies, term insurance covers you for a specific amount of time or term. It pays only if you die within that time period. It generally offers the most protection for the money paid; however, it does not build up cash value. Policy terms generally range from five to twenty-five years, although terms can be a short as one year or as long as thirty-five. Policies are usually renewable at the end of the term, although the premiums may increase, depending on your age and your health. Be sure you find out up front what the premium will be if you continue to renew the policy. Also, ask if you will be unable to renew at some point as you age.

You may be able to convert your term policy to a cash-value policy when it comes up for renewal, regardless of your health. However, the premiums for a cash-value policy will be substantially higher than those for term insurance.

Cash-Value Life Insurance

A cash-value policy charges a higher premium during the early years of the policy. It then invests the difference between the cost of the policy and the premium you pay, which builds up the cash value. You may use the cash value in your policy by taking out a loan against it. However, if you do not pay back the loan with interest, the amount you owe will be subtracted from the benefit paid to your heirs when you die.

There are several different variations of cash-value insurance, including whole life, universal life, and variable life. Let us look at the specifics of each type of policy.

- **Whole life** covers you for your lifetime, as long as the premiums are paid. Some people prefer the traditional whole life, because its premiums are fixed and savings are backed by the insurance company's investment in high-grade corporate bonds and mortgages, which also pays interest and dividends. Because insurance companies are continuously collecting money and investing it, whole life is among the few long-term fixed-income investments that keep up with and may even benefit from rising interest rates.

- **Universal life** is a flexible policy that allows you to vary your premium payments. Your premiums, minus account expenses, go into an account that earns interest. You can even adjust the face amount of your policy, although you may have to provide proof that you qualify for a new benefit amount. If your annual premium plus the interest you earn is less than the account's expense charges, the value of your account will decrease, so you may need to increase your premiums or lower your death benefit.

- **Variable life** is a policy whose value depends on how the money in the account is invested. As a policyholder, you may choose to invest in mutual funds or other types of investments that the policy allows. If the investments you choose do well, then the value of your policy will increase. If they do not do well, then your cash value may be lower or may disappear altogether. Before purchasing this type of policy, be sure you get a prospectus from the insurance company and read it carefully.

The above are the most common types of whole life policies. There are some other, less well-known policies that we should also consider.

- In a **limited-pay** policy, all the premiums are paid for a specific period of time. After that, no additional premiums are due to keep the policy in force. Common limited-pay periods are either ten or twenty years, and the cash value is paid when policyholders reach the age of sixty-five.
- An **endowment** is a policy that pays a lump sum of cash after a specific term or upon death. Some policies may even pay if the holder suffers a critical illness. An endowment policy earns money based on underlying investments. It can be cashed in, or "surrendered," early, and its value will then be determined by how much has been paid into it and its face value at the time of surrender.

- **Accidental death** insurance can be added on to a life insurance policy, or it can be purchased separately. It will pay benefits for death due to automobile or heavy-equipment accidents, plane crashes, homicide, falls, or drowning—to name a few. However, accidental death policies also have many exclusions, including suicide, acts of war, and use of drugs or alcohol.

Life Insurance and your Taxes

If your policy is structured properly, its benefits are likely either tax deferred or tax-free. Death benefits paid to your heirs are almost always tax-free. The money that builds up in your account through the investments you choose also grows tax-free. You can withdraw money from many policy accounts up to the amount you have invested without paying taxes on the withdrawal. And you can borrow against your gains without being taxed on the borrowed amount.

One type of endowment policy, called a Modified Endowment Contract, does have tax implications, however. This policy loses its tax-free withdrawal benefits if money is withdrawn before or within six months after you turn fifty-nine. Withdrawals are subject to a 10 percent income tax penalty on any gain withdrawn. However, the money remaining in the policy and death benefits are not taxable unless the entire policy lapses or is surrendered.

Advantages and Disadvantages

Many people look upon life insurance as a sort of necessary evil. But they buy it because they want to protect their families from a loss of income and major debts in case of their untimely death.

The advantages of a cash-value policy are that it builds value over time and you can borrow against it. Also, as discussed above, the death benefits are generally distributed tax-free. The major disadvantage is that the premiums are inconsistent and are likely to increase as you get older.

The advantage of a term life policy is that it is relatively cheap, especially if you purchase it when you are young and healthy. The disadvantage is that the policy is not permanent. When it expires, you must purchase another policy, often at a higher premium based on your age and health.

The main criticism about using a whole life policy as an investment vehicle is that it may be very costly for what you get. In the long term, it may be more profitable to buy term insurance at a low premium and then also invest in mutual funds or stocks that are not connected to insurance policies.

Life Insurance Questions to Ask

Do you need life insurance? If so, do you know how much and what kind you need? Before making a decision, be aware of these important questions and considerations.

- What are your life circumstances? Do you have children who need to be educated or a mortgage that must be paid?
- Can you afford the initial premium? What if the premium increases? Will you be able to keep up the payments?
- If you cancel during the early years of your policy, cancellation can cost you a lot of money. Be sure you are buying the right policy at the right price.
- Beware of agents or policies that offer free or low-cost premium financing. Ask an attorney or other expert to review anything that seems too good to be true.
- Most importantly, is the company you buy from today financially secure, and will they be able to pay the death benefit when you die?

All of these questions can be answered through careful research and with the assistance of an insurance agent whom you know and trust. In addition to working with a good agent, you should also check the rating of the company you are purchasing from. This information is provided by several agencies, including:

- A.M. Best (www.ambest.com)
- Fitch Investor's Service (www.fitchibca.com)
- Moody's Investor Service (www.moodys.com)

The purpose of having life insurance is to provide peace of mind to you and your family. By becoming an informed consumer, you will also have peace of mind about the policy and coverage you choose.

CHAPTER 19

Annuities and How to Use Them

An annuity is an investment vehicle sold by an insurance company that pays the investor a specific amount of money at regular intervals for a number of years, often for the investor's entire lifetime. Annuities come in four basic types: immediate, fixed, variable, and indexed. Immediate-income annuities provide income right away; the other types are deferred annuities that allow investors to save for retirement while deferring taxes. I will discuss the various types in detail, including the pros and cons and tax implications of each.

The main purpose of an annuity is to provide lifetime income, either immediately or down the road. People mainly choose this investment vehicle because of the safety of the funds invested, along with certain tax advantages attached to the investment.

Immediate Annuity

This type of annuity's payments generally begin immediately or within one year after you purchase it. Here is why it is of interest to many older Americans: living a long and healthy life is terrific, but many retirees worry that they will outlive their savings. Americans are living longer than ever. At the same time, the insecurity of corporate pensions, social security, and an unpredictable stock market do little to calm people's fears. One of the great features of immediate annuities is that they provide a lifetime income that you can never outlive. Even if you live to be one hundred, you are still guaranteed payment.

There are some disadvantages, however. First, you lose control of the money. An immediate annuity is irreversible. In some instances, you can choose the right of survivorship, which means that your spouse or other heirs will receive the balance of the account if you die, but the policy's monthly payout amount is usually less if you choose this option.

Deferred Annuity

In contrast to immediate annuities, deferred annuities generally have two phases: the accumulation phase and the payout phase. Your annuity will accumulate earnings on a tax-deferred basis. However, when you begin to receive a payout, part of the payout is tax-free, but you would pay taxes on another portion of the payout amount. These amounts vary from state to state, and the regulations governing them may change, so it is wise to consult a tax advisor and to work with a qualified expert, as well.

Fixed Annuity

In investment terms, a fixed annuity is similar to a certificate of deposit. It pays a fixed rate of return for a certain period of time, usually at a rate of about 2 to 4.5 percent, depending on the time period. If you choose this type of investment, make sure the annuity pays the same percentage amount for the entire term.

There is an important safety factor in both fixed and immediate annuities. Though they are state regulated, they are not FDIC insured. The money is generally invested in high-grade bonds or approved US Treasury securities. The company is required to keep a dollar-for-dollar amount in reserve, so they cannot over-leverage their investments. In addition, every company that sells annuities must be part of a re-insurance group, so if a company goes out of business, another company will pick up the obligation. There may be as many as fourteen re-insurers per company. Each state also maintains a state guarantee fund. The company pays small percentage of each annuity into a fund that will cover them in the event of multiple defaults.

A fixed annuity provides for accumulating interest on a tax-deferred basis. The interest earned is not subject to being taxed until you withdraw it. This allows for a potentially greater cash buildup than if you were paying income taxes on the interest as you earned it. If you are considering converting IRA funds to an annuity, it does not offer any advantages because an IRA is already tax-deferred—unless, of course, the annuity is offering a higher rate of return than the IRA is earning.

Variable Annuity

A variable annuity is an investment that works very much like a mutual fund. The money is invested in the market and, due to market fluctuations, cannot guarantee a specific return. In the 1990s, this type of annuity had tax advantages because it grew tax-deferred.

Today, however, the rules are different—annuity returns are taxed as ordinary income when you pull your money out, not at the more favorable capital-gains rate of 15 percent.

Investment advisors generally do not recommend this type of annuity to seniors or retirees because it often carries very high fees, many of which are not disclosed in advance or are not detailed on the account statements. Then there is a rider fee if you have opted to purchase a rider that guarantees a certain return. But you have to die to get it. These fees can be as much as 2.5 to 4 percent per year. Here is a typical example:

- Administrative fee = .5 percent per year
- Life insurance fee = 1 to 2 percent per year
- Mutual fund fees = 1 to 2 percent per year

A variable annuity is also taxed a little differently than other investments are. You do not actually know how much the annuity payment will be each month, because the market value of your investment will change based upon the market, which can be volatile. So the tax-exempt amount of each payment is determined by dividing your investment by the period over which you expect to receive the payout. In addition, this type of account is not tax-free to your heirs.

Index Annuity

The index annuity, which was created in the late 1990s, has become more popular recently. It is actually a hybrid of an immediate annuity and a fixed annuity. Its investments are regulated and must made in be high-grade bonds or treasuries. The yield is invested into the market, but the principal remains secure. So the principal is guaranteed, and if the market goes up, you gain. If the market goes down, you will have losses, but you generally will not lose your principal investment.

Some indexed annuities can be good investments, but some are not because companies will often cap the earnings. Some cap rates are high, while others are very low, so your return is not all that great. You can pull some money out of this account, but there is a stiff penalty, called a surrender charge, if you liquidate funds.

Like the other deferred annuities, indexed-annuity income grows tax-free, but it is taxed when the money is withdrawn. In all tax-deferred annuities, the way you chose to take income will determine how your taxable income is calculated. A simple partial withdrawal is usually the most desirable method, but it is treated as *interest first.* This may mean that the entire withdrawal will be taxable. However, if you set up a systematic payment, you could get some tax relief by spreading out the taxable gain over the years that annuity payments will be made. This does not reduce the total taxable amount, but it does spread it out and make the impact a little less painful.

Annuity Caveats: Let the Buyer Beware

The North American Securities Administrators Association (NASAA), the trade group for state securities regulators, has cited dishonest annuity sales practices as one of the top ten threats to investors. The main problem, they say, is not necessarily the product itself, but the way it is sold. Agents often do not explain all of the investment risk, fees, or surrender charges to the potential buyer.

According to Michael DeGeorge, vice president and general counsel for the National Association for Variable Annuities (NAVA), the industry concedes that "there have been abuses in which annuities were recommended when they weren't appropriate." He says his group is committed to matching annuities with the right buyers. "An inappropriate sale can taint the entire industry," says DeGeorge.

While much has been made about unscrupulous operators in the financial press, a recent study conducted by the Wharton School of Business concludes that "indexed annuity returns have been competitive with alternative portfolios of stocks and bonds." The study also found that the annuity design has limited the downside returns associated with declining markets and these annuities have achieved respectable returns in more robust equity markets.

As with any investment vehicle, it is the responsibility of the investor to understand both the process and the risks. And as with any profession, there are honest brokers and unscrupulous operators. A salesperson can actually learn to sell annuities in a three-day seminar, so it is important to know your advisor's level of knowledge and to make sure you are working with an expert. In the right circumstances, an annuity can be a safe and profitable investment. Get the facts and then decide if an annuity is right for you.

CHAPTER 20

Municipal Bonds

In today's financial market, there is a wide variety of investment opportunities to choose from. These vehicles all have features and benefits that may or may not be suitable for all investors. Therefore, it is important to understand which choices may prove to offer a better alternative than others based on an investor's particular goals, life stage, and risk tolerance.

What Are Municipal (Muni) Bonds?

In order to finance various capital expenditures, states, municipalities, and counties may offer a type of debt security for the purpose of raising the needed funds. Municipal bonds—or "munis" as they are often referred to—can be used for funding expenses such as the construction of schools, bridges, or highways. (1)

Municipal bonds typically fund a specific project, although this is not always the case. As an example, if a particular municipality was in need of a new community center, but it did not wish to fund the project using tax dollars from the citizens, then the municipality could sell municipal bonds to raise the needed capital.

Muni bond investors are essentially loaning their money to the issuer in exchange for a set number of interest payments during a predetermined time frame. At some point in time—typically the bond's maturity date—the original investment principal will be returned to investors.

These types of bonds are exempt from federal taxation as well as from most state and local taxes and are thus often purchased for their favorable tax implications. Because of their attractive tax status, muni bonds tend to be popular with investors in higher tax brackets.

Typically, municipal bonds pay fixed interest rates, and their maturities can range anywhere between just a few weeks to in excess of thirty years. Issued denominations of these types of bonds are usually between $1,000 and $5,000.

Comparing Bond Yields

Because of their safety, municipal bonds tend to offer lower interest rates than most other types of bonds. However, due to their tax-advantaged status, even with a lower rate of interest, an investor may still come out ahead in terms of net earnings. The tax-equivalent yield formula is use to compare taxable and nontaxable investments. The formula shows the taxable equivalent for a nontaxable investment. The formula is as follows:

Tax-Equivalent Yield = Tax-Free Interest Rate/(1 – Investor's Tax Rate)

The following example shows how this can occur:

An investor is in the 36 percent income tax bracket and he or she is purchasing a muni bond with a yield of 4.5 percent. Yet, because of the tax-free income that is received, the investor actually has an effective yield of 7.03 percent.

4.5/(1 – 0.36) = 7.03 percent

Therefore, by investing in the municipal bond with a 4.5 percent rate, the investor would net the same as they would by investing in a taxable bond paying 7.03 percent and having to pay tax on that bond's earnings.

The after-tax yield formula is essentially the same formula as the tax-equivalent yield formula above, only it does the reverse comparison. The after-tax yield formula calculates the yield after taxes are taken out of a taxable investment. The formula is as follows:

After-Tax Yield = Taxable Interest Rate x (1 – tax rate)

Using the same example above, if an investor in the 36 percent income bracket has purchased a taxable investment that yields 7.03 percent, then the after-tax yield is 4.5 percent, which is exactly what we should expect, given that we know this is the tax equivalent from the original example.

After-Tax Yield = 7.03 percent x (1-0.36) = 4.5 percent

Why Were Municipal Bonds Created?

The history of municipal bonds goes back several centuries to the early Renaissance when Italian city-states borrowed funds from wealthy families—primarily those who were in the banking business.

In the United States, the first municipal bond was recorded as issued by New York City for the funding of a canal in the year 1812. (2) During the following century, municipal bonds were used to finance a number of projects that were primarily in the areas of public education systems and urban improvements.

Once the Civil War (1861—1865) ended in the United States, a great deal of local debt was issued in order to build the massive nationwide railroad system. Because railroads were actually private corporations, the bonds that were issued at this time were quite similar to the industrial revenue bonds of more recent times. (3)

Two of the largest early issuers of muni bonds that were exempt from federal, state, and local taxes were the Triborough Bridge Authority established in 1933 and the Port of New York Authority that was established in 1921. (4)

What Type of Regulation Do Municipal Bonds Have?

Up until the 1970s, muni bonds were, for the most part, unregulated. However, that changed in the mid-70s when New York City nearly defaulted and later, when the Washington Public Power Supply System defaulted on an issue. After these events, and in accordance with the Securities Act Amendments of 1975, Congress created a body known as the Municipal Securities Rulemaking Board, or MSRB. This entity was charged with establishing a set of fair practices for both the trading as well as the underwriting of muni bonds. (5)

The MSRB is made up of fifteen members. They are divided as follows:

- Five representatives from commercial banks that deal in municipal bonds
- Five representatives from investment banking firms that trade and underwrite municipal bonds
- Five representatives from the public (6)

The Municipal Securities Rulemaking Board is essentially a self-regulating body, similar to the National Association of Securities Dealers (NASD) or the New York Stock Exchange (NYSE), and it is subject to oversight by the Securities and Exchange Commission.

A large part of the fair practices that were originally established by the MSRB focused on brokers and dealers who handle municipal bonds that were required to be registered with the Securities and Exchange Commission (SEC). Although this registration was required, the MSRB did not require any of the government muni bond issuers to abide by any type of pre-issue filing requirements like those that were already in place for corporate bonds and stocks. (7)

Under the primary rules created by the Municipal Securities Rulemaking Board, brokers and dealer must abide by several rules, including:

- Not engaging in deceptive, dishonest, or unfair practices
- Meeting the standards of professional qualification set by the MSRB
- Adhering to specific rules in the execution of muni bond transactions
- Abiding by set and detailed requirements of record keeping

Types of Municipal Bonds

Because state and local governments need to borrow funds to finance large projects, their main method of obtaining the needed capital is to issue municipal bonds. Depending upon the projects or funding necessary, these issuers can offer a number of different types of muni bonds.

The two primary types of municipal bonds are:

- **General Obligation Municipal Bonds.** In their most basic sense, general obligation bonds are issued for the purpose of raising capital to cover various expenses of a municipality. General obligation muni bonds are secure in that they are backed by the taxing power of the government issuing them. With these types of muni bonds, the funds are not tied to a certain project, and the money that is raised can, therefore, be used to fund a wide variety of different state or local activities.
- **Revenue Bonds.** Revenue bonds are primarily dependent upon the income that is expected from certain projects in order to pay the principal and interest that is due. They are typically issued for the purpose of funding certain infrastructure projects, and they are supported and backed by the income that is generated by these projects. Some project examples include water treatment plants or toll roads.

Both general obligation municipal bonds and revenue bonds are considered to be tax-exempt. In addition, these types of investment vehicles are specifically attractive to those investors who are averse to risk. This is because these bonds have a very high probability of paying back the principal to their investors.

Muni bonds may also fit into additional categories, such as:

- Taxable Municipal Bonds. Depending upon the actual project that is being funded, some municipal bonds will have federal taxable interest. The funded projects that are most likely to be taxable are those such as certain housing projects or sports arenas or those that are completed in conjunction with private companies.
- Tax-Exempt Municipal Bonds. In most cases, especially when the projects being funded are for the public good, the interest on municipal bonds will be exempt from federal income taxation and, in many cases, from state and local taxation, as well.
- Insured Municipal Bonds. In order to increase their appeal to investors who are seeking safety of principal, some municipal bonds are insured by the issuing government. These are often referred to as being Triple-A-Rated or "blue chip" muni bonds.
- Zero-Coupon Municipal Bonds. Similar to regular zero-coupon bonds, a zero-coupon municipal bond is sold at a discount. The interest from the bond is then added to its principal rather than regularly being paid out to the purchaser of the bond. (8)
- Industrial-Revenue Bond. Another type of municipal bond is the industrial-revenue bond, or IRB. These bonds provide a type of economic development incentive for private corporations. In essence, these are almost like corporate bonds that are moved though public agencies in order to make them tax-exempt due to the economic development that the funded project is providing. The companies that offer these IRBs can actually obtain low-cost financing for the project due to the fact that the bonds are issued through a government entity. The corporations are, therefore, also able to offer a low rate of interest on these bonds. (9)

Who Issues Municipal Bonds?

Municipal bonds can be issued by a number of sources, including cities, states, and counties. At the time that these bonds are issued, the issuing entity will receive a cash payment. This payment is received in exchange for the promise to repay the investors or bondholders.

Special Requirements for Municipal Bond Issuers

The requirements under which muni bonds are issued tend to vary from state to state. However, certain types of bonds may have specific issuing rules. For instance, bond measures proposed in a local county election will typically provide voters with a statement of tax rate that gives more details regarding the estimated tax rate required to levy and fund that particular bond.

In addition, in most cases, tax rules that govern muni bonds typically require that all of the funds raised by the sale of the bonds must be spent on one-time capital projects within a specific period of time. Also, there may be some exceptions that will permit an issuer to issue the bonds for the funding of other types of items, such as ongoing maintenance and operations expenses, the purchase of mortgages, and the funding of student loans. (10)

Who Can Purchase Municipal Bonds?

Investors in municipal bonds are usually seeking to preserve capital while also generating a tax-free stream of income. While there are both taxable and tax-exempt types of muni bonds, those offering tax advantages typically get the most attention.

Investors looking to obtain both capital appreciation as well as income may choose to use an active portfolio management approach. Here, the bonds are actually purchased and sold rather than being held to their maturity. With this technique, the investor will generally achieve income from the bond yields and will also obtain capital gain from selling the bond at a premium.

There are special requirements for some investors of municipal bonds. For example, investors subject to the alternative minimum tax, or AMT, are required to include the amount of interest income from some municipal bonds when they are calculating their tax.

Municipal Bonds: Advantages and Disadvantages

As with any type of investment vehicle, municipal bonds have both advantages and disadvantages. And these pros and cons may differ based on each individual investor's strategy, risk tolerance, and investment goals.

Advantages

There are a number of advantages to owning municipal bonds. These include:

- Tax-Exemption. Certainly, one of the biggest advantages to owning a municipal bond is its tax-advantaged status. Holders of muni bonds are exempt from having to pay federal income tax on these investments, and in many cases, they may also be exempt from paying state and local tax. This makes municipal bonds a very good choice for high-income investors who could end up netting more from a municipal bond—even with a lower rate of interest—in comparison to a taxable bond with a higher interest rate.
- Income. Municipal bonds are also attractive to investors due to their guaranteed income. These bonds consistently pay their investors interest—usually twice a year.
- Low Risk. Muni bonds are also considered to be low-risk investments. This is due to the fact that the issuing municipality is backing these bonds, and governments very rarely default on their payments to investors.

Disadvantages

Along with the advantages come a few disadvantages with municipal bonds. These can include:

- Credit Risk. Even with the safety of municipal bonds, investors can still run the risk of the issuer being unable to meet its financial obligations and failing to make the interest payments. To help investors in evaluating the creditworthiness of a muni bond issuer, investors can do research through rating agencies such as Standard & Poor's and Moody's. These agencies give bonds various letter ratings, with AAA being the highest and the most likely to follow through on its interest payment obligations.
- Interest Rate Risk. Because municipal bonds pay a set rate of interest, investors can often be subject to interest-rate risk. This occurs when the interest rates in the overall market go up, yet the investor is locked in to a set rate for a certain period

of time. The longer the bond's maturity, the higher the potential for interest-rate risk. This can, however, work in the opposite direction, as well. For example, if market interest rates fall and the investors are locked into a certain muni bond rate for a long period of time, their interest payments will likely be higher than they would have been if the investors were to purchase a bond at the lower, current interest rate.

- Tax Implications. Because municipal bonds generate tax-free income, they typically will pay a lower rate of interest than taxable bonds do. Therefore, those investors who anticipate a drop in their income tax rate may do better by investing in a taxable bond with a higher rate of interest.
- Call Risk. All bonds run the gamut of call risk, including municipal bonds. This occurs when the bond issuer pays back the investors' principal at a time before the bonds' maturity. When this happens, the investors' stream of income from that bond ends earlier than originally expected.
- Market Risk. When overall market conditions change, the underlying price of bonds changes, as well. So investors who plan to sell their bond prior to its maturity risk receiving back less than the amount of principal that was originally paid for the bond.

Muni Bond Investment Strategies

The investment in a municipal bond can have a long-term impact on an investor's interest-income stream. The most basic way of investing in muni bonds is to buy a bond that carries an attractive yield or interest rate return and then to hold that bond until the date of its maturity.

Muni Bond Ladder Strategy

Investors can use more advanced techniques, as well—especially if they are interested in taking advantage of the higher interest rates that are offered on the longer term maturities. For example, a muni bond "ladder" is one way to obtain higher yields without being locked in to long-term maturities with all of the bonds being purchased.

A bond ladder consists of a series of bonds that all having different maturity dates and interest rates. As each of the "rungs" on the ladder reaches maturity, the principal amount is reinvested into a new bond.

Muni Bond Bullet Strategy

When investors use a bullet strategy, they essentially purchase different municipal bonds at different times while maintaining the same maturity date for all of the bonds. In essence, this is almost the opposite of the bond ladder strategy.

With the bullet bond buying strategy, the investor would typically purchase a long-term bond first, and then later in time, they would purchase shorter term bonds with maturity dates that correspond to the first long-term bond that had been purchased. Using this type of a strategy helps investors minimize the fluctuations in interest rates because it essentially allows investors to take advantage of new, potentially favorable interest rates at varying times. (11)

Why Should Investors Purchase Municipal Bonds?

Due to the numerous advantages of municipal bonds, there are many reasons why investors may want to include these investments in their portfolios. The biggest reasons include these bonds' tax-exempt earnings status as well as their regular income payments and safety.

Many investors purchase municipal bonds due to their tax-exempt earnings. Unlike most other types of bonds, muni bonds are free of federal income taxation, and in many cases, they are also free from state and local tax.

In addition to their tax advantages, municipal bonds provide their investors with a steady source of income. This can be especially attractive to retirees who are seeking a safe and regular source of income so as to plan for expenses. Because municipal bonds typically pay interest two times per year, retirees will oftentimes purchase several munis with varying interest payment dates in order to receive an interest payment every month.

These types of bonds are also considered to be safe. Putting money into a muni bond gives investors the assurance of the issuer, which is normally a government entity. Governments rarely default on their bond payments. However, investors who wish to check the credit rating of the issuer prior to making an investment can do so via the rating agencies.

Although past performance is not a guarantee of future returns, it is still a good indicator of a bond issuer's creditworthiness. In any case, municipal bonds are typically very good investments for those who are seeking regular income, safety of principal, and tax advantages.

CHAPTER 21

Government Investments

In the financial market, a wide variety of investments are offered through the government. Oftentimes, these vehicles are considered to be safe places for investors to put their money as they are typically backed by the full faith and credit of the United States government. Before pursuing a particular type of government investment, it is a good idea to understand the differences among them as well as how each may or may not fit in with your specific financial goals and objectives.

What Are Treasuries?

US treasuries are negotiable government debt obligations. These investment instruments are issued by the United States government for the purpose of paying for government projects. (1) Here are some of the different types of treasuries available as of 2011:

Treasury Bills

Treasury bills, or T-bills, are short-term debt obligations that mature within one year. Typical maturity time frames on T-bills are one month, three months, or six months. These vehicles are sold in denominations that range from $1,000 up to $5 million.

These investments are issued via a competitive bidding process and are offered at a discount to their face value. This means that the T-bills will appreciate in value rather than paying out regular interest payments to their holders. It is in the bill's appreciation that the holder receives his or her return. (2)

Treasury Notes

Treasury notes are also issued as a debt security by the United States government. They have longer term maturities than T-bills do, and those maturities typically range from between one and ten years. These investment vehicles can be purchased either at a bank or directly from the government.

Investors who purchase Treasury notes directly from the government may participate in either a competitive or a noncompetitive bid. Noncompetitive bidding means that the investor accepts the yield on the note that is determined at the auction, whereas in a competitive bid situation, the investors specify the yield that they want on the note.

Interest on Treasury notes is paid to their holders every six months through their maturity date. This interest is subject to federal income taxation; however, it is not taxed on a state or local level. (3)

Treasury Bonds

Treasury bonds, or T-bonds, are fixed-interest debt securities that are also issued by the US government. These investment vehicles have maturity dates that are longer than ten years. They are offered in minimum denominations of $1,000 and a maximum of $5 million.

These bonds pay out interest to their holders on a semiannual basis. The interest income that is earned on Treasury bonds is not taxable at the state or local level; however, it is subject to federal income taxation. Similar to Treasury notes, T-bonds can be purchased via either a competitive or a non-competitive bidding process. (4)

Which Types of Government Investments Are Available to the Public?

A number of government investments are available for purchase by the public. These include:

- Treasury Bills
- Treasury Notes
- Treasury Bonds
- Savings Bonds
- Debt- and Asset-Backed Securities from Sallie Mae
- Debt Securities from Freddie Mac
- Loan Sales from the Federal Deposit Insurance Corporation (FDIC)
- Mortgage Backed Securities from Ginnie Mae
- Mortgage Securities from Freddie Mac (5)

Why Investors Should Consider Government Investments

Investors should consider government investments for many reasons. Some of the primary advantages include:

- Safety. Government investments—especially government bonds—are considered to be quite safe. Because these vehicles are backed by the full faith and credit of the United States government, investors can be assured that their principal is safe and that they will receive their interest payments.
- Liquidity. Government investments are also very liquid. This means that most have active secondary markets, giving investors the opportunity to buy and sell quickly and at market price.
- Tax Advantages. Many government investments are not subject to state or local income tax, giving investors a nice tax advantage on their invested capital.

Series EE US Savings Bonds

Series EE United States savings bonds are non-marketable, interest-bearing government bonds that are guaranteed to at least double the amount of the initial investment over their initial term. These bonds usually have maturities of twenty or more years.

The Series EE savings bonds were issued in 1980 for the purpose of replacing the Series E savings bonds. These bonds are considered to be low-risk investment options that can help investors save for higher education, retirement income, or other important financial goals. (6)

As of 2012, banks, credit unions, and other financial institutions no longer offer the purchase of paper EE bonds. Currently, investors may purchase these types of bonds online via the Treasury Direct website. (7)

Investors are allowed to purchase Series EE savings bonds if they have a social security number and are either a US resident or a US citizen who is living abroad. U S civilian employees are also eligible to purchase Series EE bonds, regardless of their residence. In addition, unlike most other types of securities, minors are allowed to purchase these types of bonds.

Series EE savings bonds are available in numerous denominations. The minimum amount that may be purchased is a $50 bond, and investors pay half of the face value, which is $25. The maximum denomination available on Series EE bonds is $10,000 annually (i.e., a purchase amount of $5,000). (8) Paper Series EE savings bonds are issued at a 50 percent discount to their face value, whereas those Series EE savings bonds that are purchased electronically are bought at the total amount of their face value.

Those Series EE savings bonds that have been issued since May of 2005 are actually given a fixed coupon rate. The rates on these investment vehicles are set two times each year and are paid out in the months of May and November.

Typically, the interest earned on Series EE bonds is not subject to either state or local taxation. These bonds are, however, taxed for federal income tax purposes. The coupon rates on these vehicles are assigned based on a percent of the long-term rate of Treasuries at the time they are issued.

In most cases, Series EE US savings bonds have maturities of at least twenty years and, oftentimes, longer. Should the investors in a Series EE bond wish to redeem the investment early, there are penalties. Series EE savings bonds are required to be held for a minimum of one year before they are redeemable, and those that are held for a period of less than five years will include a penalty of three months' interest at the time the bond is redeemed.

The yield on a Series EE savings bond is a component of the bond's purchase price, interest payments, and face value. It is essentially an approximate rate of return that is based on the bond's overall lifetime compound interest.

Series I US Savings Bonds

Another type of government savings bond is the Series I US Savings Bond. These, too, are backed by the full faith and credit of the United States government and so are considered to be safe investments. Series I savings bonds began being issued in 1998 to protect investors from inflation. Because of this, the Series I bond rate of return is calculated in two ways: first, using a fixed rate of interest, and then via a bond-inflation, or variable, rate.

In the past, paper Series I bonds were available online. However, today, in order to buy a paper Series I savings bond, an investor must go to a bank and obtain one in person. (9)

Series I savings bonds have some purchase restrictions in that an investor may not purchase more than $5,000 total in a given calendar year. In addition, an investor may not hold a total amount of Series I bonds in excess of $20,000.

US Series I savings bonds can be purchased in a variety of denominations, starting at $50 and going up to a maximum amount of $5,000. In addition, in early 2008, a total bond limitation of $20,000 was placed on Series I bonds. As a part of this limitation, investors are now allowed to purchase only a maximum of $5,000 of these types of bonds each calendar year.

Investors purchase Series I bonds at full face value. Therefore, someone who is buying a $50 Series I bond will pay $50 for it. These types of bonds have no guaranteed rate of return other than the fact that they are fully secured by the government and that they will never lose value.

Due to their purpose of protecting investors from inflation, Series I bond interest is calculated using two separate rates. These include a fixed rate and an inflation rate. The Series I bond's fixed rate is announced twice per year, on May 1 and November 1. This rate will apply to all of the Series I bonds issued during the six-month time period that began with the announcement date, after which the rate will stay the same for the remaining life of the Series I bond.

The Series I bond's inflation, or variable, rate is also announced on May 1 and November 1 of each year. However, this rate will change based on fluctuations in the Consumer Price Index. In addition, this rate will change on every six-month anniversary to the new variable rate that is set in the most recent month of either May or November. The fixed rate and the inflation rate on a Series I bond will then be combined in order to come up with the overall composite earnings rates. (10)

Although the interest that is earned on a Series I bond is subject to federal income taxation, these taxes can be deferred until the bond is redeemed, until it has reached its maturity, or until another taxable disposition occurs—whichever happens first. In some cases, there may be special tax benefits to owners of Series I bonds for the purpose of saving for higher education expenses. (11)

All Series I US savings bonds possess a final maturity of thirty years from their issue date. These dates are found directly on the bonds themselves. These types of bonds will place the posting of their final maturity interest on the first day of the final month of the bond's maturity. (12)

If an investor wishes to cash in a Series I savings bond prior to its maturity date, he or she will incur a penalty of three months' interest if the bond is less than five years old. In any case, a Series I bond must be at least one year old before it is eligible to be cashed in.

Investors can redeem Series I bonds at certain banks. However, not all banks offer the service of redeeming Series I savings bonds, so investors should check with their specific financial institution prior to a bond's maturity date.

Although they have a combined rate that includes fixed and inflation, Series I bonds carry guarantees that their rate of return will never drop below zero and that they will never lose value or interest to the investor.

Separate Trading of Registered Interest and Principal Securities – STRIPS

Separate Trading of Registered Interest and Principal Securities, or Treasury STRIPS, are fixed-income securities that are sold at a large amount of discount to their face value. These investments do not pay the investor any interest payments due to the fact that they instead mature at their face value in the future.

For example, a ten-year United States T-note will have twenty payments of interest, one payment every six months for ten years as well as a principal payment that comes back to the investor at maturity. When this type of security is "stripped," each of its twenty payments of interest as well as the principal payment will become separate securities and thus may be held and transferred separately. (13)

Treasury STRIPS came into existence in 1985 as a way to replace other government investments such as CATS (Certificates of Accrual on Treasury Securities) and TIGRs (Treasure Investment Growth Receipts) as the primary type of US government zero-coupon security. STRIPS are considered to be relatively safe investments that also offer some tax advantages.

The United States Treasury does not issue or sell STRIPS directly to the public or private investors. Treasury STRIPS can only be purchased and held via a government securities broker or dealer or through a financial institution.

The minimum face amount that is necessary when stripping a fixed-principal note or bond is $100. In addition, any face-value amount that is to be stripped above $100 is also required to be in a multiple of $100. (14) The minimum amount of purchase by an investor for a Treasury STRIP is $100, and the maximum is $5 million.

The price of a Treasury STRIP is quoted on a discount basis as a percentage of the investment's face value. As a STRIP is separated into its component parts, the face value needs to be an amount that, based on the interest rate that is stated, will produce a particular semiannual interest payment of a certain multiple of $100. For investors, quotes of STRIPS are stated via the yield to maturity. (15)

Because Treasury STRIPS work like zero-coupon bonds, they do not make periodic interest payments. Instead, they accumulate in value and pay out their face value at the time of their maturity.

Investors who purchase Treasury STRIPS will still be subject to federal income taxation on the amount that the STRIP has accrued during the particular tax year. This is required even though the bond has not technically paid the investor any tangible income.

Similar to other types of government securities, Treasury STRIPS have different maturity-length options. With these investment vehicles, maturities are between one year and ten years in duration.

In some cases, STRIPS can be more volatile than other types of government securities. This is especially true when interest rates rise and fall, as the price of STRIPS can rise or fall more drastically than the prices of other types of bonds can. Therefore, the investor may achieve a capital gain. However, there is also the chance that the investor could suffer a capital loss.

Because a STRIP is considered a zero-coupon bond, it does not pay regular interest to its investor. Therefore, a STRIP's overall rate of return is shown in its yield to maturity. The yield is computed by using the deep discount price of the STRIP as well as the number of years to maturity.

Treasury Inflation Protected Securities – TIPS

A Treasury Inflation Protected Security, or TIPS, is a type of treasury security that is indexed to inflation in order to help protect investors from inflation's negative effects.

These are considered to be very low risk investments because they have the backing of the United States government and because their face values tend to go up with inflation.

Treasury TIPS were created in 1997 for the purpose of allowing investors to have a debt instrument investment that is linked directly to the rate of inflation. At the time of their inception, there was a great demand for TIPS. In addition, these types of investments may also be an incentive for the United States Treasury to keep inflation in check. (16)

TIPS can be purchased directly from the government via its Treasury Direct system. These investment vehicles can be bought in increments of $100. By purchasing them in this manner, investors may be able to avoid the regular investment brokerage management fees that typically come along with other types of investments.

When purchasing TIPS, an investor is required to invest at least $100. Conversely, investors cannot purchase more than $5 million in TIPS. Investors must either be a US citizen or a US civilian employee, regardless of residence.

The value of TIPS depends upon the adjusted rate of inflation. These investments have a fixed coupon rate. The difference between TIPS and typical fixed coupon rate investments is that the amount of interest that is paid will go up as the face value of the bond is increased by the inflation factor. These investments are not, however, issued at a discount to face value.

The interest on TIPS is paid to investors semiannually. Due to the fact that the semiannual inflation adjustments on TIPS are considered to be taxable income by the Internal Revenue Service (IRS)—even though the investors in these vehicles do not actually receive the income until they sell the TIPS—federal income tax is due on the interest annually. There are not, however, state or local taxes due.

TIPS offer a variety of different maturities. These include five-year, ten-year, and twenty-year maturity options. Because TIPS can be sold in the secondary market, they can easily be sold prior to maturity. Typically, these investments will be resold to the highest bidder. At that time, based on the prevailing interest rate and thus the bond's value, the investor could end up with either a capital loss or a capital gain.

TIPS were created for the purpose of protecting investors against the financial effects of inflation. Therefore, the principal on these investments will rise and fall with inflation and deflation because their value is measured by the CPI (Consumer Price Index).

When these assets mature, they pay their investors the adjusted amount of principal or the original amount of principal, whichever amount is more. They also pay investors interest twice a year at a fixed rate. This rate is subsequently applied to the investor's amount of adjusted principal. This, along with the TIPS maturity, is all taken into consideration when calculating the investment's yield.

Agency Bonds Issued By Federal Government Agencies

Agency bonds are another type of investment offered by the US government. These, too, offer investors a great deal of safety as well as a conservative, yet consistent rate of interest or return.

Agency bonds issued by federal government agencies are typically offered for the purpose of financing activities related to public purposes. Some examples include providing agricultural assistance or increasing home ownership by citizens. In addition to providing funding for public-related projects, these bonds offer investors a way to invest safely, with their investment dollars backed by the full faith and credit of the United States government.

Some agency bonds may be structured for a particular type of issuer or a certain class of investors. Therefore, some of these bonds may not be suitable for all investors—primarily due to the minimum investment amounts that may be required.

Agency bonds issued by federal government agencies can usually be purchased through most financial brokers and brokerage institutions. It is important to note that the buying and selling of investments in this manner may include transaction costs.

Agency Bonds Issued By Government Sponsored Enterprises (GSEs)

Agency bonds issued by government-sponsored enterprises, or GSEs, offer financing to fund loans for entities that have been created by the US Congress for certain groups of borrowers. These may be home owners, farmers, or students. (17)

A GSE is a privately held corporation with a public purpose. They are created by Congress in order to reduce the cost of capital for specific sectors of borrowers in the economy. Investment in GSEs carries the backing of the US government. However, they are not direct obligations of the government.

The purpose of these bonds is to obtain financing for particular projects that will benefit a certain section of the public good at a reduced price. Examples include agencies such as Freddie Mac and the Federal Farm Credit Bank. (18)

Most investors are eligible to purchase agency bonds that are issued by government-sponsored enterprises. In many cases, there is a minimum investment amount of $5,000, and then additional funds in $1,000 increments can usually be added.

Oftentimes, large financial brokerage houses will purchase large blocks of agency bonds that are issued by GSEs. Most bonds issued by GSEs to investors are purchased through brokerage houses and financial institutions.

SECTION 6

Financial Planning

CHAPTER 22

The Power of Compounding

Compounding is one of the most important concepts in finance. Understanding how it works is crucial to appreciating how money grows and wealth is created.

What is compounding?

The key to understanding compounding is first understanding your investment base. An investment base is the dollar value of your investment that is earning interest. If you put \$100 in the bank today, then your investment base is \$100. If you put \$500 in the bank, then your investment base is \$500. The concept is simple, but it is very important that you grasp it to understand the powers of compounding.

Next, I will look at the rate of interest. This is the percentage at which your investment base will increase. This percentage is usually stated on an annual basis. The result of the calculation shown below is the resulting value after the interest is added to, or in financial terms, compounded, to the investment base (the initial investment) at the end of the year.

Investment Base x (1 + interest rate) = dollar value of investment at end of one year

$$Co \times (1 + r) = C1$$

Co = initial investment base

r = interest rate for compounded period

C1 = investment at the end of the year

Example:

\$100 put in the bank for one year at 10 percent interest. The investment base is \$100.

$$\$100 \times (1+ 0.10) = ?$$

$$\$100 \times (1.10) = \$110$$

Now I am going to look at the power of compounding. Remember, compounding means that the earned interest is added to the investment base. This is usually done on an annual basis, but in the real world, there are many instances where compounding is done semiannually (twice a year), quarterly (4 times a year), monthly, weekly, daily, and on even a notion called continuously, which I will discuss in detail later. Let us look at these rules with regard to compounding

Rule #1: The investment base changes every time we add interest to it.

Example: In the example above, our initial investment base was $100, but the new investment base at the end of the compounding period, which was one year, became $110 because the interest ($10) was added to the initial investment base ($100).

Rule #2: You have to divide the annual interest rate by the number of times interest compounds each year. If compounding occurs once per year, then you do not need to divide. If it occurs twice a year, you must divide the interest rate by 2.

Example: The investment has an annual interest rate of 10 percent.

Compounding once: 10 percent/1 = 10 percent each time interest is compounded

Compounding twice: 10 percent/2 = 5 percent each time interest is compounded

Compounding ten times: 10 percent/10 = 1 percent each time interest is compounded

Now that you have these rules, take a look at some real-life compounding examples. In each example, pay attention to the number of investment bases and the interest rate when the investment base is compounding.

We are going to assume that the initial investment base in each of our examples is $100 and that the annual interest rate is 10 percent. Look at what happens when the number of compounding periods (how many times compounded) increases.

Annual

We are assuming that the interest is compounded once per period in this case.

Compounding period: 1 time

Interest rate per compounding period: 10 percent

$$\$100 \times (1+0.10) = ?$$

$$\$100 \times (1.10) = \$110$$

Semiannual

We are assuming that the interest is compounded twice per year.

Compounding period: 2 times

Interest rate per compounding period: 5 percent

First period

$100 x (1+ 0.05) = ?

$100 x (1.05) = $105

Second period

$105 x (1+ 0.05) = ?

$105 x (1.05) = $110.25

See how the investment base changed? In the first period, it was $100, but then when the interest at the end of the period was added to it, the new base became $105. Then at the end of the second period, the amount of the total investment had grown to $110.25. We earned an extra $0.25 because of that one additional compounding period.

Before I move on to more additional compounding periods, I am going to modify the formula to make it more practical for our purposes. I do not know about you, but I do not want to write down each new investment period, new investment base, and the interest rate. If you are one of those individuals who must do so, that is okay, but when you have daily compounding (that is 360 or 365, depending on the financial institution), the figures become unwieldy. The new formula is as follows:

FV = Co x (1+r)^t

Co = initial investment base

r = interest rate for the compounding period

t = time period(s) to compound initial investment base

FV = future value of the initial investment base at the end of the compounding period(s)

This new formula may look a little complicated, but it is very similar to the formula we were working with before. The C1 is replaced by FV, because we might be interested in compounding more often than once a year. The *t* determines how many times that the investment will be compounded. We can have *t* equal days, months, years, or whatever other period we choose. Let us take a look at our semiannual compounding example with e new formula.

Co = $100

r = 10 percent/t (times compounded) or 10 percent/2 = 5 percent.

Look familiar?

t = 2 times.

FV = $100 x (1+0.05)^2

FV = $100 x (1.05)^2

FV = $100 x 1.1025

FV = $110.25

The new equation results in the same answer that we received before, which we expected, but the formula is more flexible for when we compound multiple times. Let us move on to some more complicated compounding to fully appreciate this formula.

Daily

We are assuming that the interest is compounded 365 times.

Co = $100

r = 10 percent/t (times compounded) or 10 percent/365 = .0274 percent. In decimal form, this is 0.000274. This is what you will input in your calculator or computer. By the way, I rounded a little bit, so your calculations might be slightly different than mine. Remember, this is the rate per period.

t = 365 times.

FV = $100 x (1+0.000274)^365
FV = $100 x (1.000274)^365
FV = $100 x 1.105167
FV = $110.52

The final investment at the end of that year with 365 times compounding was an extra $0.52. That might not seem like much to you, but imagine if the base had been

$10,000, $100,000, or a million dollars. The results would be an extra $52, $520, and $5,200 respectively. Notice that we made more money because we compounded more times.

This is the power of compounding. The more we compound, the more money we get at the end of the investment period. This concept is very important in investing. That is why, in many cases, it is important to stay invested over many decades and to let your money compound. If you remove your money every year, spend the interest, or take away from your investment, then you are not making as much money as you would have if you had let it all ride (compound). It really is amazing how much money can be made by letting your investment be reinvested *and* grow over a period of time. Despite the ups and downs in the market, it has continued to grow over time. Take a look at the Dow Jones Industrial Average's historical closing prices over time.

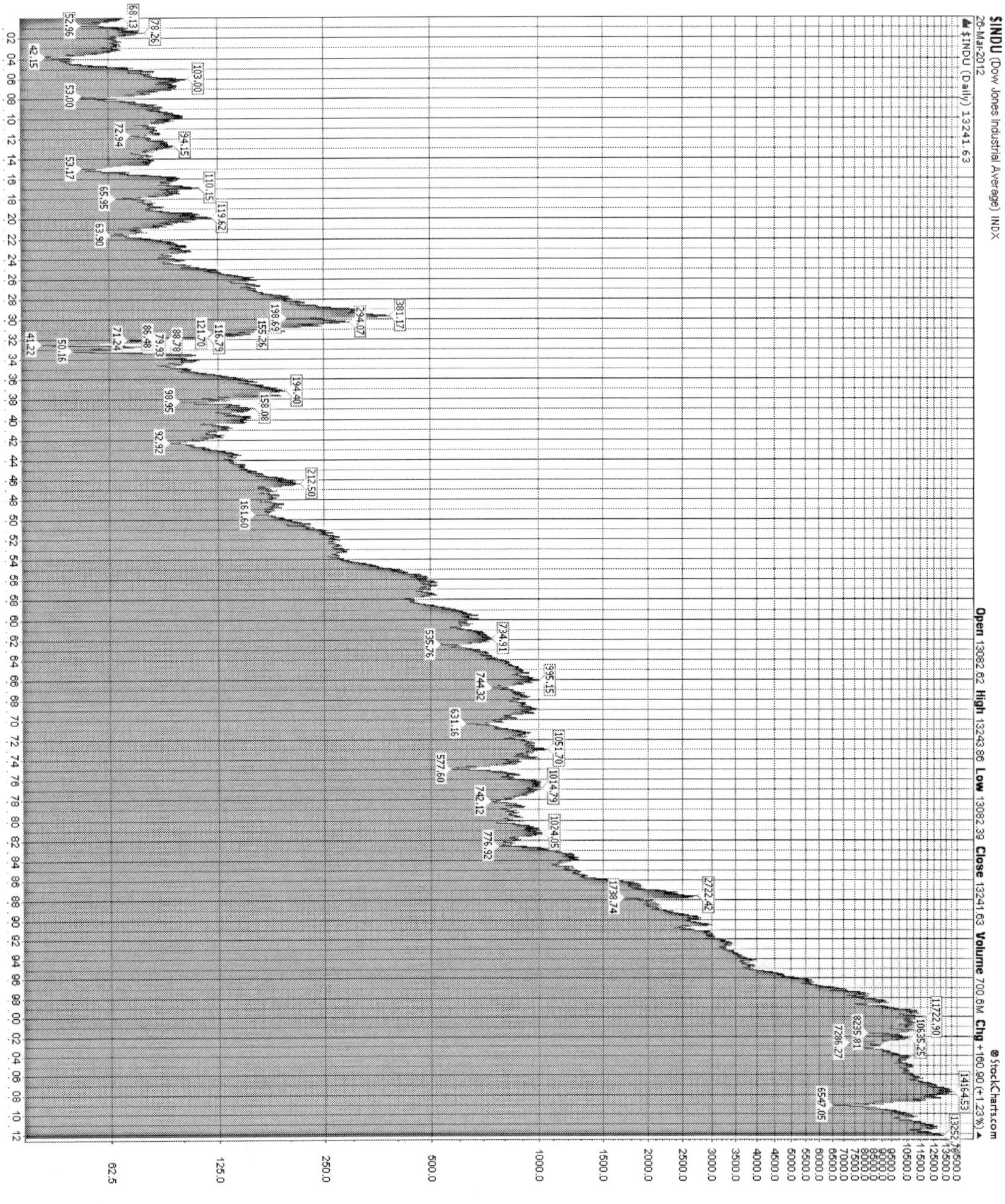
$INDU (Dow Jones Industrial Average) INDX
26-Mar-2012
$INDU (Daily) 13241.63
Open 13082.62 High 13243.86 Low 13082.39 Close 13241.63 Volume 700.6M Chg +160.90 (+1.23%)
@StockCharts.com

CHAPTER 23

Investment Programs Introduction

Retirement plans can be funded by an individual, an employer, or another qualified contributor per the various plan requirements. A myriad of terminology comes into play when discussing investment programs and retirement. Understanding these terms is key to participating wisely.

Pension Benefit Guaranty Corporation (PBGC)

ERISA is the federal law that regulates the implementation and management of the private-sector retirement plans. The law does not require employers to establish a pension plan nor does it guarantee a minimum level of benefits. Instead, the act establishes the rules for business pension plans when a company chooses to create one. ERISA establishes the acceptable standards for participation, vesting, benefit accrual, and funding in an employer-sponsored retirement plan.

The PBGC, established by ERISA in 1974, will pay benefits up to a certain amount if an insured plan is terminated for any reason and promised benefits are not adequately funded. However, defined contribution plans like the 401(k) are not insured. Compared to government pension funds that will be covered by public funds, a private 401(k) can lose significant value, have no fallback for restoration, and leave pensioners without adequate retirement income.

Defined Benefit Plans

A defined benefit plan provides a fixed and specific amount of benefit to the employee at retirement time. This is usually referred to as the traditional pension benefit retirement plan. The plan usually has provisions to calculate benefits based on formulas taking into consideration the employee's base compensation and years that they worked for the employer.

Funded Plans:

Funded pension plans set aside funds or monies each year in order to ensure that the amount of the pension benefit will be paid out as per the plan requirements.

Unfunded Plans (PAYGO):

Unfunded plans, usually found in the public sector, allow an employer to pay out benefits as they come due. Although there are usually resources to ensure that such plans can be paid when due dates arrive, there are still a lot of risks posed in fulfilling an unfunded plan as oppose to a funded plan. An unfunded plan can also become challenging for an employer if an employee requests a lump sum payment at retirement instead of requesting benefits to be paid out over his or her retirement lifetime. This is also known as a pay-as-you-go (PAYGO or PAYG) plan. ERISA prohibits the private sector from establishing these types of plans because some companies might go out of business or declare bankruptcy before paying out benefits.

Defined-Contribution Plans (e.g., IRA, 401(k) plans, and 403(b) plans)

In a defined-contribution plan, an employer makes a specified annual contribution to an employee retirement plan. The employer does not guarantee any future benefits to the employee under this plan. Therefore, the account will likely fluctuate with economic and market conditions.

Participation in employer plans stipulates that all employees be covered if they meet age and employment requirements. Generally, an employee should be at least twenty-one years old and have worked at least a year to qualify.

Vesting

Vesting refers to how long an employee has to work for an employer before he or she can have a claim on the contributions that the employer has been making to the retirement program on his or her behalf. A vested employee has earned a non-forfeitable right to benefits funded by employer contributions.

The Pension Protection Act of 2006 requires that employer contributions made to a defined-contribution plan started after 2006 be 100 percent vested after a period of three years in most plans. However, if the plan is created under a graduated vesting schedule of more than three years (usually six years), then the employer's contributions must be 20 percent vested after two years of employee service and 100 percent vested at the end of the graduated period.

Even if an employee leaves before he or she is fully vested in the retirement plan, he or she can still have a legal claim on a percentage of the contributed funds based on the plan terms. So check carefully with your employer if your retirement information is not clear.

Retirement Accounts-tax Deferability

And like most people who invest in retirement accounts that offer tax deferments, you may assume that at retirement, your tax base will be substantially lower, which means you will pay comparatively lower taxes and will have more funds to keep than you did when you were younger.

Contributions

An individual can contribute to his or her retirement account in various ways, regardless of the type of account. Some accounts require only contributions by the account owner, while others allow for contributions by relatives, spouses, employers, organizations, and even friends. Indeed, an individual can use many retirement accounts to prepare for retirement based on income, risk, and other individual personal qualifiers.

Also while it may be a good idea to have different types of retirement accounts, some retirement accounts look at the total contributions you have made to all qualified retirement accounts in order to determine if you have me maximum limits and, more importantly, whether any penalties will be assessed against your account. Therefore, it is important to note accounts that may be in conflict with your contribution strategy and which are more aligned with your strategy.

In addition, some retirement accounts allow the account owner to make contributions with pretax or after-tax dollars. There are many debates over the benefits that the government receives when it allows pretax dollars to go to retirement accounts. Many argue that the individual and hence the government is better off in the long term because these retirement amounts are funds that the individual will not necessarily be relying on the government for later in life. However, the short-term-focused individual's argument is that the government is losing much-needed tax revenues by allowing pretax contributions of any kind, including retirement.

Whatever the case, the options for both pretax and post-tax contributions are currently available. Therefore, you should speak with a qualified and trusted financial consultant or attorney in regard to how these different types of accounts can affect your long-term financial goals. Following are some general potential benefits of each tax option.

Pretax contributions Potential Benefits

Reduced Taxable Income During the Current Tax Year

Current taxable income reduced by pretax contribution, which means more monies after taxes, all things being equal for you.

Lower Taxable Income in Retirement Tax Year

Since the average person's tax bracket will be lower by the time her or she retires and has begun distributions, there is additional benefit of being taxed at a lower rate after retirement than being taxed when the deposit was made. So your initial contribution, gains, and any related income are hopefully all growing tax-deferred at a higher compounding rate, relatively speaking. That should give you a moment's pause to reflect on how good that can be for you in the long term; of course, we can only hope that the economy will also cooperate during this time of your investment account's growth.

After-tax Contributions' Potential Benefits

Lower Taxable Income in Retirement Tax Year

Since taxes are already levied against post-tax-dollars contributions, the good news is that you potentially will not be assessed similar taxes when the time comes for the distribution of those funds. Taxes, however, will be assessed on any gains in the account, albeit usually at a lower tax bracket.

Waived Future Withdrawal Penalties

Some accounts provide means to withdraw post-tax-dollar contributions without incurring a penalty. Of course, there are still usually hoops to jump through, such as age and vested period restrictions, to avoid all penalties. Nevertheless, the option is there in case it is needed.

More Money Kept from Your Paycheck Today

Sometimes, your current financial situation does not allow you to fully participate in a retirement plan on a pretax basis because you need the money today. If that is the case, the decision is understandable, but you should understand the amount of potential benefits that you might lose.

Employer-Matching and Retirement Plan Contribution Level

Higher contribution amounts usually mean more money working for you over the long term, and those dollars are generally growing on a tax-deferred basis. So assuming that the economy is doing well and that you are earning income, it would make sense to contribute as much as possible to your retirement accounts. In addition to the tax benefits for doing so, there is also another reason to possibly increase your retirement contributions: employer matching contributions.

Employer Matching Contributions

Employers are not presently mandated to contribute to their employees' retirement accounts. However, in a competitive job market environment, even the most frugal employer will extend some sort of incentive in order to attract talented employees.

Most employers who do make matching contributions match anywhere from 1 percent to 15 percent of the employees' contributions. Employers, however, have to be mindful that their contributions along with the employees' contribution do not go above stipulated limits. Although this is unlikely to happen, it is best to keep track of all contributions made to all your retirement accounts so that you will know when limits are reached on those accounts.

All things being equal, it is usually good practice to contribute at least the maximum amount that your employer will match. In doing so, you will have double the funds working for you rather than just your own contributed funds.

Example

Lisa's employer matches employee-retirement contributions up to 10 percent of their eligible contribution amounts. Assuming that Lisa's salary is $50,000 and that she has no other retirement accounts, what is the total contribution to her retirement under the following scenarios? It should be $3,000 if she contributes 3% of her annual salary with the employer matching 100% of her contribution and a $10,000 total contribution for a 10% match. High matching percentages are rare, and most employers tend to match 0% to 6% of their employees' contributions to the retirement plans.

Employer Matching Scenario

Annual Salary: $50,000	**Annual**
She contributes 3%	
Lisa's contribution	$1,500
Employer's Contribution	$1,500
Total Contribution	**$3,000**
She contributes the maximum 10%	
Lisa's contribution	$5,000
Employer's Contribution	$5,000
Total Contribution	**$10,000**

Types of IRA-Qualified Investments

Eligible Investments

- Stocks
- Bonds
- Mutual funds
- Qualified unit investment trusts (UITS)
- Limited partnerships
- Government securities
- US government–issued gold and silver coins
- Annuities

Ineligible Investments

- Collectibles (antiques, stamps, art, etc.)
- Life insurance (cash value or term life)
- Municipal bonds
- Unqualified unit investment trusts (UITs)

Speculative practices in retirement accounts

Speculation in retirement accounts is generally frowned upon. The purpose of retirement accounts is to ensure that funds are available upon retirement. Therefore, the government tries to limit the amount of risk-taking strategies that can be employed in managing these retirement accounts.

Of course, many participants in the financial industry have pushed for and enabled changes that are detrimental to the average investor. But because the rules and regulations are constantly changing, it is wise to consult with a competent qualified financial advisor or attorney to ensure that your best interest is preserved.

Traditionally, these have been the three worst offenders when it comes to risky strategies that should be avoided in your retirement accounts:

- **Margin account trading:** Borrowing money from a broker to buy stocks
- **Short selling:** Selling a security that you do not own with a goal of purchasing it at a lower price
- **Speculative options strategies:** Entering into options that add unnecessary risk to your account

Rollovers

Every twelve months, a qualified retirement owner has the option of transferring the account funds to another qualified custodian, such as a new bank or brokerage firm. Typically, 100 percent of funds must be transferred to the new account, or the owner risks being subject to tax and penalties as if an actual distribution was made from the account. Also, the account owner must have the transfer complete within sixty calendar days, which is considered to be a sufficient time frame to receive the proceeds and complete the necessary paperwork to effect the change in custodian of the retirement account.

Tax Deductions Benefits

Some retirement plans allow the account holders to deduct portions of their contributions pretax (before taxes are taken out of earnings). These individuals must still meet eligibility requirements subject to the modified adjusted gross income (MAGI) limits mandated by the government. The adjusted income is compared to current available IRS amounts to determine deductibility of contributions and how much is deductible.

Adjusted Gross Income (AGI)

Adjusted gross income is used on the IRS standard tax filing 1040 Form to determine an individual's tax liability.

AGI = Total gross income - Certain deductions and exemptions
Total gross income = All income you receive in the form of money, goods, property, and services that is not tax-exempt

Modified Adjusted Gross Income (MAGI)

These adjustments to the AGI will determine if an individual's IRA contribution is eligible for tax deductions. MAGI adds certain items that may have been excluded in the calculation of the total gross income or AGI.

MAGI = AGI + selected previously excluded items (such as tax-exempt interest, selected Social Security benefits, etc.)

Per the IRS, MAGI should be as follows:

<u>AGI without:</u>

- Any passive loss or passive income
- Any rental losses (whether or not allowed by IRC § 469(c) (7))
- IRA, taxable Social Security
- One-half of self-employment tax (IRC § 469(i) (3) (E))
- Exclusion under 137 for adoption expenses or
- Student loan interest

- Exclusion for income from US savings bonds (to pay higher education tuition and fees)
- Qualified tuition expenses (tax years 2002 and later)Tuition and fees deduction
- Any overall loss from a PTP (publicly traded partnership)

Tax-deferred Growth

Capital gains and other income are usually allowed to grow tax-free within qualified retirement accounts.

Distributions

All things being equal, accounts with pretax contributions carry more restrictions than accounts where the monies have already been taxed before they were transferred to the retirement account. In general, to avoid penalties, it is most prudent to know when the required age is to begin optional distribution and the age to begin mandatory distribution for the various retirement accounts. Benefits can be received without penalty at age fifty-nine even though some Americans are working way past the legal retirement age due to economic conditions, delay of government benefits, and longer life expectancy as well as personal financial resources. Also, Social Security benefits usually begin at age sixty-five, or later, as the age is projected for future generations.

Penalties

Penalties are assessed to a retirement account for a variety of violations to the terms of the plan requirements. Most penalties vary in amount and apply to violations involving contribution amounts, specific early withdrawal amounts, non-distribution at specific age's requirements, rollover requirements, and other plan-specific considerations.

CHAPTER 24

Traditional IRA Retirement Plans

Traditional IRA plans come in a variety of options that may appeal to your retirement and investment plans in different ways. I will discuss these different plans and how they might relate to your investments.

Individual Retirement Account (IRA)

Who is it for?

Individuals with earned income.

What it is:

Individual retirement accounts were formed with the goal of enabling individuals to save for their retirements. These accounts are open to all working individuals. Individuals can select among different types of IRAs, which offer various tax benefits as well as qualified contributions options. The four main types of individual retirement accounts available are the traditional IRA, which I will discuss shortly, and the Roth IRA, SEP IRA, and the Coverdell ESA.

Contributions

These maximums are slated to increase annually to keep pace with inflation. From what I have seen, most individuals tend to wait until April or during the tax season to decide on the maximum contributions to make to their retirement accounts.

Maximum Annual Contribution (as of 2010):

- $5,000 per individual or up to 100 percent of your income if your earned income is $5,000 or less
- $10,000 between spouses filing joint tax returns
- Tax deductions phased out gradually for individual-filer modified adjusted gross income (MAGI) between $ 55,000 and $65,000
- Tax deductions phased out gradually for joint-filer modified adjusted gross income (MAGI) between $89,000 and $109,000

Please check with the IRS as well as a competent and qualified tax consultant, financial advisor, or attorney for recent updates to all plans and information presented. The maximum is a total of all your IRA accounts.

Maximum Tax-deductible Examples:

Individual Tax Returns for workers under fifty years old:
Jane: Annual Earned Income $50,000: Maximum allowed contribution: $5,000
John: Annual Earned Income $25,000: Maximum allowed contribution: $5,000
Anna: Annual Earned Income $3,000: Maximum allowed contribution: $5,000
Paul: Annual Earned Income $1,000: Maximum allowed contribution: $1,000
Joint Tax Returns for couples under fifty years old:
Dan and Michelle: Annual Earned Income $50,000: Maximum allowed contribution: $10,000

Notice the tax-deductible maximum per individual is currently capped at 5,000 per individual. Of course, contributions in excess of the maximum can be made to the IRA account, but it will not be tax-deductible and will be subject to penalties. Also, the maximum amounts apply to the combined total of all your IRA accounts.

Catch-up Contributions

If an IRA owner happens to be fifty years of age or older, then the government has made it possible to add more funds to the traditional IRA as well as the Roth IRA and still retain its benefits. These additional amounts are referred to as catch-up contributions and represent the amounts above what the IRA owner was qualified to contribute over the years. As of 2010, the maximum catch-up amount was $1,000.

Tax-deferred Growth

What also makes the traditional IRA attractive to a lot of investors is the fact that there are numerous tax benefits associated with this account. In addition to the tax-deductible contributions, capital gains and other income received in this account are effectively tax-deferred until the funds are distributed. This means that potentially more monies will be in the account, which can lead to faster accumulation relative to other similar accounts. And like most retirement accounts that offer tax deferments, there is an assumption that at retirement, your tax base will be substantially lower, allowing you to keep more than you could have when you were younger.

Distributions

So hopefully the financial markets have treated your account well over the many years since you have started your IRA account and you have reached the age of fifty-nine and half. At that age, you are allowed to start making withdrawals without penalty from your IRA account. You can also keep making contributions to your account until six months after your seventieth birthday. However, at that age, contributions to the IRA account are no longer allowed, and mandatory distributions will begin the April after you turn seventy and a half. Please be aware that any distributions made before age fifty-nine and a half are subject to a 10 percent penalty and applicable taxes.

Qualified Early Withdrawals

In cases of financial emergencies that require funds that cannot be obtained from other sources, some people might turn to their IRA to get these monies. In general, there are penalties associated with withdrawals made before the predetermined retirement age selected for retirement plans. However, there are exceptions to this rule. Following are some of the qualified early withdrawals that can be made within a specific limited set of requirements.

- **Education Expenses:** Funds can be used for educational expenses of the account owner, a spouse, a child, or a grandchild.
- **First-time Primary Residence Home Purchase (maximum $10,000):** The home must be the account owner's primary residence, and no more than $10,000 can be withdrawn for these purposes without incurring potential penalties.
- **Total Disability of Account Owner:** If the account owner is legally and totally disabled, then withdrawals can be made without penalty.
- **Medical Expenses Above 7.5 percent AGI:** The account owner can also make penalty-free withdrawals to cover qualified medical expenses that are over 7.5 percent of his or her adjusted gross income.
- **Death of account owner:** Upon the death of the account owner, qualified parties may withdraw funds without penalty.

Rollover

A rollover is basically a transfer of funds from an existing retirement account to another account, typically another IRA account. Although a rollover can be made into any account, bear in mind that there might be penalties and fees associated with doing unqualified transfers of qualified retirement funds. So speak with a competent qualified advisor before making this decision.

There are many reasons that individuals choose to roll over to or into an IRA. One reason is to consolidate similar retirement accounts held at different companies into a single manageable account. Many choose to do a rollover when they have left a job. Rather than leaving their retirement funds with that company, they decide to move it to an individual retirement account, where they can supposedly have more control of it. However, there are advantages to keeping the retirement account at your old company, even if you do decide to leave the job. Some of these advantages can be:

- **Control and Accessibility**: Some companies allow ex-employees who are current account owners access that is comparable to that of current employees. Some even allow you manage your account in much the same way as you did when you were working for them. Of course, do a little check and see what options your (former) company allows.
- **Access to Exclusive Funds and Investments:** Sometimes, you may have funds in your employer's retirement account that are not available once you transfer funds to an IRA. Of course, a similar fund or portfolio can be created, but definitely do some research first to compare.

Whatever your reason for rolling over your IRA, the government allows individuals to make one rollover every twelve months, but the process must be completed within sixty days. If it is not done within the allotted time, then the amount being transferred can be treated like a withdrawal and hence can be subject to various penalties and taxes. Therefore, if you want to do a rollover, make sure that it is done by a reputable firm and in a timely manner. It is always wise to do a little research and even speak with a qualified financial advisor or tax attorney before making long-term financial decisions.

IRA Benefits

- Contributions can be tax-deductible
- Unlimited trustee-to-trustee transfers

- Qualified withdrawal options

IRA Drawbacks

- Distribution can be taxed.
- Distributions must begin at age seventy and a half
- No contributions after age seventy and a half

IRA Income and Capital Gains Treatment

Tax deferred until withdrawal

IRA Penalties

You might be penalized for the following:

Early withdrawal

Early withdrawals are unqualified withdrawals before age fifty-nine and a half. The penalty is 10 percent plus applicable taxes.

Excess Contribution

A 6 percent penalty is assessed on all amounts contributed above the maximum-allowed contribution level. There are two ways to possibly reverse this penalty:

1) Withdraw the extra contribution and related earnings before taxes' due date

2) Apply excess contributions to next year contribution

Insufficient Distribution Penalty

If a withdrawal is not made after age seventy and a half, then a penalty is assessed on the required withdrawal amount up to 50 percent on amounts you are required to withdraw.

How to Create Plan: Contact a qualified, trusted, and reputable broker, bank, investment house, etc.

Roth Individual Retirement Account (Roth IRA)

Who is it for?

Individuals with earned income

What it is:

In the 1990s, taxpayers were fed up (well, more than usual) with taxes, an unbalanced budget, and declining tax-deductible amounts for their IRAs. They were finally able to get some relief when President Clinton signed into law the Taxpayer Relief Act of 1997 and the Balanced Budget Act of 1997. These pieces of legislation ushered in comprehensive changes to the tax system and much-needed, albeit temporary, relief for taxpayers. The Roth Individual Retirement Account (Roth IRA) was one of the new forms of accounts created by the new tax laws. The Roth IRA was named after Senator William Roth, finance chairman at the time, who was instrumental in the tax law changes and the creation of this new IRA.

Contributions

The Roth IRA gave individuals an additional way to save for their retirements. The 1997 law allowed nondeductible contributions up to $2,000 a year for individuals. Today, that amount is $5,000.

These maximums are also slated to increase annually to keep pace with inflation. Please be aware that the maximums for the Roth IRA can differ based on other IRA contributions totals.

Maximum Annual Contribution (as of 2010):

- $5,000 per individual or up to 100 percent of your income if your earned income is $5,000 or less
- $10,000 between spouses filing joint tax returns.
- Phased out gradually for individual-filer modified adjusted gross income (MAGI) between $105,000 and $120,000
- Phased out gradually for joint-filers modified adjusted gross income (MAGI) between $167,000 and $177,000

The maximum is the total of all your IRA accounts.

<u>Examples:</u>

Individual Tax Returns for workers under fifty years old.
Jane: Annual Earned Income $50,000: Maximum allowed contribution: $5,000
Makes contributions as follows:
Traditional IRA $3,000 + Roth IRA $2,000 = $5,000 maximum contribution

Joint Tax Returns for couples under fifty years old.
Dan and Michelle: Annual Earned Income $50,000: Maximum allowed contribution: $10,000

Makes contributions as follows:

Traditional IRA $6,000 + Roth IRA $4,000 = $10,000 maximum contribution

Catch-up Contributions

If a Roth IRA owner happens to be fifty years of age or older, then the government has made it possible to add more funds, similar to the traditional IRA allowance. This means that individual can add amounts in addition to maximum allowed for individuals under age fifty without being penalized. As of 2010, the maximum catch-up amount was $1,000.

Tax-deferred Growth

The Roth IRA also defers taxes on capital gains and other income received in this account. And since the initial contributions are made with after-tax funds, the proceeds are also tax-deferred when a qualified distribution is made. Of course, the catch is that the funds were held for at least five years in the account. Either way, the tax deferability of capital gains and other income usually means higher comparable growth compared to non-deferred accounts.

Distributions

Since Contributions to the Roth IRA are not tax-deductible, they are usually withdrawn tax-free, also. However, early withdrawal penalties still apply for unqualified withdrawals similar to those to the traditional IRA.

Qualified Early Withdrawals:

- Education Expenses
- First-time primary residence home purchase (maximum $10,000)
- Total disability of account owner
- Medical expenses above 7.5 percent AGI.
- Death of account owner

Six months after turning age fifty-nine, you are allowed to start making withdrawals without penalty from your Roth IRA account. You can also keep making contributions to your account until age seventy and a half. However, at age seventy and half, contributions are no longer allowed in the Roth IRA account, but withdrawals are not mandatory.

Roth IRA Benefits:

- Potentially tax-free distributions
- Distribution does not have to begin at age seventy and a half
- Unlimited trustee-to-trustee transfers
- Assets can be passed to heirs

Roth IRA Drawbacks:

- Contributions are monies that have been taxed already
- Income limits before eligibility phases out on amounts that can contribute to Roth IRA

Penalties

You might be penalized for the following:

Early Withdrawal

Unqualified early withdrawals are assessed a 10 percent penalty plus applicable taxes.

Excess Contribution

A 6 percent penalty will be assessed on any amounts contributed to the account above maximum allowed contribution.

There are two ways to possibly reverse this penalty.

1) Withdraw the extra contribution and related earnings before taxes' due date.

2) Apply excess contributions to the next year's contribution.

How to Create Plan: Contact a qualified, trusted, and reputable broker, bank, investment house, etc.

CHAPTER 25

Retirement Plans in the Workplace

In today's world, people are living longer than ever before. While longevity can mean many more years spend enjoying retirement, it also means that individuals will need to save for the possibility of living twenty, thirty, or even more years without income from an employer or business.

Depending upon an individual's employment status and employer, a variety of retirement plans may be available. Many of these plans have differing features, contribution limits, and tax advantages, so it is important to understand the benefits of each, especially if one or more of these plans are an option to build your retirement savings.

Retirement Plans for Small Business Employees

Prior to setting up a retirement plan, small business owners should determine the answers to a few questions and then decide which plan may work best for them, their business, and their employees. These criteria are:

- Can the small business afford a match for its employees?
- Do the small business owners want to allow their employees to contribute to the retirement plan?
- If so, will some of the employees want to contribute more than $11,500 annually (indexed for inflation)?
- Will the small business owner and/or the employees need the flexibility to access their funds for potential emergencies prior to retirement?
- How important is the management of future taxes versus tax needs of today?

Once these factors have been determined, the small business owner should then move forward with the retirement plan that best fits the situation. There are several retirement plans available to small business employees.

SEP IRA

A Simplified Employee Pension, or SEP, is a popular plan for small businesses. These plans, a variation of the Individual Retirement Account, can be set up to provide retirement benefits for both the employer and the employees of a company.

Participation Rules

When offering a SEP, an employer must offer participation in the plan to employees who meet all of the following criteria:

- The employee is at least twenty-one years of age
- The employee has been employed by the employer for at least three of the last five years
- The employee has earned at least $550 in compensation from the employer (in 2011) (1)

Contribution Limits and Funding

One key feature of a SEP IRA is that the contributions are funded entirely by the employer. In fact, employee contributions are not allowed at all. In addition, the contribution made by the employer into the employee's SEP IRA account is immediately 100 percent vested.

For 2011, the maximum amount of annual contribution per employee was an amount up to 25 percent of the employee's annual compensation, up to $49,000. Unlike Individual Retirement Accounts, SEP IRA plans do not allow an additional amount of catch-up contributions for employees who are age fifty or over. (2)

Tax Treatment

Similar to traditional IRA accounts, the contributions that are made by the employer to an employee's SEP IRA go into the plan on a pretax basis, and are, therefore, taxable as ordinary income at the time of withdrawal. While in the account, the funds in a SEP grow tax-deferred.

Distribution Rules

Withdrawals from a SEP are permitted at any time and are subject to federal income taxes. And a penalty applies if the employee withdraws funds prior to the time they turn age fifty nine and a half. In addition, by April 1st of the year following the time when the employee turns age seventy and half, he or she is required to begin receiving distributions from the SEP plan. In addition, unlike some other types of retirement plans, SEP plans do not allow loans. (3)

Penalties

Employees who take a distribution from the SEP IRA prior to reaching age fifty and a half will not only be taxed, but they will also be subject to an additional IRS penalty of 10 percent of the full amount that is withdrawn. (4)

Advantages and Disadvantages

The primary advantage of a SEP IRA is that it can easily be set up. It is also simple to maintain. These types of plans also offer higher contribution flexibility than some of the other retirement plans available to small businesses. Therefore, more funds can be growing toward an employee's retirement.

Along with the advantages, SEP IRA plans also have some disadvantages. Some people see a downside to the fact that SEP IRAs are limited to the contributions of the employer. In addition, SEP IRAs are also subject to taxation on earnings. So, even though all of the distributions will eventually be taxed at the rate that will apply at that time, this is still taxation that could be avoided through the use of an alternative type of retirement plan.

SIMPLE IRA

A SIMPLE IRA plan is a type of salary reduction plan that qualifying small businesses are allowed to offer to their employees. The term SIMPLE stands for Savings Incentive Match Plans for Employees.

Participation Rules

SIMPLE IRA plans may be offered by employers with no more than one hundred employees. These employees must earn at least $5,000 annually, have done so for at least any prior two years, and be reasonably expected to earn at least that amount in the current year. Employers who offer SIMPLE IRA plans are not allowed to offer any other type of retirement plan. (5)

Contribution Limits and Funding

Both the employee and the employer may make contributions into a SIMPLE IRA plan. In 2011, the maximum amount that may be contributed by an employee was $11,500 annually. However, for employees who are age fifty or over, an additional catch-up contribution of up to $2,500 may be made. (6)

Employers are allowed to match the employee contributions up to 100 percent of the first 3 percent of compensation that is deposited by the employee. Alternatively, the employer may simply contribute 2 percent of each of the eligible employee's compensation. In either case, 100 percent of both the employee and employer contributions are immediately vested. (7)

Tax Treatment

The deferral contributions of the employee go into the SIMPLE IRA plan on a pretax basis, and the funds inside of the account grow tax-deferred. Upon withdrawal, funds will be taxed at the employee's then-income tax rate.

Distribution Rules

Withdrawals from a SIMPLE IRA plan are permitted at any time; however, these withdrawals will be subject to federal income taxation. Any withdrawals taken before the employee has reached age fifty-nine and a half will also be subject to an additional IRS penalty.

Penalties

If an employee withdraws funds from a SIMPLE IRA plan before reaching age fifty-nine and a half for anything other than for a qualified emergency or other IRS exception, the funds will be subject to an IRS penalty of 10 percent of the amount that is withdrawn. (8)

If, however, an employee who is under age fifty-nine and a half withdraws funds from a SIMPLE IRA without first participating in the plan for at least two years, the IRS penalty jumps to 25 percent of the amount that is withdrawn.

Advantages and Disadvantages

The key advantage to a SIMPLE IRA is that it allows salary reduction with very little administrative paperwork for the employer. SIMPLE IRAs allow employee participants to contribute the amount of their choice, up to a maximum contribution limit.

Certainly, one of the biggest drawbacks to a SIMPLE IRA is the 25 percent early withdrawal penalty that is assessed on funds withdrawn prior to age fifty-nine and a half if they are taken out within the first two years of participation in the plan.

SARSEP

A SARSEP plan is a Salary Reduction Simplified Employee Pension Plan. These plans allow employees of small businesses to contribute to a SEP account with pretax dollars and to reduce their net income in the year of contribution. These retirement plans are for employers who have twenty-five or fewer employees. Another name for a SARSEP is a 408(k) plan.

Participation Rules

Employees meeting all of the following requirements are eligible to participate in a SARSEP plan.

- The employee is at least twenty-one years of age
- The employee has worked for the employer for at least three of the past five years
- The employee has earned a minimum of $550 in compensation from the employer (in 2011) (9)

Some employees may be excluded from a SARSEP plan. These employees include those who are covered by a union agreement and whose retirement benefits have been bargained for by the employees' union as well as by the employer. In addition, an employer may also exclude from participation any nonresident aliens who do not have any source of compensation in the United States from the employer.

Contribution Limits and Funding

SARSEP plans, like other retirement plans, have contribution limits. For 2011, employees in a SARSEP plan may defer the lesser of the following amounts:

- $16,500
- 25 percent of their compensation

In addition, employees age fifty and over are allowed to make an additional catch-up contribution of up to $5,500 (in 2011).

Employees who defer more than the maximum limit will be required to withdraw the excess amount as well as any earnings that are attributed to that amount. In addition, the amount of the excess deferral will be included as additional taxable income in the year it was deferred.

The employer may also make contributions to a SARSEP on behalf of employees. There are, however, no matching contributions allowed by the employer in a SARSEP plan. (10) The maximum amount of the employer contribution is the lesser of:

- 100 percent of the employee's compensation (up to $245,000 in 2011)
- $49,000

Tax Treatment

Employee contributions to a SARSEP are pretax via salary reduction. The funds inside the account will grow tax-deferred until withdrawn. At the time of withdrawal, funds will be taxed at the employee's most recent income tax rate.

Distribution Rules

The distributions from a SARSEP are taxable as ordinary income. Should an individual make a withdrawal prior to reaching age fifty-nine and a half, an additional IRS penalty will be required. SARSEP participants are required to begin taking distributions from the plan at age seventy and a half.

Penalties

Should an employee take a distribution from his or her SARSEP plan prior to reaching age fifty-nine and a half, he or she will be penalized by the IRS at a rate of 10 percent of the amount that is withdrawn. In addition, individuals who have reached age seventy and a half without taking at least the required minimum amount of distribution will also be penalized. (11)

Advantages and Disadvantages

SARSEP plans are easy for an employer to set up and administer. In addition, the administrative costs to the employer are typically on the low side. Also, because a SARSEP does not have fixed contribution requirements, it can be a good plan for those who have cash-flow issues.

On the downside, discrimination rules apply to these plans. Therefore, highly compensated employees may not choose a SARSEP as their first choice for retirement plan, as they will be limited on contribution amounts.

Safe Harbor 401(k)

A Safe Harbor 401(k) plan is typically intended to encourage plan participation among the rank-and-file employees as well as to ease administrative burden to the employer. These plans are very desirable for companies with highly compensated employees wishing to contribute more than they may be allowed to invest in other types of retirement plans. Employers with one or more employees are eligible to offer a Safe Harbor 401(k) plan.

Participation Rules

Employers who offer Safe Harbor 401(k) plans must generally allow all employees who are at least twenty-one years of age and who have worked a minimum of 1,000 hours in a previous year to participate in the plan. (12)

Contribution Limits and Funding

Safe Harbor 401(k) plans have an annual contribution limit of $16,500 (in 2011); however, employees who are age fifty or over may also make an additional catch-up contribution of $5,500. (13)

Tax Treatment

The funds contributed to a Safe Harbor 401(k) plan are considered to be salary reductions and thus go into the plan on a pretax basis. When the funds are withdrawn, they are taxed at the individual's ordinary income tax rate at that time.

Distribution Rules

Withdrawals from a Safe Harbor 401(k) plan are typically permitted to occur following a certain event, such as retirement. The withdrawals are taxable as ordinary income. These plans may also permit the employee to withdraw funds from the plan in the form of a loan or as a hardship withdrawal.

Penalties

In most cases, if an employee takes a withdrawal prior to turning age fifty-nine and a half, they will be subject to an IRS penalty of 10 percent of the amount withdrawn. If, however, the distribution is based on a hardship or other specific emergency situation, the individual may be exempted from this penalty. (14)

Advantages and Disadvantages

One of the key advantages of a Safe Harbor 401(k) plan is that the contributions by both employee and employer are usually 100 percent vested. In addition, these types of retirement plans permit a high level of salary deferral by employees without being subject to annual discrimination testing.

Retirement Plans for Employees of Large Corporations

One of the perks of working for a large company is that these companies typically offer a benefits package to their employees. One of these benefits is usually a retirement savings plan. A number of different types of retirement plans may be offered by large companies.

401(k)

The 401(k) is likely the most popular type of retirement plan offered by large organizations. A 401(k) plan allows employees to defer a certain percentage of their salary on a pretax basis into an account where the funds will grow tax-deferred. However, in some cases, these deferrals may be made on an after-tax basis. In addition, the employer often provides an additional amount of matching contribution into employees' accounts based on a percentage of the individual employee's contribution amount. Any employer with one or more employees may offer a 401(k) plan.

Participation Rules

Any employee who is at least age twenty-one and who has worked for the employer for at least one year must be eligible to participate in the plan. However, in order to receive employer contributions, two years of service from the employee may be required. (15)

Contribution Limits and Funding

Similar to most other retirement plans, 401(k) plans also have annual contribution limits. For 2011, the limit is $16,500. However, for employees who are age fifty or over, an additional $5,500 catch-up contribution may also be made. (16)

Tax Treatment

In most cases, the funds that go into an employee's 401(k) plan are pretax. Therefore, upon withdrawal, these funds will be subject to income taxation. The funds within the account are allowed to grow tax-deferred as long as they remain there.

Distribution Rules

Withdrawals from a 401(k) plan are permitted following a specific event such as the employee's retirement or plan termination. In addition, these plans do allow loans to be taken. Distributions may also be taken as hardship withdrawals based on various qualifying circumstances.

Penalties

Should an employee take a distribution of funds from his or her 401(k) plan prior to turning age fifty-nine and a half—other than for a qualifying event or hardship—then the IRS will impose a penalty of 10 percent of the amount withdrawn. This is in addition to the taxes that will also be due on the amount of withdrawn funds. (17)

Advantages and Disadvantages

One of the primary advantages to a 401(k) is that they allow a high level of salary deferral by employees. In addition, the tax deferral of funds within the account allows for a higher potential for growth over time.

Although there are many advantages to investing through a 401(k) plan, one of the key drawbacks is that the employee is truly not in control of the funds until retirement. In addition, the employer decides which investment options will be available through the plan.

Money Purchase Plan

Another retirement plan that may be offered by large companies is a money purchase plan. This type of pension plan allows both employees and the employer to contribute to the plan based on a percentage of the employee's annual earnings. At the time of retirement, the total amount of funds in an employee's account may then be used to purchase a lifetime annuity that will provide retirement income to that individual. Employers of any size may offer money purchase plans.

Participation Rules

Regarding participation, money purchase plans are mandatory. This means that the sponsoring employer must guarantee that a certain amount of contribution will go into each employee's account each year.

Contribution Limits and Funding

Similar to profit sharing plans, the maximum contribution limit for a money purchase plan is 25 percent of an employee's total compensation up to $49,000 (for 2011). This limit is typically adjusted annually for inflation. There are also penalties to the employer for either underfunding or overfunding the plan.

Tax Treatment

The contributions to a money purchase plan go in on a pretax basis and are, therefore, excluded from the employee's taxable income amount. The earnings in this type of plan grow on a tax-deferred basis. Upon withdrawal, all funds will be taxed at the individual's ordinary income tax rate at that time.

Distribution Rules

Distributions may be taken upon the employee's retirement. Early distributions may be taken for various situations such as the employee's disability or death as well as after a separation from service after reaching age fifty-five.

Penalties

Employees who take a withdrawal from their money purchase plan prior to attaining age fifty-nine and a half—other than for a qualified disability or other hardship—will be responsible for a penalty of 10 percent of the amount withdrawn to the individual.

Advantages and Disadvantages

One advantage of money purchase plans is that sponsoring employers are allowed to also offer other retirement plans to their employees. In addition, these plans may allow participants to grow a larger account balance than other types of arrangements may allow.

One disadvantage that may be seen in money purchase plans is that benefits need to be tested in order to be sure that the plan is not discriminating in favor of higher compensated employees. In addition, an excise tax will be levied on the employer if minimum contributions are not made for the participating employees. (18)

Employee Stock Ownership Plan (ESOP)

An Employee Stock Ownership Plan, or ESOP, is a qualified retirement plan that is specifically designed to invest in the sponsoring employer's stock. In essence, the employer is actually aligning the employees of the company with the interests of its stockholders. This is done in order to encourage employees to do what is in the best interest of the company, as the employees/stockholders will benefit from better performance of the company's stock.

Participation Rules

In most cases, employers must offer participation in an ESOP plan to all employees who are at least twenty-one years of age. Some allocation may also be made with regard to the employee's income amount. In addition, employees must become vested in their plan funds within three to six years.

Contribution Limits and Funding

An employer can deduct up to 25 percent of the employee's eligible compensation to contribute to an ESOP. The combined contributions of the employee and the employer for an ESOP plan may not exceed 100 percent of the employee's annual pay up to a maximum of $49,000.

Tax Treatment

ESOP plans have a number of tax-related benefits, including:

- The contributions of company stock to the participating employees are tax-deductible
- The contributions of cash are also tax-deductible

- The dividends that are paid out on the stock shares are also tax-deductible

Distribution Rules

When employees leave the employer, they are given their stock. At this time, the company must then buy back the stock from the employee at the stock's current fair market value, unless there is a public market for the shares.

Employees may begin withdrawing their funds at the time of retirement. At that time, the funds that are withdrawn will be subject to ordinary income tax rates at the individual's then-current rate.

Penalties

Employees making a withdrawal from their ESOP plan prior to reaching age fifty-nine and a half will be subject to a 10 percent IRS penalty on the total amount of funds that are withdrawn.

Advantages and Disadvantages

One of an ESOP's unique advantages is the tax deductibility to the employer of the contributions used to repay plan loans that were used to buy company shares. In addition, the gains that are accumulated over time in an employee's account will actually be taxed as a capital gain versus being taxed as income at the time they are withdrawn.

There are also a few drawbacks to ESOP plans. One such disadvantage is the inability of partnerships and many professional corporations to use such a plan. In addition, these plans tend to be quite costly for an employer to set up. (19)

Defined Benefit Plan

Although their popularity has been fading over the years, defined benefit retirement plans are still offered by some large employers. Oftentimes, these plans offer employees the potential for a greater benefit amount at retirement than a defined contribution plan could. This is because, as the name implies, a defined benefit plan provides a fixed and specific amount of benefit to the employee at retirement time. However, defined benefits plans are often complex to establish and are likely more expensive to maintain in comparison to other types of retirement plans. Any employer with one or more employees may have a defined benefit plan.

Participation Rules

ERISA regulations stipulate that most defined benefit plans must allow employees to begin participating in the plan no later than when the employee attains the age of twenty-five or when the employee completes one year of service with the employer. (20)

Contribution Limits and Funding

Unlike most other retirement plans that are deemed as defined contribution plans, there are no contribution limits in a defined benefit plan, per se. This is because the contribution—funded primarily by the employer—is determined annually, based on a formula that is used to decide how much an employee will receive at the time of retirement. Employees are also allowed to make contributions, depending on how the plan is set up. (21)

Tax Treatment

The distributions that are taken from a defined benefit plan will be taxed at the individual's ordinary income tax rate. Likewise, the employee is allowed to take a deduction on his or her tax return for the amount of employer contributions that are made into the plan on behalf of the employee.

Distribution Rules

The payment of benefits from a defined benefit plan may occur at the employee's retirement or after some other specified type of qualifying event. Distributions may also be taken as a loan by an employee.

Penalties

If an employee takes a distribution from a defined benefit plan—other than for a qualifying hardship or other exception—then, similar to distributions from other qualified retirement plans, those funds will be levied an IRS penalty of 10 percent of the amount. (22)

Advantages and Disadvantages

One big advantage of a defined benefit plan is that, depending upon the amount of retirement benefit allocated for the employee, it can potentially allow for larger contributions than a defined contribution plan could. Conversely, a defined benefit plan setup may be more costly to the employer.

Retirement Plans for Self-Employed Business Owners

Like large and small businesses, self-employed individuals are also allowed to have retirement plans. Many of these plans offer substantial advantages over simply contributing to an individual retirement account for the self-employed individual.

SEP IRA

Just like the Simplified Employee Pension Plan, or SEP IRA, for the small business, the SEP IRA for self-employed business owners is an easy, low-cost plan to set up. The rules regarding participation, taxation, and distribution for a self-employed business owner's SEP plan are the same as those for the SEP IRA that is set up for the small business. However, a primary difference with a self-employed individual owning a SEP is that rather than the employee making contributions into the plan with a match from the employer, the employer—which, in this case, is the self-employed individual—will make the entire contribution. (23)

SIMPLE IRA

The SIMPLE IRA plan that is allowed for small businesses may also be set up by a self-employed business owner. Here, too, the tax treatment and other rules are similar to those governing the SEP IRA, other than the fact that the self-employed business owner will also fund the employer's contribution as well as the employee's contribution. (24)

Defined Benefit Plan

Because a defined benefit plan can be set up for employers of one or more, a self-employed business owner may also set up such a plan, and the rules for small businesses and self-employed business owners tend to be the same as those for SEP and SIMPLE plans, except the funding of the plan is done solely by the self-employed individual for the part of the employee and employer. (25)

Solo 401(k)

Solo 401(k) plans are a recent addition to the array of retirement plans available to self-employed individuals and owner-only businesses. In addition, those business owners who have a spouse who works either as a full- or part-time employee may also qualify for inclusion in a solo 401(k).

Participation Rules

These plans allow only the self-employed business owner as well as a qualified spouse to join the plan. In addition, self-employed individuals may also establish a solo 401(k) if they have W-2 employees who work less than 1,000 hours annually. (26)

Contribution Limits and Funding

Similar to regular 401(k) plans, a solo 401(k) has annual contribution limits. For 2011, these were up to $16,500, depending on the amount of total compensation that the business owner earns. The business owner's qualifying spouse could also contribute. Solo 401(k) account participants who are age fifty or over may also contribute up to an additional $5,500 as a catch-up contribution. (27)

Depending upon their income, business owners may actually be able to contribute even more to their solo 401(k) plan. Similar to a SEP IRA owner, a solo 401(k) participant can contribute 25 percent of his or income as profit sharing in addition to the tax deferred contributions.

Tax Treatment

Contributions to a solo 401(k) are typically pretax. Therefore, upon withdrawal, these funds will be taxed at the account holder's ordinary income tax rates at the time of withdrawal. Funds in the account grow on a tax-deferred basis.

Distribution Rules

Distributions may be taken at the account owner's retirement. The distributions from pretax contributions as well as the account earnings will be taxed at the then-current ordinary income tax rate for the individual. (28)

Penalties

If a solo 401(k) account holder withdraws funds from the account prior to reaching age fifty-nine and a half, unless they are subject to a qualified hardship withdrawal or other exception, they will be accessed an IRS penalty of 10 percent of the entire amount that is withdrawn. (29)

Advantages and Disadvantages

The key advantage to a solo 401(k) is that the business owner may be able to make higher contributions at the same income level that he or she could in other types of plans. In addition, solo 401(k) plans also have a tax-free loan feature that allows the individual to use the account's balance as loan collateral.

Another advantage to a solo 401(k) is that these plans offer both a traditional and a Roth option. If an individual chooses the Roth option, contributions will go in after tax; however, the distributions will be taken tax-free.

While there are numerous advantages to having a solo 401(k), there are also some drawbacks. These plans are only available to business owners—and possibly their spouses—who have no full-time employees. In addition, the accounting and administrative costs can be quite high with these types of plans.

Retirement Plans for Employees of Nonprofit and Religious Organizations

Although there are many different types of retirement plans offered to businesses and self-employed individuals, there are differing rules for the plans of religious entities and nonprofit organizations, partly because these types of organizations themselves have differing tax rules.

403(b)

The 403(b) retirement plans are similar to 401(k) plans. These plans are utilized primarily by educational entities and other types of 501(c)(3) organizations. Funds in a 403(b) plan are invested into one of the options that are offered by the employer.

Participation Rules

All employees of a participating organization may participate in a 403(b) plan if it is offered. (30)

Contribution Limits and Funding

Similar to a 401(k) plan, the annual deferred contribution limits for an employee 403(b) are $16,500 (for 2011), and those employees who are age fifty or over may make an additional catch-up contribution of $5,500. Depending upon the employee's income, the combination employee/employer contribution could be as high as $49,000 or 100 percent of the employee's income, whichever is the lesser amount. (31)

Tax Treatment

Deferred contributions to a 403(b) plan will not be included in the employee's taxable income. Therefore, these funds will be taxed as ordinary income tax rates upon withdrawal. Earnings in the account will grow on a tax-deferred basis and will also be taxed at the individual's ordinary income tax rates upon distribution.

Distribution Rules

Withdrawals by the individual may be taken at retirement. In addition, qualified hardships such as disability may also allow the employee to withdraw funds without incurring a penalty for early withdrawal. The employee is required to begin receiving at least a minimum amount of withdrawal as of the April 1st that follows their attaining the age of seventy and a half. In addition, 403(b) plans can be used as loan collateral. (32)

Penalties

If an employee takes a withdrawal from his or her 403(b) plan prior to attaining the age of fifty nine and a half and that withdrawal does not qualify as a hardship withdrawal, then the funds being distributed will be assessed a 10 percent IRS penalty. (33)

Advantages and Disadvantages

Some advantages of the 403(b) plan include the fact that an employee could be eligible to defer a high amount of compensation. In addition, these types of plans could allow a designated Roth program.

Disadvantages include the fact that the employee is not allowed to withdraw funds penalty free before reaching age fifty-nine and a half, unless they qualify for a hardship withdrawal.

457(b)

457(b) plans also have some similarities to 401(k) plans. These retirement plans are used primarily by state and local government entities, which include public school employees as well as police officers and firefighters. There are also some non-government organizations, such as unions, charities, and hospitals, that are tax-exempt and also use these types of plans.

Participation Rules

There are differing participation rules depending on whether a 457(b) plan is being used in a government entity or a tax-exempt (but non-religious) organization. For example, if the plan is being offered by a government organization, then the following employees may participate:

- Common-law employees
- Independent contractors

If the plan is being offered by a non-religious, tax-exempt entity, then the following people may participate:

- Independent contractors
- A select group of management or highly compensated employees

In neither case does there need to be a minimum coverage test, thus allowing all other employees to also participate. (34)

Contribution Limits and Funding

Contributions to a 457(b) plan are done on a salary-deferral basis. The employer may also contribute on behalf of the employees. For 2011, the maximum allowable amount of annual contribution was $16,500. However, if an employee is age fifty or over, he or she is allowed to contribute an additional catch-up amount of $5,500.

The 457(b) plan also has a catch-up provision called the "final three year" provision. This is for employees who are near their retirement time and have not contributed the maximum amount during previous years. This final three year provision allows these employees to make contributions that are higher than the regular limits in the three years just prior to their retirement. (35)

Tax Treatment

Similar to other retirement plans contributions, the funds that are contributed to a 457(b) plan are pretax. Therefore, they are not includable in the employee's annual taxable compensation. Likewise, upon withdrawal at retirement, these funds—as well as the tax-deferred earnings—will be taxed at the individual's income tax rate at the time of withdrawal.

Distribution Rules

Withdrawals from a 457(b) plan are allowed after the employee's severance from employment. In addition, the employee must begin receiving at least a specified minimum amount of distribution by the April 1st that follows the year of the employee's retirement or their attainment of age seventy and a half.

In a 457(b) plan that is offered by a government entity, loans and hardship withdrawals are allowed. However, those plans that are offered by other tax-exempt organizations may not permit loans. In addition, special rules apply to independent contractors who are participating in the plan. (36)

Penalties

In any case, short of an exception or hardship withdrawal, an employee who withdraws funds from his or her 457(b) plan prior to the attainment of age fifty-nine and a half will be hit with a 10 percent IRS penalty on the entire amount of withdrawal. This penalty is in addition to the taxes that will be owed. (37)

Advantages and Disadvantages

One big advantage to a 457(b) plan is that it may permit a high level of salary deferral for the participating employees. In addition, the 457(b) plans that are offered by government organizations may also include a designated Roth program. A primary disadvantage to a 457(b) plan is the inability to roll the plan assets over to an IRA. In addition, loans are often not permitted with these types of retirement plans.

401(a)

A 401(a) is a type of money-purchase retirement plan. These plans allow for contributions by an employer, an employee, or both. These plans are similar to 401(k) plans, except that they are specific to nonprofit organizations. Employees who participate in a 401(a) may also participate in a 457(b) plan.

Participation Rules

Any employee—regardless of whether they work full or part time—may participate in a 401(a) plan, as long as they work more than twenty hours per week. In addition, the employee must have at least one year of service with the employer and have worked a minimum of 1,000 hours within the year of joining the plan. In addition, participants in other types of retirement plan may be eligible to also take part in a 401(a) plan after three months of service with the employer—as long as they are not actually receiving benefits from the other retirement plan. (38)

Contribution Limits and Funding

Funds are contributed to a 401(a) plan in one of three ways. These include:

- The employer contributes a specific dollar amount or percentage amount, either without or in conjunction with a required employee contribution
- The employer matches a fixed percent of the contribution of the employee
- The employer may match the employee's contribution within a given range

In a 401(a) plan, employees can make tax-deferred contributions. The employer may also make a contribution either in the name of the employee or in the form of a matching amount. The contributions that are made by employees may be required or voluntary.

Employees may contribute up to 100 percent of their gross income to a 401(a) plan after the subtraction of any mandatory employee contributions that are made with pretax dollars, which are not to exceed $49,000 (in 2011). This amount includes both the employee and employer contributions. (39)

Tax Treatment

Contributions to a 401(a) plan are not considered to be taxable. Upon withdrawal, funds are taxed at the individual's tax rate. Funds in the account grow on a tax-deferred basis.

Distribution Rules

Employees are not allowed to make early withdrawals if they are still employed with the contributing employer. If, however, they retire or leave the employer, funds may be distributed. Upon retirement, the funds will be taxed as income.

Penalties

If a participant in a 401(a) plan withdraws funds prior to turning age fifty-nine and a half, they will be subject to a 10 percent IRS penalty on the entire amount of funds that are withdrawn. There are, however, some exceptions, such as an employee hardship or disability. (40)

Advantages and Disadvantages

One big advantage to the 401(a) plan is that the employee is always 100 percent fully vested in their contributions. In addition, even if an employee is participating in a 401(a) plan, they are also allowed to participate in a 457(b) plan. A disadvantage to the 401(a) plan is that, in some cases, the employee participant may be required to make a contribution.

CHAPTER 26

Investments for Children

You are never too young to have an investment portfolio, though you may be too young to actually make the investments if you are a child. Unfortunately, many parents do not think of investing for their children, except for savings accounts and college funds. Children, defined as people under the age of eighteen for investment purposes, do have outlets to begin building financial security for adulthood and even retirement.

Parents who teach children how to manage money and finances are to be commended. Using various types of financial vehicles, a child can build a significant portfolio before leaving home, which enables him or her to start life with assets. Let us face it, many of us would be much better off now if we had begun investing as children. The fact is that most workers have saved something for retirement, but very little—less than $25,000. In addition, 68 percent of workers are not sure that social security will be able to continue providing the same level of benefits it provides now by the time they retire. (1)

Before selecting investment vehicles for your children, you should be aware of the legal restrictions concerning minors. Minors cannot enter legal contracts. Another important fact to know is that children do need to file a tax return if they earn income or have investment income. If their income from dividends, interest, and other investments is greater than $1,900, the IRS rules say that part of the investment income may have to be reported on the parent's income tax return. (2)

The following are some ways parents can help their children prepare for their education and future financial life.

IRAs

An IRA, or Individual Retirement Account, is a government-created investment account meant to encourage savings. There are two types of IRAs: traditional and Roth. In 2011, the amount that could be contributed to the account was the lesser of $5,000 or taxable earned income for the year. You can split the contributions between a traditional and Roth IRA, but the combined total cannot exceed $5,000.

Parents can give the child money to contribute to an IRA as long as the child has earned income, and allowance money and household chores money do not qualify. The contributions simply cannot exceed the child's annual earned income. It could be difficult to convince an eleven-year old child to part with all of his or her lawn-mowing money earned through the summer, so it is nice to know parents can add to the contributions.

Since these are investments made with earned income, you can open the account in the child's name. However, a brokerage firm will require the parent or legal guardian to cosign on the account and act as custodian until the child reaches the age of eighteen or twenty-one because children are not allowed to enter into legal contracts. The guardian or parent will maintain ownership of the IRA account until the child turns eighteen or twenty-one, depending on the state in which you live.

Traditional IRA

The contributions made to a traditional IRA account are not taxed. However, the money deposited must be earned income, so a child cannot open a traditional IRA until he or she works and earns money. The contributions cannot be more than $5,000 a year, and the income used for contributions is tax-deductible. When the contributions are withdrawn after the age of fifty-nine and a half, the contributions are taxed. The contributions can also be withdrawn for college expenses with no penalty, but income taxes must be paid. Earnings are tax-free if they are used for education expenses.

Roth IRA

The Roth IRA is an option for a child who has earned income. Earned income is just what it implies—money that was earned by doing work. Many children work at various jobs, and even babysitting money or lawn-mowing money qualifies for deposit into a Roth IRA. You must keep a good record of the amount of money the child earned and how it was earned. The amounts contributed to the Roth IRA are after-tax, and the investment grows tax-free.

The Roth IRA is a powerful investment tool that can turn small account contributions into large tax-free savings accounts by retirement. The contributions can be withdrawn at any time without paying penalties or owing taxes, since you invested with after-tax earned income. The earnings on contributions, however, cannot be withdrawn tax and penalty free.

Education Savings Plans

Coverdell Education Savings Account (ESA)

The Coverdell Education Savings Account used to be called the Education IRA. It was created to give parents a way to save for their child's college education. Contributions to the Coverdell ESA are not tax-deductible and can be made until the child is eighteen years old. Family and friends can open an account and contribute money as long as they meet the income eligibility requirements as defined by the IRS. The really good news is that the earnings on the contributions are tax-free.

The parent or legal guardian will control the account and decide when funds are withdrawn. Withdrawals can be made at any time, but to be tax-free, the funds must be used for qualified educational expenses. They must also be used before the child reaches the age of thirty. Qualified expenses include educational fees, tuition, books, equipment, and supplies plus some room and board expenses. Some elementary and secondary education expenses also qualify.

The annual contribution limit is $2,000 per child for all Coverdell ESAs. If the child does not use the funds, the money can be rolled over to an account for another child in your family who is under the age of thirty. There are case-specific rules and guidelines that a financial advisor can explain.

Section 529 Plans

The Section 529 Plan was designed to encourage parents to save for college expenses. They are managed by an educational institution or the state. Each state has one or more Section 529 Plan. The plan, in effect, allows the prepayment of higher education expenses at certain educational institutions. The parent or guardian of the child opens the account, and there is no income restriction for contributors. The only catch is that the contributions cannot be greater than the qualified higher education expenses, which include tuition, fees, room and board, and books. Some states allow 529 accounts to be opened for potential students within their state or out-of-state, as well. It is important to discuss the case-specific advantages and disadvantages for these plans, and in general, you should always discuss investment and financial plans with a qualified financial advisor.

The parent or legal guardian, not the child or beneficiary, owns the account, but anyone, bearing certain restrictions, can contribute to the account once it is opened. The contributions are after-tax, but earnings are tax-free as long as they are used for eligible expenses. The amounts of contributions vary by state, with some having capped annual limits and others having unlimited annual contributions as long as certain restrictions are met.

Example of Contributions in New York:

Minimum contributions per beneficiary account of $15/$25 can be deducted by payroll each pay period.

Contributions can be made until the total balance of the entire beneficiary's program accounts has reached a maximum of $375,000. (3)

These monies may be invested in money market funds or bond and stock mutual funds, which do add some risk to the earnings potential. Data has shown that some of these accounts lost money after the stock market collapse connected to the 2008 recession.

Some schools have a prepaid 529 savings plan that is the equivalent of prepaying tuition credits, so this setup does not carry the same risk of market loss since money is not invested in an account. However, these accounts do not offer the benefit of earning like a regular invested 529 savings plan would. Another limitation of the prepaid 529 savings plan is that a student choosing to attend a different college than was originally planned may or may not get the same return on their money, depending on the tuition rates at the new school.

Uniform Gifts to Minors Act (UGMA) or Uniform Transfer to Minors Act (UTMA)

The Uniform Gifts to Minors Act (UGMA) or Uniform Transfer to Minors Act (UTMA) custodial accounts give parents the right to transfer up to $13,000 in assets or investments to a child each year in most cases. UGMA accounts were the preferred education investment vehicle prior to the establishment of the 529 plans. They were ideal, because they provided for educational expenses and enabled investments earnings to be taxed at a lower tax rate (that of the minor). In other words, the child claims the investment earnings.

The assets or investments that are transferred become the property of the child, although it is still under the control of the parent or guardian while the child is still a legal minor. However, once the child assumes control of the account, withdrawals can be made both for educational as well as non-education purposes. Until age eighteen or twenty-one, however, the parent or legal guardian is in control, and all withdrawals must be for the benefit of the child the account was opened for. It is important to note that the child will also have to legally claim the income, which could impact financial aid eligibility.

Education Trust Fund

An education trust fund can be established for a child. Trusts are accounts managed by a trustee according to the guidelines established by the person funding the trust, who is called the grantor. Trust funds are often established for estate-planning purposes. Once a trust fund is transferred to the beneficiary, it is no longer part of the grantor's estate. Another reason for establishing a trust fund is to ensure that the money is set aside for a child's educational expenses while also having the ability to establish guidelines on how the money can be withdrawn and spent. A trust fund can be established in a way that makes it eligible for the annual gift tax exclusion. The IRS has established two such plans:

- Section 2503 trust – Trust principal and income is used for the child until he or she reaches the age of twenty-one, and then account is paid out in full.
- Section 2503(b) – Income is paid annually to the child, and money can be placed in a custodial account if the child is young.

One of the advantages of establishing a trust fund is that you are able to establish controls on how and when the money in the fund is spent. The child cannot take control of the trust until a specified age. The trustee can ensure that the account's funds are spent as the grantor intended until the child takes control of the account.

A living trust is created while the grantor is still alive. A trust account can also be created by provisions in a will. In other words, the testamentary trust is established after the person dies. Most trust accounts are large, but there are no dollar limits on the amounts. The trust guidelines will include specific instructions on what the money should be used for and what will happen to the fund should the child forgo higher education.

Savings Account

Surely one of the slowest growing types of investment vehicles is a savings account. That is especially true since the 2008 recession led to the reduction of banks' savings interest rates to less than 0.05 percent in some cases. However, a savings account can make a good investment vehicle for children for several reasons:

- The account earns interest, so parents can teach about money growth
- Account has a statement the child can learn to read

- The child experiences physically depositing money
- Saving teaches a child how to plan financially

In addition, you should not underestimate the power of compounding over time. A $100 deposit and $50 added each month for ten years earning a small 3 percent interest has a future value at a payout of $7,122 to be exact! This could be quite helpful when it is time to pay college expenses.

Most banks and credit unions have special accounts just for children. Of course, the parent or legal guardian will have to be a cosigner on the account.

Government Savings Bonds

Unlike stocks and bonds, minors can own US Savings Bonds Series EE bonds. They are low-risk investments that are backed by the government. They are often purchased to finance education. They earn a fixed rate of return that is determined on May 1st and November 1st each year. The interest accrues monthly but compounds semiannually. The bonds must be held for at least five years to avoid an interest penalty. (4)

You are Never Too Young to Invest

You are never too young to start investing. A lot of people today wish they had started much younger saving for retirement. Fortunately, the government has created so many investment opportunities that children can participate in. Parents and guardians can teach children the importance of being financially savvy and of thinking about the long term. Smart financial planning can generate the money needed to pay for an education, prepare for financial necessities and emergencies, and enjoy retirement. Remember, lessons learned as children become part of their repertoire that shapes their core values they will rely on as they get older and become adults.

CHAPTER 27

Bankruptcy and Retirement Plans

Since the start of the 2008 recession, people around the country have been waking up to headlines like this: "The Next Crisis: Public Pension Funds." (1) In the past, the words "security" and "public pension funds" were almost synonymous, but now, the word "crisis" is paired with "public pension funds." Just as worrisome is the fact that private pension funds seem to be more at risk than those public funds because of the higher risk that is naturally associated with the private market. If the government entities cannot keep up with retirement plan funding when they have taxing authority, what hope is there for private plans?

Pension funds are subject to the uncertainties of the financial markets because they are invested in a variety of ways, including the stock market, bonds, and US Treasuries. Revenues come from three main sources, which are employer contributions, employee contributions, and investment earnings. If any of these falls below pension payout requirements according to actuarial calculations, the fund can literally go broke.

Complicating the issue is the fact that companies, unions, and some government entities can go bankrupt. The federal government can print money, so there is no risk of bankruptcy, but federal pension plans can be significantly underfunded over time. That is when you wake up and read the newspaper or Internet headlines that use the words "crisis" and "pension funds" in the same sentence.

What happens when a public fund is underfunded and cannot meet its obligations to retirees or a public entity files bankruptcy? We saw this happen in the 2011 bankruptcy filing of Jefferson County in Alabama. What happens when a business files bankruptcy and reorganizes or goes out of business? In the following sections, I will briefly discuss the relationship of bankruptcy first to public funds and then private funds.

Bankruptcy and Public Funds

Public pension funds are those offered or funded by a government entity, which may be a city, county, state, or the federal government. The problem that has arisen with public pension funds is that they often promise participants too many benefits based on contributions and investments. Before the current recession, investments have typically included real estate, stocks, hedge funds, and even riskier assets like derivatives.

For government entities, pension funds are a type of asset called off-balance-sheet debt. The liability exists based on obligations to future pensioners, but the money to fund them does not actually exist in entirety. The higher the amount of unfunded liabilities, the more the government must contribute to keep the fund solvent. If a fund gets close to being exhausted, the government entity must borrow the funds to cover the withdrawals.

Any time the government funds a pension plan with borrowed money, the financed portion of the pension obligation moves to the balance sheet. Unfunded or unfinanced pension funds can literally drive a government entity into bankruptcy. Then what?

When a government entity is insolvent, it can mean one of two things:

- Total liabilities are greater than total assets
- Assets are greater than liabilities, but there are still not enough funds available to pay liabilities as they accrue

A government bankruptcy might necessitate the trimming or discharging of pension obligations. Though pension fund obligations are seldom—if ever—eliminated by a bankruptcy court, they can be significantly reduced for future pensioners. This is especially true if they are out of line with private pension funds. A municipality, county, or city that declares bankruptcy when it has pension funds will be instructed by the court on how to manage unfunded pension liabilities and future pension requirements.

Currently, only municipal, county, or city governments can declare bankruptcy. A state is not allowed to file bankruptcy according to the US Constitution because states are granted sovereign immunity. This means they cannot be sued. The state must cover the pension withdrawals with cash, whether that process takes place through the sale of assets, bond sales, or raising taxes. Clearly, though, there is an untested scenario in which a state may be unable to sell enough assets or is unable to collect enough taxes to cover pension withdrawals. In that case, the courts would be most likely to determine the resolution, assuming the federal government does not step in.

Private Pensions and Bankruptcy

In a business bankruptcy, the intent is to identify the total assets, set priorities for distribution of those assets to various creditor classes, and then discharge the liabilities. The current law protecting employee retirement plans is referred to as ERISA or the Employee Retirement Income Security Act of 1974. This act establishes the rules for business pension plans when a company chooses to create one.

Basically, ERISA requires that employers provide adequate funding for the pension plan. There are accountability requirements, and plan participants can sue if the plan is mismanaged and benefits cannot be paid. (2) Because of provisions set forth in current bankruptcy laws, pension fund assets are never liquidated in a Chapter 13 bankruptcy, nor are they taken and redistributed like other assets in a Chapter 7 bankruptcy. This is the result of a change made to bankruptcy laws in 2005 that virtually exempts pension funds from bankruptcy. (3)

Defined benefit plans or traditional pension plans may be insured by the federal government through the Pension Benefits Guaranty Corporation (PBGC). If an insured plan is terminated for any reason and promised benefits are not adequately funded, the PBGC will pay benefits up to a certain amount. However, defined contribution plans like the 401(k) are not insured. (4) Compared to government pension funds that will be covered by public funds, a private 401(k) can lose significant value, have no fallback for restoration, and leave pensioners without adequate retirement income—with or without government bankruptcy laws.

It is important to understand the terms of your pension funds. Though bankruptcy will not liquidate a pension fund, it can impact the value of a pension fund through changes in future benefit payouts or fund losses.

SECTION 7

Government

CHAPTER 28

Social Security Benefits

When social security was created by President Franklin D. Roosevelt (FDR) in 1935, it was considered one of the best systems available to provide income to retirees as well as certain types of financial support for the disabled and the widowed.

At that time, the system had ample funding due to the many workers paying into the program. And while it offered a financial safety net for its recipients for several decades, Social Security is now facing a number of hurdles that could even deem the system insolvent in the years to come.

What is Social Security?

Social security is technically defined as the United States's version of social insurance and benefits. The program began in 1935, and since its inception, it has become one of the largest government programs globally, paying out billions of dollars to recipients every year. (1)

The program has an effect on nearly all families in the United States. As of 2011, approximately 54 million people receive benefits from Social Security, and over 150 million working individuals pay into the program via payroll tax. (2)

Why Social Security Was Created

Originally, Social Security was created as part of President Franklin D. Roosevelt's New Deal program. This program was meant to help the United States out of the Great Depression and to provide financial security to retirees as well as to other qualifying beneficiaries. (3)

Regardless of the safety net provided by Social Security, the program was never intended to replace 100 percent of a retiree's pre-retirement earnings. In fact, it is estimated that the income received by Social Security retirement benefits only replaces roughly 40 percent of an average income earner's income after they are retired. (4)

Therefore, it is important to understand how benefits are calculated and approximately how much you will be receiving after retirement so that you can plan for additional retirement income sources.

The Components of Social Security

Social Security is often thought of as the program that pays out benefits to retirees. While this is true, Social Security also offers disability income benefits, death benefits, and survivorship benefits to the qualifying spouses and children of its beneficiaries. Social Security, along with Medicare coverage, is also paid for out of the payroll taxes of workers.

Who is Eligible for Social Security?

Contrary to what many believe, retirees are not the only ones who are eligible to receive Social Security benefits. Those who have worked, paid taxes, and accumulated enough eligibility credits may be entitled to any or all of the following benefits from Social Security:

- Retirement income
- Disability income
- Survivors benefits
- Dependents benefits

In addition to paying taxes into the system, an eligible individual must have accumulated at least forty working "credits" to be entitled to full Social Security benefits. One credit is equal to one quarter of a year of work. Therefore, those who have worked at least ten full years—or forty quarters—will have accumulated enough working credits to be eligible.

What Are the Primary Benefits of Social Security?

Social Security pays out benefits in a variety of different ways. Most of the recipients are receiving retirement income benefits. However, others who receive income from the program can include disabled persons, the spouse or child of someone who is receiving Social Security, the spouse or child of someone who has passed away, or the dependent parent of an eligible worker who has passed away.

Retirement Benefits

When the program was first established, those who had reached the age of sixty-five were considered to have reached what Social Security deems "full retirement age." This is why so many people today still consider age sixty-five to be the age at which they will retire; however, that is no longer the case for everyone.

Participants may begin receiving Social Security retirement benefits as early as age sixty-two. However, anyone who begins receiving benefits prior to their full retirement age will receive a reduced amount—even after reaching their full retirement age. This reduction in benefits is calculated by reducing roughly one-half of one percent for every month that the individual begins receiving benefits prior to reaching full retirement age. (5)

Over the years, due to solvency issues, the Social Security program has had to make a number of adjustments with regard to stretching its funds, including extending the age at which retirees are considered to have reached full retirement age. Although a limited amount of benefit is still allowed when an eligible individual reaches age sixty-two, a worker is now considered to have reached full retirement age based on the year of their birth.

Year of Birth	Minimum Retirement Age for Full Benefits
1937 or Before	65
1938	65 + 2 months
1939	65 + 4 months
1940	65 + 6 months
1941	65 + 8 months
1942	65 + 10 months
1943 to 1954	66
1955	66 + 2 months
1956	66 + 4 months
1957	66 + 6 months
1958	66 + 8 months
1959	66 + 10 months
1960 or Later	67
Source: SSA Publication 05 -10024, Aug. 2011	

Eligible recipients may also decide to delay their retirement benefits. By doing so, the amount that they are eligible for will increase by a certain percentage that is based upon the year in which they were born. This increase in benefits will be added in every month from the time the person reaches full retirement age until he or she either begins taking benefits or reaches age seventy, whichever comes sooner. (6)

Disability Benefits

For those who are under retirement age, but need financial assistance due to a disability, Social Security can provide income benefits to those who qualify. In fact, qualified disabled individuals as well as certain family members might actually be eligible.

Similar to the receipt of Social Security retirement benefits, those who are disabled must meet specific criteria in order to receive this income. The disability must be expected to last for at least twelve months or to result in the individual's death. In addition, the individual must earn a certain number of work-related credits. This number will be dependent upon the age at which the individual actually becomes disabled.

Provided they meet the other eligibility requirements, a disabled individual may receive Social Security disability benefits at any age. If they are still receiving disability payments at the time of reaching their retirement age, the payments will convert to retirement benefits.

Certain family members of the disabled individual may also be eligible to receive at least some amount of benefit from Social Security, as well. These family members can include:

- Unmarried children who are under the age of eighteen (or age eighteen if they are a full-time elementary or high school student)
- Unmarried children who are age eighteen or older who become disabled prior to the age of twenty-two
- The disabled individual's spouse, provided that he or she is either at least age sixty-two, or any age if they are caring for a child who is either younger than age sixteen or is disabled and is also receiving Social Security disability benefits

The amount of benefit paid by Social Security for a disability is also dependent upon the individual's lifetime average earnings that are covered by Social Security. In order to qualify, the potential beneficiary must provide an official medical report from a doctor, clinic, or hospital that offers information about the disability as well as the estimated time that the disability may last.

The qualification criteria also include the extent of the disability. For example, the potential benefit recipient must not only be unable to do his or her previous type of work, he or she must also be incapable—relative to age, work experience, and education—of engaging in any other kind of substantial work that exists in the national economy. According to Social Security, when considering the inability to perform certain work-related tasks, it is immaterial as to whether such work actually exists in the individual's immediate area or whether a job vacancy is likely to exist.

Survivors Benefits for Spouse and Children

If a Social Security recipient passes away, qualifying survivors may also receive benefits. Provided that the individual has enough work credits, eligible family members are entitled to receive survivors benefits, regardless of the age of the individual at his or her time of death.

The amount of survivors benefits is based on the amount of retirement benefits that the individual would have received had he or she reached the full retirement age. Should the person pass away prior to reaching full retirement age, then the survivors benefit will be calculated by considering the individual's lifetime earnings as well as a factor that corresponds to the number of years that he or she would have been expected to participate in the workforce.

Eligible survivors can include the deceased individual's:

- Spouse
- Children
- Parent(s)

Medicare

In addition to the payroll taxes that are paid into the Social Security program, there is an additional amount that goes toward funding the Medicare program. Medicare is the basic health insurance program that has been set up for those who are age sixty-five and over as well as individuals with certain disabilities. It should be noted, however, that Medicare is not run by the Social Security Administration but rather by the Centers for Medicare and Medicaid Services.

Medicare consists of the following parts:

- Part A – Hospitalization Coverage
- Part B – Doctors' Services
- Part C – Medicare Advantage
- Part D – Prescription Drugs

Individuals who are eligible to receive Medicare benefits include those who are age sixty-five and are also receiving Social Security retirement benefits or who have at least worked long enough to be eligible for Social Security retirement benefits. In addition, people age sixty-two or older may also qualify to receive Medicare benefits based on their spouse's earnings record.

Those who are younger than age sixty-five but have been receiving Social Security disability benefits for at least twenty-four months or who have worked long enough and have met the requirements of Social Security disability may also be eligible for Medicare benefits. In addition, individuals who have a chronic kidney disease that requires either dialysis or a kidney transplant may also be able to receive Medicare benefits, regardless of age.

How is the Social Security Program Funded?

The Social Security program is funded via payroll taxes that are collected by the government from companies and individual workers. The funds are then placed into the Social Security Trust Fund and are subsequently managed by the government in conjunction with the Federal Reserve Board.

Most people who work for an employer are required to pay into the Social Security program. Social Security and Medicare taxes are typically deducted directly from workers' paychecks. These tax contributions are then sent to the IRS, along with an additional amount of contribution from the employer.

Those who are self-employed or who run their own business must report earnings and pay their Social Security and Medicare taxes directly to the IRS. In 2011, the Social Security tax rate was 13.3 percent on the income of self-employed individuals, up to a maximum of $106,800. For income that exceeds this amount, the individual will only be required to pay the Medicare portion of the Social Security tax, which, in 2011, was 2.9 percent, on the remaining amount of his or her earnings. (7)

Social Security and Medicare Taxes (2011)		
For employed individuals:	**Social Security Tax**	**Medicare Tax**
Individual Portion	4.20%	1.45%
Employer Portion	6.20%	1.45%
For self-employed:		
Self-Emp. Individual Portion	10.40%	2.90%

Must All Workers Pay Into the Social Security Program?

Those who earn less than $400 in a given year are not required to pay into the Social Security program, although they may if they choose to do so. In addition, some alternate types of income are not required to be counted toward Social Security and thus are not required to be included in figuring an individual's net earnings in a given year. This includes:

- Income received from a limited partnership
- Interest income received from loans (unless the individual operates a business that loans money as a part of its regular operations)
- Income received from rental real estate (unless the individual is a real estate dealer or they regularly provide real-estate-related services to tenants)
- Dividend income that is received via stocks (unless the individual is a dealer in stocks or securities)
- Interest income that is received from bonds (8)

The Social Security Budget–Current and Future Projections

Over the past few decades, Social Security has faced some major solvency issues. Because the funds used to pay out benefits are collected from current workers, these same individuals may not have benefits available to them at the time of their own retirement.

For the past several decades, the number of retirees receiving Social Security benefits has grown much faster than the tax-paying workforce paying into the system to fund it. Due to declining birth rates, increasing life expectancies, and the compounding effect of the cost-of-living adjustments, the Social Security system is now facing some serious challenges. And it is estimated that the number of workers per beneficiary will continue to decrease over time.

Number of Workers Contributing to One Social Security Recipient's Benefits	
Year	**Tax-Paying Workers Per 1 Recipient**
1945	35
1995	3
2030	2 (estimated)

For the fiscal year 2012, the Social Security Administration requested $12.522 billion, which includes an increase of nearly $300 million over the previous year, in order to meet their fixed costs that include the meeting of the rising number of customers and growing workloads. (9) Due to the economic downturn, which includes lower income for many in the taxpaying workforce, the Social Security program saw a $49 billion deficit in the year 2010 and has estimated a $46 billion deficit for 2011. (10) Over the long term, the program is estimated to continue in the red.

Will Social Security's Funding Be Sustainable?

Based on future projections, the deficit in the Social Security program is expected to be in the range of $20 billion for the years 2012 through 2014. With an anticipated strengthening of the economy after that time, the deficit is expected to shrink. However, the program will still likely continue to operate at a loss based on the growing number of program beneficiaries along with the decreasing number of taxpaying workers per beneficiary recipient. (11)

The Social Security Administration estimates that through the year 2022, the annual cash deficits will be made up by redeeming trust fund assets from the General Fund of the United States Treasury. As these redemptions are likely to be less than the interest earnings within the trust, the balances are projected to continue growing. (12)

After the year 2022, the assets in the trust fund are estimated to be redeemed in amounts that will far exceed the earnings from interest in the fund. Current projections estimate that the reserves in the trust fund will be completely exhausted in the year 2036. After this time, the tax income entering the Social Security program is expected to be only sufficient enough to pay approximately 75 percent of the program's scheduled benefits through the year 2085. (13)

Issues and Amendments Regarding Social Security

In order to help keep the Social Security program solvent, the government has considered numerous amendments to the program over the past several years. This reform—whether it has been via legislation, privatization, or changes in the tax law—has been a serious political issue that has brought with it some extremely strong opinions from a variety of demographic segments.

Just some of the overall amendments to the Social Security program over the years have included those in the areas of:

- Universal Coverage
- Benefit Computation
- Tax Treatment of Benefits
- Surviving, Divorced, and Disabled Spouses Benefits
- Revenue Measures
- Mechanisms to Assure Continued Benefit Payments
- Long-Term Provisions (14)

Criticisms of the Social Security Program

Certainly, any program that involves millions of individuals will run into its share of criticisms. One of the biggest issues with Social Security has been its projected outlook regarding the payment of benefits—especially in light of the shrinking workforce in relation to the growing number of benefit recipients.

Because Social Security is considered a pay-as-you-go system, each generation of current workers is actually paying the benefits of current retirees. In a population where the number of taxpaying workers grows at the same pace as retirees, this system would appear to be adequate.

However, given the demographic projections both currently and for the future, the Social Security program will essentially become unsustainable. So a large number of analysts are in favor of moving Social Security to more of a pre-funded system where workers are able to save some of their own taxes in a private account for their future retirement benefits.

How Will Social Security Remain Solvent?

Social Security is facing the real threat of becoming insolvent. Due to longer life expectancies, inflation, and a large number of baby boomers entering retirement age, the system may be unable to sustain the payment of all benefits that are due.

Under currently scheduled financing, the projected long-run costs of the Social Security program, as well as Medicare, will not be sustainable. In order to correct this issue and to avoid disruptive consequences for taxpayers and program beneficiaries, legislative corrections will likely be required. Otherwise, privatization of the system may be essential. In any case, those who are planning to retire in the future should not depend completely upon Social Security as their sole or even primary source of retirement income.

CHAPTER 29

Tax Rates Comparison

Practically every national and regional government on the planet levies taxes on its citizens in order to pay for public utilities and services, including oversight agencies, road maintenance, and military protection. Social Security, federal medical programs, and other public funds also require a substantial amount of tax revenue to function properly.

Every member nation of the Organization for Economic Co-operation and Development (OECD) relies on taxation for a substantial portion of their government's funding. The OECD, which was founded in the 1960s, is dedicated to advancing and evaluating tax policies in developed countries. There were thirty-four member nations in the OECD as of 2011. These nations include the United States, most of Europe, and a handful of countries in Eastern Asia and South America. (1)

When many European and American taxpayers hear the word "taxes," they think of the single largest tax that they are subject to: the federal income tax. However, income tax levied by the national government is only one part of the picture. Citizens of most developed nations pay numerous taxes throughout the year, including consumption taxes, property taxes, and local income taxes.

To determine an individual's real tax rate, all of these other taxes must be taken into account. Tax rates vary extensively between countries, so the citizens of some nations pay a much greater portion of their annual income in taxes than those of other countries. In larger nations, like the United States, the individual tax burden can vary significantly, depending on the policies of different states or provinces, which makes a simple rate comparison even more convoluted.

Some high-income businesses and individuals rely on tax havens to shield their money from the hefty tax rates in the countries where they conduct business. Tax havens are often small, independent nations that offer corporations and other entities an extraordinarily friendly business environment for taxation and management purposes.

Real Tax Rate

An individual's real tax rate is the percentage of his or her annual income spent on taxes during that fiscal year. Citizens of the United States, as well as a few other developed countries, are subject to various taxes on several distinct levels: federal, provincial, and local. Federal taxes are levied by the central, national government. Provincial taxes in the United States are enforced at the state level, while smaller jurisdictions, like cities and counties, can also levy taxes independently of state or federal tax policies.

The bulk of federal taxation in the United States is collected as personal income tax, social insurance tax, and taxes on goods, like the excise tax. (2) An individual's personal income tax rate is calculated based on his or her total taxable income. The rate at which income is taxed depends on the total amount of money generated by a person, business, or married couple. As the total income increases, so does the rate at which that income is taxed up to the maximum (marginal) rate. There are a few exceptions to this rule. Countries with a flat tax policy, like Hungary, enforce a single income tax rate regardless of a taxpayer's total income.

As of 2011, the marginal rate on personal income in the United States was 35 percent, so any income in or above the top bracket is taxed at this rate. This rate only applies to income of $379,150 or more. Individuals with an income between $174,400 and $379,150 are taxed at a rate of 33 percent. The lowest bracket, individuals whose income is between $0 and $8,500, are taxed at a 10 percent rate. (3) In 2010, the average single US citizen earning average wages was taxed at an "all-in" rate of 22.9 percent. The all-in rate includes federal and state income taxes as well as contributions to Social Security. (4)

A 2007 report by the Tax Foundation found that, in 2004, the average household paid a total of $17,338 in federal taxes and $9,400 in state and local taxes. (5) According to the report, $7,069 was contributed to social security and Medicare per household, $7,062 was claimed as federal income tax, and $2,155 was paid as corporate income tax.

A paper published in 2006 through Boston University revealed some interesting information regarding the real tax rate of US individuals. The total rate of taxation was between 35 percent and 45 percent for working, single individuals across most age groups and income levels. Individuals earning roughly $250,000 paid between 41.5 and 44 percent of their income in taxes each year. Individuals with an income of around $100,000 paid a total tax rate of 36.1 to 38.8, while those earning $40,000 paid between 37.7 and 42.9. (6)

Tax Rate Comparison by US State

While most state governments levy consumption and income taxes, a few jurisdictions do not. This means that the burden of state-level taxation is not shared equally throughout the country. Some states have a distinctly higher average tax burden than others do. The vast majority of state-level taxation takes one of three forms: property, income, and consumption taxes.

Income Taxes

Seven states in the United States do not levy an income tax: Alaska, Florida, Nevada, South Dakota, Texas, Washington, and Wyoming. Two states, New Hampshire and Tennessee, only levy taxes on income from dividends and interest. Of the remaining forty-one states, Hawaii, Oregon, California, Iowa, and New Jersey boast the highest marginal income tax rates in the country.

Five states with the highest marginal income tax rate[7]:

1. Hawaii	11.00%
2. Oregon	11.00%
3. California	9.30%
4. Iowa	8.98%
5. New Jersey	8.97%

Property Taxes

Property taxes are levied as a percentage of the property's value, which fluctuates between rural and urban environments. The following lists rank states based on the percentage of their residents' total income that was paid in property taxes in 2009. Rates reflected in the chart represent the percentage of the average home owner's income that was paid in property taxes, not the percentage of property value.

States with the lowest property taxes[8]:

1. Louisiana	0.45%
2. Alabama	0.78%
3. West Virginia	1.03%
4. Arkansas	1.10%
5. Mississippi	1.11%

States with the highest property taxes[8]:

1. New Jersey	7.45%
2. New Hampshire	6.34%
3. Vermont	5.55%
4. Connecticut	5.51%
5. Illinois	5.11%

Sales and Excise Tax

While the federal government enforces some excise taxes on products like gasoline, cigarettes, and alcohol, state governments are also allowed to enforce their own taxes on goods or services. Prices of cigarettes, for example, may differ significantly from one state to the next, depending on each jurisdiction's excise tax laws.

States with the highest combined sales tax rate[9]:

1. Tennessee	9.43%
2. Arizona	9.12%
3. Louisiana	8.84%
4. Washington	8.79%
5. Oklahoma	8.66%

Five states do not have any state-level sales tax on goods or services purchased within their jurisdiction: Delaware, Alaska, Montana, New Hampshire, and Oregon. (9)

Table: U.S. states with the highest excise tax on cigarettes, gasoline, and alcohol[9]

Commodity	**#1** *($ per unit)*	**#2** *($ per unit)*	**#3** *($ per unit)*	**#4** *($ per unit)*	**#5** *($ per unit)*
Cigarettes (20-pack)	Rhode Island (0.03)	Connecticut (0.03)	Hawaii (0.03)	New York (0.03)	New Jersey (0.03)
Spirits (gallon)	Alaska (0.13)	Florida (0.07)	New York (0.06)	New Mexico (0.06)	Hawaii (0.06)
Wine (gallon)	Alabama (2.50)	Florida (2.25)	Iowa (1.75)	Alabama (1.70)	New Mexico (0.02)
Beer (gallon)	Alaska (0.01)	Hawaii (0.01)	South Caro. (0.01)	North Caro. (0.01)	Alabama (0.01)
Gasoline (gallon)	California (0.00)	New York (0.00)	Hawaii (0.00)	Connecticut (0.00)	Illinois (0.04)

Tax Rate Comparison by OECD Country

Marginal Income Tax Rate

Countries with the lowest marginal income tax rate:

1. Switzerland	13.20%
2. Slovakia	19.00%
3. Mexico	30.00%
4. Turkey	35.00%
5. United States	35.00%

Countries with the highest marginal income tax rate:

1. Sweden	56.50%
2. Netherlands	50.10%
3. United Kingdom	50.00%
4. Finland	48.20%
5. Denmark	48.10%

Property Taxes

The following property tax lists compare the ratio of each government's income from property taxes to their gross domestic product (GDP). Property tax rates are variable, depending on the location and purpose (commercial or domestic) of the property.

Countries with the lowest property tax to GDP ratio:

1. Mexico	0.30%
2. Estonia	0.30%
3. Czech Republic	0.40%
4. Slovakia	0.40%
5. Slovenia	0.40%

Countries with the highest property tax to GDP ratio:

1. United Kingdom	4.20%
2. Canada	3.60%
3. France	3.40%
4. United States	3.30%
5. Korea	3.00%

Sales Tax (2011)

Federal sales tax often takes the form of a value-adjusted tax (VAT), which applies to each stage of the production and distribution of goods and services. The United States is currently the only member of the OECD that does not enforce a federal sales tax or VAT policy.

Countries with the lowest federal sales tax:

1. United States	(None)
2. Japan	5.00%
3. Canada	5.00%
4. Switzerland	8.00%
5. Australia	10.00%

Countries with the highest federal sales tax:

1. Iceland	25.50%
2. Norway	25.00%
3. Sweden	25.00%
4. Hungary	25.00%
5. Denmark	25.00%

Source: Tax data for international comparisons taken from OECD: Tax Database

Selected References and Resources

SECTION I: Credit

Good and Bad Debt

Citations:

1. "The Big Payoff: Education: Educational Attainment and Synthetic Estimates of Work-Life Earnings." (2002, July). Retrieved from US Census Bureau: http://www.census.gov/prod/2002pubs/p23-210.pdf

2. "How much student loan debt can I afford?" (2011). Retrieved from Columbia College: http://www.ccis.edu/offices/financialaid/howmuchdebt.asp

The Benefits of Consumer Credit

Citations:

1. Indiana Consumer Credit. (2011). Retrieved from Indiana Department of Financial Institutions - Consumer Credit Division: http://www.in.gov/dfi/incredit.pdf

2. "Financial Capability in the United States."(2009, December). Retrieved from FINRA Investor Education Foundation: http://www.finrafoundation.org/web/groups/foundation/@foundation/documents/foundation/p120535.pdf

3. "More work to be done on credit cards." (2009). Retrieved from Consumers Union: http://www.creditcardreform.org/learn.html

4. *Guide to Consumer Credit.* (2010, May). Retrieved from Massachussetts Attorney General Office: http://www.mass.gov/ago/docs/consumer/consumer-credit-050510.pdf

Credit Cards: The Consumer and Debt

Citations:

1. US Federal Reserve, (2012, February 7). *Consumer Credit - G.19 (December 2011).* Retrieved from Board of Governors of the Federal Reserve System: http://www.federalreserve.gov/releases/g19/Current/

2. US Census Bureau (2012) 2012 *Statistical Abstract of the United States, Table 1188 – Credit Cards.* Retrieved from US Census Bureau: www.census.gov/compendia/statab/2012/tables/12s1188.pdf

3. Ibid

4. Ibid

5. Ibid

6. The Nilson Report. (January 2012). *Discover Financial Services - Discover Card Results 2011 vs. 2010.* Carpinteria, CA: The Nilson Report.

7. Office of Inspector General. (2011). *Credit Cards Fees.* Retrieved from Board of Governors of the Federal Reserve System: http://www.federalreserve.gov/creditcard/fees.html

8. US Federal Reserve. (2012). *Charge-Off and Delinquency Rates on Loans and Leases.* Retrieved from Board of Governors of the Federal Reserve System: http://www.federalreserve.gov/releases/chargeoff/delallsa.htm

9. US Federal Reserve. (2010, March 11). *New Credit Card Rules Effective Feb. 22.* Retrieved from Board of Governors of the Federal Reserve System: http://www.federalreserve.gov/consumerinfo/wyntk_creditcardrules.htm

10. Jennifer Acosta Scot. (2012). "Students, credit cards and the new reform law: the fine print." Retrieved from CreditCards.com: http://www.creditcards.com/credit-card-news/college-student-credit-card-law-1279.php

11. Richard Cordray. (2012). "Learn About the Bureau - Core Functions." Retrieved from Consumer Financial Protection Bureau: http://www.consumerfinance.gov/the-bureau/

The Debate over Payday Loans

Citations:

1. Uriah King and Leslie Parrish. (2007). "Springing the Debt Trap." Durham, NC: Center for Responsible Lending.

2. Payday Lending. (n.d.). Retrieved from Georgia.gov Department of Banking and Finance: http://dbf.georgia.gov/00/article/0,2086,43414745_46389324_70709483,00.html

3. Credit.com's State-by-State Payday Loan Summary. (2012). Retrieved from Credit.com: http://www.credit.com/credit_information/credit_law/PaydayLoanLaws.jsp

4. FTC. (2008, March). "Payday Loans Equal Very Costly Cash: Consumers Urged to Consider the Alternatives. Retrieved from Federal Trade Commission." http://www.ftc.gov/bcp/edu/pubs/consumer/alerts/alt060.shtm

5. APR Matters on Payday Loans. (2009, June 23). Retrieved from Center for Responsible Lending: http://www.responsiblelending.org/payday-lending/research-analysis/apr-matters-on-payday-loans.html

6. Wei Li, Leslie Parrish, Keith Ernst, and Delvin Davis. (May 26, 2009). "Predatory Profiling: The Role of Race and Ethnicity in the Location of Payday Lenders in California." Durham, NC: Center for Responsible Lending.

Selected Resources:

Turning Poverty into a Multibillion-Dollar Industry (2010)

http://www.npr.org/templates/story/story.php?storyId=127236038

SECTION 2: Personal Finance

A Budget for all Your Needs

Citations:

1. AFSA Education Foundation. (2011). Consumer Budget Planner. Retrieved from American Financial Services Association Education Foundation: http://www.afsaef.org/BudgetPlanner.cfm

2. NFCC. (n.d.). "More Than One-Third of Americans Give Themselves Low Grades on Their Understanding of Personal Finance." Retrieved from National Foundation for Credit Counseling: http://www.nfcc.org/consumer_tools/consumertips/TipsUnderstandingPersonalFinance.cfm

3. Internal Revenue Service. (2011, June 15). 529 Plans: Questions and Answers. Retrieved from IRS: http://www.irs.gov/newsroom/article/0,,id=213043,00.html

Learning to Respect Debt: The Reduction Plan

Citations:

1. Federal Reserve. (2012, January 9). Consumer Credit - G.19 (November, 2011). Retrieved from Board of Governors of the Federal Reserve System. http://www.federalreserve.gov/releases/g19/Current/

2. Federal Reserve. (2012, January 9). Charge-Off and Delinquency Rates on Loans and Leases at Commercial Banks (3rd quarter 2011). Retrieved from Board of Governors of the Federal Reserve System. http://www.federalreserve.gov/releases/chargeoff/chgallnsa.htm

3. FinAid. (2012). Loan Forgiveness. Retrieved from FinAid - The Smart Student Guide to Financial Aid. http://www.finaid.org/loans/forgiveness.phtml

4. "Three Reasons to Pay Off Your Mortgage Early." (2011, November 2). Retrieved from *US News Money*: http://money.usnews.com/money/blogs/the-smarter-mutual-fund-investor/2011/11/02/three-reasons-to-pay-off-your-mortgage-early

5. Office of Judges Programs - Statistics Division. (2011). 2010 Report of Statistics Required by the Bankruptcy Abuse Prevention and Consumer Protection Act of 2005. Washington, D.C.: Administrative Office of the United States Courts.

Fear of Generic Products

Citations:

1. "Does Generic Food Have the Same Health Vitamins For You?" (2011, June 14). Retrieved from *Live Strong.com*: http://www.livestrong.com/article/305078-does-generic-food-have-the-same-healthy-vitamins-for-you/

2. Veronica Liljander, Pia Polsa, and Allard van Riel. (2009). "Modelling consumer responses to an apparel store brand: Store image as a risk reducer." *Journal of Retailing and Consumer Services*, 16 (4), pp. 281-290.

3. "What Are Generic Drugs?" (2009, May 12). Retrieved from US Food and Drug Administration:
http://www.fda.gov/Drugs/ResourcesForYou/Consumers/BuyingUsingMedicineSafely/UnderstandingGenericDrugs/ucm144456.htm

Why Banks Nickel and Dime You

Selected Resources:

Center for Responsible Lending. Big Bank Payday Loans: High-interest loans through checking accounts keep customers in long-term debt. Available at
http://www.responsiblelending.org/payday-lending/research-analysis/big-bank-payday-loans.pdf

"Big Bank Payday Loans: High-interest loans through checking accounts keep customers in long-term debt." Rebecca Borné, Joshua Frank, Peter Smith, and Ellen Schloemer. July 2011. http://www.responsiblelending.org/payday-lending/research-analysis/big-bank-payday-loans.pdf

Federal Reserve. Balance Sheet of Households and Nonprofit Organizations available at http://www.federalreserve.gov/releases/z1/current/z1r-5.pdf

http://online.wsj.com/article/SB10001424052970203733504577021972358085822.html

http://www.cbo.gov/doc.cfm?index=666&type=0&sequence=5

www.consumerreports.org

http://www.reuters.com/article/2012/01/12/us-banking-unbanked-idUSTRE80B1J220120112

http://money.cnn.com/galleries/2011/pf/1101/gallery.least_evil_banks/index.html

http://www.nytimes.com/2011/10/16/business/online-banking-keeps-customers-on-hook-for-fees.html?pagewanted=all

Leasing vs. Buying . . . The Discussion Continues

Citations:

1. "Keys to Vehicle Leasing - Up-Front, Ongoing and End-of-Lease Costs." (2003, May 5). Retrieved from Federal Reserve: http://www.federalreserve.gov/pubs/leasing/resource/consider/upfront.htm

2. "How to Buy a Certified Pre-Owned Vehicle." (2009, April 29). Retrieved from *Edmunds.com*: http://www.edmunds.com/certified-cars/how-to-buy-a-certified-pre-owned-vehicle.html

3. Car Buyer's Bill of Rights FFVR 35. (2011) Retrieved from California Department of Motor Vehicles: http://dmv.ca.gov/pubs/brochures/fast_facts/ffvr35.htm

4. Mortgage Settlement Costs. (2010, August 18). Retrieved from The Federal Reserve Board: http://www.federalreserve.gov/pubs/settlement/

5. John Wasik. (2010, October 11). "Don't hold your breath on home appreciation." Retrieved from *Reuters*: http://blogs.reuters.com/reuters-money/2010/10/11/dont-hold-your-breath-on-home-appreciation/

SECTION 3: Real Estate

Real Estate Investing: Buying a Home

Citations:

1. HUD. (1997). *Settlement Costs and Helpful Information.* Retrieved from HUD.gov: http://portal.hud.gov/hudportal/HUD?src=/program_offices/housing/ramh/res/sc3sect d

2. Federal Reserve Board. (2010, August). *A Consumer's Guide to Mortgage Settlement Costs.* Retrieved from The US Federal Reserve Board: http://www.federalreserve.gov/pubs/settlement/

3. "How much does the typical title insurance cost?" (2009). Retrieved from *Ask For Insurance*: http://www.askforinsurance.com/title-and-mortgage-insurance/how-much-does-the-typical-title-insurance-cost.html

4. Debora Vrana. (n.d.). "3 ways to pay lower real-estate commissions." Retrieved from *MSN Real Estate*: http://realestate.msn.com/article.aspx?cp-documentid=13108435

5. National Endowment for Financial Education. (2012). "Prepare for the Costs of Home Maintenance." Retrieved from SmartAboutMoney.org: http://www.smartaboutmoney.org/LifeEventsFinancialDecisions/MajorLifeEvents/BuyingaHome/HomeMaintenance/tabid/349/Default.aspx

6. Bell Mortgage. (202). "Minnesota first time home buyer programs." Retrieved from *Homes of Minnesota*: http://www.minnesotafirsttimehomebuyer.com/minnesota-programs.php

7. IRS. (2011, December 22). Topic 505 - Interest Expense. Retrieved from Internal Revenue Service: http://www.irs.gov/taxtopics/tc505.html

International Real Estate Investing

Citations:

1. Luis Resendiz. (2008, April). "The Dilemma Surrounding International Real Estate: To Lend or Not to Lend?" *Real Estate Finance , 24* (6), pp. 1-3.

2. AIPP. (2012). "Consumer Buying Guide and Advice." Retrieved from Association of International Propety Professionals: http://www.aipp.org.uk/consumer/buying-guide-and-advice/

3. Kayleigh Kulp. (2011, February 18). "What You Need to Know Before Buying Foreign Property." Retrieved from *Fox Business News*: http://www.foxbusiness.com/personal-finance/2011/02/18/need-know-buying-foreign-property/

Refinancing

Citations:

1. The Federal Reserve Board. (2008, 28 August). A Consumer's Guide to Mortgage Refinancings. Retrieved 2011, from The Federal Reserve Board: http://www.federalreserve.gov/pubs/refinancings/default.htm

2. Julie Garton-Good. (2004). "All About Mortgages." Chicago: *Dearborn Trade Publishing.*

3. Jessica Silver-Greenberg. (2011, October 8). "Refinance Now? Maybe Not." Retrieved from *The Wall Street Journal*: http://online.wsj.com/article/SB10001424052970204010604576597423407158588.html

SECTION 4: Education and Jobs

Financial Education for Kids

Selected Resources:

dfi.wa.gov: a resource packed with information about financial education in schools

payjr.com: a site with quizzes and educational material aimed at teens and young adults

http://hsfpp.nefe.org: is a site that has student and parent sections and offers courses designed specifically to address the needs of both

usmint.com: the home of the US Mint has teaching tools for educators and kids.

childrensfinancialnetwork.com: has a wealth of information for children and parents and also has books for sale that will help in the educational process

familyeducation.com: wealth of information for children and parents covering various topics

Higher Education: Will Your College Degree Pay Off?

Citations:

1. W. Symonds, R. Schwartz, and R. Ferguson. (2011). "Pathways to Prosperity: Meeting the Challenge of Preparing Young Americans for the 21st Century." Report issued by the Pathways to Prosperity Project, Harvard Graduate School of Education

2. David W. Kirkpatrick. "Student Aid and College Tuition: The Upward Spiral" (November 01, 2007) Retrieved from: http://www.schoolreport.com/schoolreport/articles/College_Tuition_11_07.htm

Selected Resources:

Ashenfelter, O. and Cecilia Rouse, C. (1999). "Schooling, Intelligence, and Income in America: Cracks in the Bell Curve," National Bureau of Economic Research, Working Paper 6902.

Barclay, S. (2011). "Voluntary Midlife Career Change: Integrating the Trans Theoretical Model and the Life-Span, Life-Space Approach." *Career Development Quarterly, 59*(5), 386.

Carnevale, A., Rose, S., and Cheah, B. (2011). Georgetown University Center on Education and the Workforce, *The College Payoff.*

The College Board (2012). [Online.] Available: www.collegeboard.org.

Goodwin, Cathy (2011). 3 Reasons to Get an MBA for Career Growth. [Online] Available: www.cathygoodwin.com.

Kuzma, A. T., Thiewes, H. F., and Kuzma, J. R. (2010). "An Examination Of Business Students' Student Loan Debt And Total Debt." *American Journal Of Business Education*, *3*(4), 71-77.

Reed, M., and Institute for College Access and Success. (2011). Student Debt and the Class of 2010. *Project On Student Debt.*

US Department of Labor, Bureau of Labor Statistics, (1998). "Number of Jobs, Labor Market Experience, and Earnings Growth: Results from a Longitudinal Survey." Press Release USDL 98-253.

"Paying for College," (2012). *US News* [Online]. Available: http://www.usnews.com/education.

http://www.thecrimson.com/article/2000/6/5/1946-1950-harvard-and-beyond-bpfont-size21946fontbpbseptemberbbr4/

http://colleges.usnews.rankingsandreviews.com/best-colleges/rankings/national-universities

Student Loans and Bankruptcy

Citations:

1. Bureau of Labor Statistics. (2012). *Labor Force Statistics from the Current Population Survey - Household Data Not Seasonally Adjusted as of January 2012.* Retrieved from United States Department of Labor: http://bls.gov/web/empsit/cpseea13.htm

2. Duke Chen. (July 26, 2007). "CRS Report for Congress - Student Loans in Bankruptcy." Washington, D.C.: Congressional Research Service (CRS) - Library of Congress.

3. Institute for College Access and Success. (2011, November 3). "Student Debt and the Class of 2010." Retrieved from *Project on Student Debt*: http://projectonstudentdebt.org/pub_view.php?idx=791

4. US Department of Education. (2011, September 12). *Default Rates Rise for Federal Student Loans.* Retrieved from Ed.gov: http://www.ed.gov/news/press-releases/default-rates-rise-federal-student-loans

5. Kim Clark. (2011, October 29). "College costs climb, yet again." Retrieved from *CNN Money*: http://money.cnn.com/2011/10/26/pf/college/college_tuition_cost/index.htm

6. College Board. (2011). "Trends in College Pricing." Retrieved from *College Board Advocacy and Policy Center*: http://trends.collegeboard.org/

7. Josh Higgins. (2012, February 1). "Colleges get less from state." Retrieved from *Collegiate Times*: http://www.collegiatetimes.com/stories/19147/colleges-get-less-from-state

8. Larry Abramson. (2011, October 19). "Why is College So Expensive?" Retrieved from *NPR*: http://www.npr.org/2011/10/19/141505658/why-is-college-so-expensive

9. Megan Eckstein. (2009, January 29). "Education Ranks 7th Among 'Industries' in Spending on Federal Lobbying." Retrieved from *The Chronicle of Higher Education*: http://chronicle.com/article/Education-Ranks-7th-Among/42336

Salary Trends: Compensation in America

Citations:

1. Retrieved from ABC News: http://abcnews.go.com/Business/walmart-ceo-pay-hour-workers-year/story?id=11067470

2. Megan McArdle. (2012, January 26). "How Rich Is Warren Buffett's Secretary?" Retrieved from The Atlantic: http://www.theatlantic.com/business/archive/2012/01/how-rich-is-warren-buffetts-secretary/252056/

3. Scott Shane. (2010, November 15). "How Much Money do Small Business Owners Make?" Retrieved from Small Business Trends: http://smallbiztrends.com/2010/11/how-much-money-do-small-business-owners-make.html

Selected Resources:

Edwards, C. (2010) Federal Pay Continues Rapid Ascent, *Cato@Liberty,* [Available] Online: www.cato-at-liberty.org.

Georgia State University (2011).

Hellman, C. (2011). "America's 25 Highest Paid CEOs," *Forbes.*

Karim, A. (2008). "How Much Money Should a CEO Make?" *Wise Bread* [Available] Online: www.wisebread.com

Knapp, A. (2011). "Govs' Salaries Range from $1 to $206,500." *Stateline,* [Available] Online: www.stateline.org.

Labor Law Center (2010). Federal Minimum Wage Increase, [Available] Online: www.laborlawcenter.com

Moriarty, J. (2009). "How Much Compensation Can CEOs Permissibly Accept?" *Business Ethics Quarterly, 19*(2), 235-250.

Penn State University (2011). www.livingwage.geog.psu.edu

Spires, S. (2011). "CEO Compensation as an Ethical Issue." Georgia State University. [Available] Online: www.gsu.edu.

http://online.wsj.com/article/S61019MEMOS.html?mod=RSS_Startup_Journal&sjrss=wsj

http://usgovinfo.about.com/od/uscongress/a/in-recession-congress-pay-increased.htm

Insurance Overview

Citations:

1. http://money.cnn.com/retirement/guide/insurance_life.moneymag

Selected Resources:

"What's Wrong with Using Insurance as an Investment?" (2010). *CNN Money Online,* Available: http://money.cnn.com/retirement/guide/insurance_life.moneymag

Ramsey, Dave (2011). "The Truth about Life Insurance." [Online], Available: http://www.daveramsey.com/article/the-truth-about-life-insurance

"Buying Homeowners' Insurance." (2011). *MSMoney.* [Online], Available: http://www.msmoney.com/mm/life_purchases/insurance

"How Much Does DI Cost?" (2010). National Association of Health Underwriters. [Online], Available: http://www.nahu.org/consumer/DI-Cost.pdf

"Factors that Affect Your Car Insurance Premium." (2011). CarInsurance.com. [Online], Available: http://www.carinsurance.com/Articles/content6.asp

Understanding Life Insurance

Selected Resources:

Baldwin, B. G. (2008). "Life Insurance Considerations in a Rapidly Changing World." *Journal of Financial Service Professionals,* 62(5), 48-60.

Lankford, K. (2011). "Life (Insurance) Begins at 50." *Kiplinger's Personal Finance,* 65(6), 56-58.

National Association of Insurance Commissioners. (2011). Consumer Guide. [Online]. Available: http://www.naic.org/documents/consumer_guide_life.pdf

Annuities and How to Use Them

Selected Resources:

Babbel, David F., Marrion, Jack, and VanderPal, Geoffrey (2010). "Real World Index Annuity Returns, Wharton Financial Institutions Center." [Online], Available: http://www.advisorsexcel.com/downloads/Wharton_Study.pdf

Langford, Kimberly (2007). "The Great Annuity Ripoff." [Online]. Available: http://www.kiplinger.com/magazine/archives

Mellberg, Josh (2011). "Which Annuity is Right for You?" [Online]. Available: http://www.seniorannuityalert.com

The Motley Fool (2010). Annuity Taxation [Online]. Available: http://www.fool.com/retirement/annuities/annuities01.htm

Municipal Bonds

Citations:

1. http://www.investopedia.com/terms/m/municipalbond.asp

2. http://en.wikipedia.org/wiki/municipal_bond

3. Ibid

4. "The Fundamentals of Municipal Bonds: The Bond Market Association," by Judy Wesalo Temal (2001)

5. http://www.publicbonds.org/major_players/regulators.htm

6. Ibid

7. Ibid

8. http://www.ehow.com/point/facts_5065490_types-municipal-bonds.html

9. http://www.publicbonds.org/bond_basics/municipal_bonds.htm

10. http://www.fourmilab.ch/ustax/www/t26-A-1-B-III-103.html

11. http://www.ehow.com/print/way_5761448_ladder-bullet-strategy.html

Selected Resources:

www.investopedia.com

www.publicbonds.org

"The Fundamentals of Municipal Bonds: The Bond Market Association," by Judy Wesalo Temal (2001)

Government Investments

Citations:

1. http://www.investorwords.com/5057/Treasuries.html

2. http://www.investopedia.com/terms/t/treasurybill.asp#axzz1kapcxii4

3. http://www.investopedia.com/terms/t/treasurynote.asp#axzz1kapcxii4

4. http://www.investopedia.com/terms/t/treasurybond.asp#axzz1kapcxii4a

5. http://www.usa.gov/shopping/investments/investments.shtml

6. http://www.savingsbonds.com/buying-us-savings-bonds.cfm

7. Ibid

8. Ibid

9. Ibid

10. Ibid

11. Ibid

12. Ibid

13. http://www.treasurydirect.gov/instit/marketables/strips.htm

14. http://www.bondtrac.com/professional/information/education/treasurystrips.xml

15. Ibid

16. http://www.efttrends.com/2009/09/tips-etfs-your-questions-answered/

17. http://www.investinginbonds.com

18. http://www.investopedia.com/terms/g/gse.asp

Selected Resources:

www.investopedia.com

www.usa.gov

www.savingsbonds.com

Treasury Direct

SECTION 6: Financial Planning

The Power of Compounding

Selected Resources:

http://www.math.ufl.edu/~mgluck/MGF1107/Lecture%20Notes/4B%20The%20Power%20of%20Compounding.pdf

http://mupfc.marshall.edu/~schroederm/4b.pdf

http://www.investopedia.com/terms/c/compounding.asp#axzz20o5hrTWm

http://www.wellsfargoadvantagefunds.com/wfweb/wf/education/101/principles/compounding.jsp

Investment Programs Introduction

Selected Resources:

http://www.dol.gov/ebsa/faqs/faq_compliance_pension.html

http://bls.gov

http://www.irs.gov

Traditional IRA Retirement Plans

Selected Resources:

http://www.irs.gov/pub/irs-pdf/p590.pdf

http://www.dol.gov/ebsa/publications/wyskapr.html

http://www.irs.gov/retirement/article/0%2C%2Cid=111413%2C00.html

http://www.irs.gov/publications/p590/index.html

Retirement Plans in the Workplace

Citations:

1. IRS Publication 3998 (2010). "Choosing a Retirement Plan for Your Small Business." (http://www.irs.gov/pub/irs-pdf/p3998.pdf)

2. IRS Publication 3998 (2010) "Choosing a Retirement Plan for Your Small Business." (http://www.irs.gov/pub/irs-pdf/p3998.pdf)

3. IRS Publication 4484 (2010). "Choose a Retirement Plan." (http://www.irs.gov/pub/irs-pdf/p4484.pdf

4. IRS Publication 4484 (2010). "Choose a Retirement Plan." (http://www.irs.gov/pub/irs-pdf/p4484.pdf

5. IRS Publication 3998 (2010). "Choosing a Retirement Plan for Your Small Business." (http://www.irs.gov/pub/irs-pdf/p3998.pdf)

6. IRS Publication 3998 (2010). "Choosing a Retirement Plan for Your Small Business." (http://www.irs.gov/pub/irs-pdf/p3998.pdf)

7. IRS Publication 3998 (2010). "Choosing a Retirement Plan for Your Small Business." (http://www.irs.gov/pub/irs-pdf/p3998.pdf)

8. IRS Publication 4484 (2010). "Choose a Retirement Plan." (http://www.irs.gov/pub/irs-pdf/p4484.pdf

9. http://www.irs.gov/retirement/article/0,,id=112859,00.html

10. http://www.irs.gov/retirement/article/0,,id=112859,00.html

11. http://www.irs.gov/retirement/article/0,,id=112859,00.html

12. IRS Publication 3998 (2010). "Choosing a Retirement Plan for Your Small Business." (http://www.irs.gov/pub/irs-pdf/p3998.pdf)

13. IRS Publication 3998 (2010). "Choosing a Retirement Plan for Your Small Business." (http://www.irs.gov/pub/irs-pdf/p3998.pdf)

14. IRS Publication 3998 (2010). "Choosing a Retirement Plan for Your Small Business." (http://www.irs.gov/pub/irs-pdf/p3998.pdf)

15. IRS Publication 4484 (2010). "Choose a Retirement Plan." (http://www.irs.gov/pub/irs-pdf/p4484.pdf

16. IRS Publication 4484 (2010). "Choose a Retirement Plan." (http://www.irs.gov/pub/irs-pdf/p4484.pdf

17. IRS Publication 4484 (2010). "Choose a Retirement Plan." (http://www.irs.gov/pub/irs-pdf/p4484.pdf

18. http://www.irs.gov/retirement/article/0,,id=108949,00.html

19. http://www.en.wikipedia.org/wiki/Employee_Share_Ownership_Plan

20. IRS Publication 4484 (2010). "Choose a Retirement Plan." (http://www.irs.gov/pub/irs-pdf/p4484.pdf

21. IRS Publication 4484 (2010)). "Choose a Retirement Plan."(http://www.irs.gov/pub/irs-pdf/p4484.pdf

22. IRS Publication 4484 (2010)). "Choose a Retirement Plan." (http://www.irs.gov/pub/irs-pdf/p4484.pdf

23. IRS Publication 4484 (2010)). "Choose a Retirement Plan." (http://www.irs.gov/pub/irs-pdf/p4484.pdf

24. IRS Publication 4484 (2010)). "Choose a Retirement Plan." (http://www.irs.gov/pub/irs-pdf/p4484.pdf

25. IRS Publication 4484 (2010)). "Choose a Retirement Plan." (http://www.irs.gov/pub/irs-pdf/p4484.pdf

26. http://solo401krules.com/

27. http://solo401krules.com/

28. http://solo401krules.com/

29. http://solo401krules.com/

30. IRS Publication 4484 (2010)). "Choose a Retirement Plan." (http://www.irs.gov/pub/irs-pdf/p4484.pdf

31. IRS Publication 4484 (2010)). "Choose a Retirement Plan." (http://www.irs.gov/pub/irs-pdf/p4484.pdf

32. IRS Publication 4484 (2010)). "Choose a Retirement Plan." (http://www.irs.gov/pub/irs-pdf/p4484.pdf

33. IRS Publication 4484 (2010)). "Choose a Retirement Plan." (http://www.irs.gov/pub/irs-pdf/p4484.pdf

34. IRS Publication 4484 (2010)). "Choose a Retirement Plan." (http://www.irs.gov/pub/irs-pdf/p4484.pdf

35. IRS Publication 4484 (2010)). "Choose a Retirement Plan." (http://www.irs.gov/pub/irs-pdf/p4484.pdf

36. IRS Publication 4484 (2010)). "Choose a Retirement Plan." (http://www.irs.gov/pub/irs-pdf/p4484.pdf

37. IRS Publication 4484 (2010) Choose A Retirement Plan (http://www.irs.gov/pub/irs-pdf/p4484.pdf

38. http://financial-planning.bestirarescue.com/401a-plan-rules.html

39. http://financial-planning.bestirarescue.com/401a-plan-rules.html

40. http://financial-planning.bestirarescue.com/401a-plan-rules.html

Selected Resources:

IRS Publication 4484 (2010)). "Choose a Retirement Plan." (http://www.irs.gov/pub/irs-pdf/p4484.pdf

IRS Publication 3998 (2010). "Choosing a Retirement Plan for Your Small Business" (http://www.irs.gov/pub/irs-pdf/p3998.pdf)

Investments for Children

Citations:

1. Choose to Save. (2011). Retrieved from Employee Benefit Research Institute's Education and Research Fund: http://www.choosetosave.org/asec/index.cfm?fa=about

2. Topic 553 - Tax on a Child's Investment Income. (2011). Retrieved from IRS: http://www.irs.gov/taxtopics/tc553.html

3. New York's 529 College Savings Direct Plan (2011). Retrieved from IRS: https://uii.nysaves.s.upromise.com/content/programfeatures.html

4. EE Savings Bonds in Depth. (2011). Retrieved from Treasury Direct: http://www.treasurydirect.gov/indiv/research/indepth/ebonds/res_e_bonds.htm

Bankruptcy and Retirement Plans

Citations:

1. Roger Lowenstein. (2010, June 25). "The Next Crisis: Public Pension Funds." Retrieved from *The New York Times*: http://www.nytimes.com/2010/06/27/magazine/27fob-wwln-t.html

2. US States Department of Labor. (n.d.). "What is ERISA?" Retrieved from United States Department of Labor: http://webapps.dol.gov/dolfaq/go-dol-faq.asp?faqid=225

3. Bankruptcy Law Network. (2011). "Will My Retirement Account Be Taken in Bankruptcy?" Retrieved from Bankruptcy Law Network: http://www.bankruptcylawnetwork.com/will-my-retirement-account-be-taken-in-bankruptcy/

4. United States Department of Labor. (2011). Fact Sheet: Your Employer's Bankruptcy - How Will It Affect Your Employee Benefits? Retrieved from United States Department of Labor: http://www.dol.gov/ebsa/newsroom/fsbankruptcy.html

SECTION 7: Government

Social Security Benefits

Citations:

1. http://www.investopedia.com/terms/s/socialsecurity/asp
2. http://www.ssa.gov/pubs/10024.html
3. http://www.investopedia.com/terms/s/socialsecurity/asp
4. http://www.ssa.gov/pubs/10024.html
5. Ibid
6. Ibid
7. http://www.ssa.gov/pubs/10022.html
8. Ibid
9. http://www.ssa.gov/budget/
10. http://www.ssa.gov/OACT/TRSUM/index.html
11. Ibid
12. Ibid
13. Ibid
14. http://www.ssa.gov/history/1983amend2.html

Selected Resources:

Social Security Administration

SSA Publication No. 05-10024, August 2011, ICN 454930

SSA Publication No. 05-10022, January 2011, ICN 454900

Social Security Administration Fiscal Year 2012 Budget Overview

www.investopedia.com

http://www.ssa.gov

http://www.investopedia.com/terms/s/socialsecurity/asp

http://www.ssa.gov/pubs/10024.html

http://www.ssa.gov/pubs/10022.html

http://www.ssa.gov/budget/

http://www.ssa.gov/OACT/TRSUM/index.html

http://www.ssa.gov/history/1983amend2.html

Tax Rates Comparison

Citations:

1. OECD: About the Organization for Economic Co-operation and Development (OECD). http://www.oecd.org/pages/0,3417,en_36734052_36734103_1_1_1_1_1,00.html

2. Tax Foundation: America Celebrates Tax Freedom Day. http://www.taxfoundation.org/taxfreedomday/

3. Tax Policy Center: 2011 Individual Income Tax Rates, Standard Deductions, Personal Exemptions, and Filing Thresholds. http://www.taxpolicycenter.org/taxfacts/content/pdf/individual_rates.pdf

4. OECD: Tax Database www.oecd.org/ctp/taxdatabase

5. Chamberlain et al. Tax Foundation: "Special Report: Who Pays America's Tax Burden, and Who Gets the Most Government Spending?" March 2007. http://www.taxfoundation.org/files/sr151.pdf

6. Kotlikoff et al. Boston University. "Does it Pay, at the Margin, to Work and Save?" December 2006. http://www.bu.edu/econ/files/2011/01/2006_48_Kotlikoff.pdf

7. Federation of Tax Administrators: "State Individual Income Taxes." February 2011. http://www.taxadmin.org/fta/rate/ind_inc.pdf

8. Tax Foundation: "Property Taxes on Owner-Occupied Housing by State, 2004-2009." September 2010. http://www.taxfoundation.org/taxdata/show/1913.html

9. *Tax Foundation*. "State Sales, Gasoline, Cigarette, and Alcohol Tax Rates by State, 2000-2010." April 2010. http://www.taxfoundation.org/taxdata/show/245.html

Made in the USA
Monee, IL
08 November 2026

68156252R00192